SHAGGY JACK

Titles by Barb Bissonette

Shaggy Jack
The Christmas Field
Nobody's Dog
Just a Bit of Magic
Leave a Light On for Christmas
A Winter Town
Among Little Faces

SHAGGY JACK

BARB BISSONETTE

Shaggy Jack
Copyright © 2025 Barb Bissonette

No part of this publication may be reproduced, stored in a retrieval system, or transmitted in any form or by any means, electronic, mechanical, photocopying, recording, scanning, or otherwise, without the prior written permission of the author, except by reviewers, who may quote brief passages in a review.

To request permissions, contact the publisher at
jennifer@entouragemedia.ca.

Editing and Cover Design: Jennifer Goulden
Editing and Interior Design: Chris Arnold
Cover Art: Jeanette Obbink

ISBN (Paperback): 978-1-0689121-6-0
ISBN (e-Book): 978-1-0689121-7-7
First Edition Printed in Canada: October 2025
1 2 3 4 5 6 7 8 9 10

ENTOURAGE
...
Published by Entourage Media
www.entouragemedia.ca

This book is dedicated to the memory of my mother,
Betty Van Vliet

"Not all mothers are mothers. Some mothers are aunts by blood, or by royal appointment. Some are best friends with safe spaces for laps and listening ears so large they can hear silent cries. Some are teachers who will be remembered lifelong for all the right reasons. Not all mothers are mothers. And if you have one in your life, you are blessed. They have much love to give. And they are walking around this earth with nurture flowing out of their fingertips. Not all mothers are mothers, but oh, they mother so very well."

—Donna Ashworth

Contents

Author's Note ix
Chapter One 1
Chapter Two 10
Chapter Three 23
Chapter Four 29
Chapter Five 36
Chapter Six 44
Chapter Seven 48
Chapter Eight 52
Chapter Nine 56
Chapter Ten 62
Chapter Eleven 67
Chapter Twelve 77
Chapter Thirteen 93
Chapter Fourteen 102
Chapter Fifteen 108
Chapter Sixteen 121
Chapter Seventeen 140
Chapter Eighteen 146

CONTENTS

Chapter Nineteen 161
Chapter Twenty 170
Chapter Twenty-One 175
Chapter Twenty-Two 179
Chapter Twenty-Three 182
Chapter Twenty-Four 191
Chapter Twenty-Five 198
Chapter Twenty-Six 205
Chapter Twenty-Seven 213
Chapter Twenty-Eight 221
Chapter Twenty-Nine 228
Chapter Thirty 237
Chapter Thirty-One 250
Chapter Thirty-Two 258
Chapter Thirty-Three 267
Chapter Thirty-Four 275
Chapter Thirty-Five 282
Chapter Thirty-Six 293

Author's Note

In writing this book, I would like to make it very clear that in no way, shape, or form was my intention to make light of the diagnosis of dementia. My sisters and I have experienced firsthand this horrific journey with both of our parents. Thus, we are well aware of the frustration and grief it entails, not to mention the complete and utter loss of losing your loved one bit by agonizing bit every day.

My mother became almost catatonic for the last two years of her life and was non-verbal for most of this time. My father, however, always a sociable man, remained quite jolly and congenial even in the throes of adject confusion.

One day I was visiting him in the nursing home with a friend of mine, whom he had known and liked very much, for many years. He proceeded to make a wildly inappropriate comment about a certain part of her anatomy. We giggled all the way to the elevator, mainly because he had always been a gentleman and had never said anything untoward in all the years she'd known him.

It made me think about people who lost their inhibitions and were therefore free to say whatever—anything really—that entered their head at any given moment.

Hence, Doc came into being. Old age and dementia is so depressing, but I wanted to write something to capture the funny side of it all. So, I made Doc sweet and lovable, I hope, in spite of his diagnosis. At least I fell in love with him, with the idea of him. I hope you do, too.

BARB BISSONETTE

As for the others characters, they just came along for the ride. Thank you for reading my story.

Chapter One

THERE'S a story I'd like to tell you. It all happens around June, a middle-aged lesbian woman (who doesn't realize she's a lesbian; not yet anyway), Jed, a retired doctor grappling with old age and bouts of memory loss (some of the time; some of the time his mind is razor sharp), a young boy, Nicholas, who has completely lost his way, and a very shaggy dog, Jack, the biggest dog imaginable.

There is no conventional or logical starting point to this tale. It roams about all over the place in a similar fashion to the dog. And the boy.

But if it were to have a proper beginning, it may well have started one bright spring afternoon. June emerged from her front door to encounter the first day of the rest of her life.

She paused on the porch, admiring the welcome glow of the sun, basking gratefully in its warmth.

June resided in what had always been referred to locally as "the old boarding house," although it no longer functioned as such. It stood well back, barely visible to passersby, the last of a handful of homes scattered along a winding country road.

Strands of ivy vines clung doggedly to the old, grey walls, softening their harsh lines, thus making the house appear both sheltered and hidden. A rambling, herbaceous garden bordered the front of the house, tentative blooms springing up here and there, easing their way into the comfort of spring.

At the front of the lawn, a pair of maple trees had stood for as long as June could remember, spreading their protection from the sun with broad, sturdy branches. Sometime over the years, an old crab apple tree had happened along between them, growing more gnarled and grouchier with the passing of time.

At the far side of the property, a copse of birch trees stood in stark contrast, their white bark smooth and elegant. Late afternoon beams of sunlight filtered through their slender branches, creating a dapple pattern on the grass. The rustling of gossamer leaves in the gentle breeze and the occasional flutter of bird wings added to the peaceful ambiance of the day.

Not a fancy place by any stretch of the imagination, not even a very well-kept one, but perhaps one that emanated something appealing just the same, something homey and comforting, not unlike its owner.

June Howard had been trampled down by life through no fault of her own, or so she believed. Even so, sometimes she couldn't help but feel bitter about certain things.

She was sixty-three years old, an age at which she felt she should have been considerably more established in life than she actually was, further ahead on the coveted path of achieving a state of comfortable wealth. Or at least freer from financial struggle. Yes, she would have settled for that. Furthermore, she would have liked to have become a better human being than she perceived herself to be.

She wanted to be patient and wise. She wanted to be calm and self-controlled. But how did one become these things? She didn't know. She would have blamed her appearance on her crusty disposition if pressed to do so. She was short and squat, almost as wide as she was tall, and this had been the general shape she'd inhabited for most of her life.

SHAGGY JACK

Grey, wispy hair framed her round face, which usually sported a severe countenance. If, perchance, you caught June in the throes of a genuine smile, ten years fell away from her face.

However, on this particular afternoon, her features darkened into a decided scowl at the unbelievable sight unfolding before her eyes.

An enormous dog, the biggest one June had ever seen in her whole life, was sauntering unceremoniously across her front lawn. His massive paws happily trampled through her garden with utter disregard for the new plants sprouting to life beneath them.

He carried something in his mouth. June squinted her eyes to get a better look. The thing in the dog's mouth was more than half obscured by enormous amounts of scraggly hair, but she could still see enough of it to know it looked familiar. Not a bunny. Definitely not, or she would wallop him. Who gave him the right to kill bunnies on her property? It wasn't a bird. She was positive about that, too. No feathers. Then the smell hit her nostrils.

"Where did you get that roast?" June hollered at the top of her lungs. "You drop that right this minute!" She motioned wildly at him from the porch as if to scare him into listening. "Do you hear me, you wretched beast? Drop it!"

The dog paused, startled by the outburst, but was not startled enough to drop the scrumptious roast of beef he'd found cooking away on a barbecue down the road, just lying there, up for grabs.

He clenched the meat firmly between his jaws and stared at the woman. She was mad. He could tell. He knew all about people. Especially the mad ones. And he did, in fact, understand what "drop it" meant. However, there was not one bone in his canine body that had any intention of dropping such a delicious find.

"What's all the yelling about, Junie dear? Are you alright?" Dr. Jed McIntyre, a retired local doctor, appeared from the doorway behind her.

June pointed at the animal. "That dog has a roast!!"

"That dog?" Doc asked, pointing in momentary fascination. "Well, I think that's the biggest dog I've ever seen in my life."

"Yes, that dog," she snapped impatiently. "That monstrosity of a dog. Look at that roast he's got in his mouth. Those things aren't cheap."

"Was that going to be our dinner?"

"No, it's not our dinner!" She exploded. "But it's *somebody's* dinner! Or it was before this ruthless animal stole it."

"He can't be that ruthless," Doc observed. "Or he would have devoured it by now."

"And you're commending him for that, are you?"

Doc shrugged noncommittally.

June shook her head in exasperation, wondering how on earth she was going to rectify this mess. The roast must have been snatched from Fred Wilson's barbecue. He was the only neighbour close enough. And just like June, he would be furious. And his wife, the long-suffering Martha, would remember "the day of the great roast theft" and bring it up at regular intervals for the rest of June's life. Maybe even longer.

It wasn't beyond Doc to charm the dog into surrendering the choice cut of beef. Or even to expect her to finish cooking it and then offer a portion to this mutt. June bristled at the very thought.

Even though he was too nice for his own good, June held no animosity toward Doc. None. And she had never regretted her decision to board him at her house. He had been, and still was, a sweet-natured man, asking for little and pleased with everything she did for him (which really wasn't a whole lot besides providing him with a home base, meals, and clean clothes). He was quite capable of looking after his personal needs and was ever ready to lend a helping hand.

He had served the old-fashioned, rural village of Laventra well for many years. It encompassed a willy-nilly scattering of nearby fields, farms, and trees.

Doc had always been knowledgeable and kind, caring for Laventra's citizens with competence and compassion. Then, sadly, the effects of his advancing years forced him to step down from his beloved practice. His mind wasn't what it used to be, and that was unacceptable to him. What was once sharp was now foggy at times. There were whispers of "dementia" and "Alzheimer's" among the villagers, but no one knew for sure. They only knew they would miss being able to turn to their beloved Doc when they needed help.

Disease of the mind is a funny journey. There were many days in which Doc could not remember what he'd had for breakfast or even the name of the nurse who had worked alongside him for thirty years. Other days, he could recall events from yesteryear with startling accuracy, possessing an uncanny memory for dates and numbers. Recently, Doc's decline had begun to affect more than just his knack for facts and figures. He had begun to utter wildly inappropriate remarks, totally out of character and often amusing.

No one had, as yet, been found to replace him in Laventra. Even if the village did manage to attract another medical professional, Dr.

Jed McIntyre would always be affectionately referred to as "Doc" by all who have known him.

He stood lean and lanky, an upright figure even now. His hair, a thick mop of white, framed a face marked with gentle wrinkles and deep laugh lines, each one telling a story of wisdom and warmth. His blue eyes, twinkling behind round, steel-rimmed spectacles, held a world of kindness. He was known for his soft-spoken manner and ready sense of humour.

Although the Howard homestead no longer functioned as a boarding house per se, its five bedrooms remained in relatively decent repair, largely because they stood unused, receiving only a perfunctory dusting from June. She despised housework with every fibre of her being.

So, when Doc had started to run into difficulty, wandering a little and losing his way home, June had agreed to take him in. After caring for everyone else in the community for so many years, it just wasn't right that Doc had neither chick nor child in the world to care for him. He'd always been an agreeable soul, and not a lick of trouble.

Until today. Until he stood in front of her, hand shading his eyes against the afternoon sun, quietly contemplating this dog from God only knew where, with a smile on his face.

"Maybe this young fellow can help us out. Does this dog belong to you, my friend?"

June wondered if he had begun to hallucinate until she followed his gaze and beheld a young, bedraggled-looking boy stepping through the trunks of the old maple trees.

First, the dog and now a boy. This was the most action her

property had seen in years. She stared, transfixed, trying and failing to comprehend the surreal scene unfolding before her.

A ragamuffin of a boy child had materialized on her lawn. Quite literally. Tattered clothes hung from his string-bean body. Scraps of stained fabric strung together with laces sufficed as shoes. Smears of dirt smudged his face and bare appendages.

In spite of his attire, he shone in that beautiful, young way of boyhood. Bright eyes, brimming with curiosity, illuminated a scrawny, tanned face; unkempt hair, bleached from the sun, framed a pleasing, well-defined set of features.

He regarded June with undisguised fascination, which unsettled her greatly. She knew, for a fact, that she was not in the least bit fascinating.

June struggled to decipher her current situation. Time seemed to have frozen in its tracks; the shaggy dog still coveting his juicy bounty, Doc trying to understand the uncanny turn of events in his gentle, muddled way, and this boy staring at her fiercely, his eyes seeming to penetrate her very being.

"Is this your dog, my boy?" Doc inquired again.

The boy shook his head.

"What's your name?"

"Nicholas," he replied, not taking his eyes from June's face.

"Nicholas, well, well. That's a great name. Very dignified."

Anyone appearing less dignified than this wayward child could scarcely be imagined, but Nicholas nodded his head as if conceding this fact as a matter of course.

"People sometimes call me Nicky."

"Ah!" Doc nodded his head in approval. "Then we shall call you Nicky. And what is your dog's name, Nicky?"

"He only joined me this afternoon. So, I don't know his name yet."

"Oh really? Well, he seems to have made off with a roast. Thought maybe he was bringing it for your supper. You do look a little hungry, if you don't mind my saying so. I'm sure you could use a good meal."

June noticed the truth of this remark and her heart softened a little, in spite of herself. She was not without empathy for her fellow creatures, especially those so obviously down on their luck as this boy child.

"Who are you? And why are you here on my front lawn? What's going on?"

"I don't know what's going on. Not really. But are you—"

"Am I what?"

"Are you—are you June Howard?"

"Oh yes," Doc jumped in, delighted to be of assistance. "Yes, this is June. I board here with her."

"You do?"

"Yup, for a while now. I can't remember how long, but Junie runs a most wonderful boarding house."

"It's not actually a boarding house, not anymore," June snapped. She did not want this strange, inquisitive boy getting any wild ideas about boarding here.

"Did it used to be?" the boy asked.

"It did, but that was a long time ago. Years and years ago, when my grandparents owned it. No one's been here since they died."

"But you're here," the boy pointed at Doc.

"Well, yes, he is, but it's *my* family home. I lived here with my mom after my dad took off. And then she died, too."

"You sound bitter," the boy observed.

"I'm not bitter."

"I don't know. You sound kind of bitter." He turned to Doc for affirmation. "Doesn't she?"

Doc considered, then admitted, "Maybe a little bit."

"For the love of God!" June erupted, feeling this whole turn of events spiralling out of her realm of control. "I am not bitter. And it's none of your business if I am or not, anyway. Just exactly who on earth are you, and how do you know my name?!"

The shaggy dog, seemingly absorbed in the drama of the scene, lay on the grass now, regarding the trio with interest. He tore juicy strips of meat from the remainder of the roast, which he seemed to be consuming with great gusto.

"What did you say the dog's name was, Nicky?" Doc asked. "I just forget what you said."

"I don't know the dog's name, but I think you're my aunt, June Howard."

Chapter Two

"His aunt! Oh, now this is wonderful news!" Doc exclaimed. "You're lucky, Nicky. Junie is great. She'll be a wonderful aunt."

"Doc, calm down," June told him, utterly bewildered now. "I think you're mistaken, Nicky. I'm not aware that I possess any nephews in this world."

"So, it's a great surprise then," Doc gleefully interjected. "How old are you, Nicky?"

"Thirteen."

June gasped. He looked much younger.

"A great age to be! Hey, maybe you can stay here and board with us."

June groaned. "Doc! This isn't a boarding house. Just hang the hell on for a minute."

"I thought you said it *was* a boarding house," the boy protested.

"But you're his aunt, Junie. You can't turn him away."

"I said it *used* to be a boarding house. And I'm no one's aunt."

June turned to the boy, her face stern and unyielding. "What on earth gave you the idea that I was your aunt?"

Just as the child was about to explain, yells of rage erupted, followed by Fred Wilson's appearance on June's lawn. He was waving his barbecue tools in anger and turning the air blue with his choice selection of words.

June understood his fury and was not without sympathy for his plight. She assured him, "This has nothing to do with me! I have no idea who on earth this dog belongs to or where the hell he came from!"

SHAGGY JACK

"He wouldn't even have to jump up to reach my barbecue," Fred roared. "Look at the size of that thing. He could have just leaned his head over and grabbed it."

"I know. He's bloody huge. But I'm sorry, I don't know where he came from. He just turned up here on my lawn."

"Well, he's enjoying *my* supper, that's all I know," Fred pointed a finger that shook with rage at the offending creature.

"Yes, he sure is," Doc agreed, still amused at the scene unfolding on June's front lawn.

Martha, Fred's wife, churlish and negative by nature, hastened into view, following her husband and puffing from unaccustomed exertion. "Groceries are bloody expensive, you know!!"

"They sure are. I know that fine well," June sighed. "But I fail to see how any of this is my fault."

Martha's lips curled in a most unbecoming fashion. "How can it not be your fault, June Howard? Did everyone just choose today to show up on your lawn?"

June looked around her. "I guess they did."

"So you *are* June Howard!" Nicholas cried, aiming an accusing finger in June's direction.

"I never denied it."

"She didn't," Doc agreed. "And Martha, maybe we have something in the freezer that would suffice for your dinner. In lieu of the roast, I mean."

He turned to June, his smile broad and well-intentioned, and asked, "Do we, Junie dear?"

After much convoluted dialogue and attempted unruffling of Martha's feathers, things got straightened out in the dinner department.

June apologized for any part she might have played in the barbecue mishap—although for the life of her, she couldn't see what that could possibly have been—and the Wilsons headed home. Martha's grumbling could be heard trailing behind them as they made their way back down the road.

To June's relief, Fred had refused to accept any donations for dinner that might have been lurking in the depths of her freezer. Donations that Doc had so graciously offered, much to her chagrin.

Because Martha Wilson was dead right about one thing. Groceries were very expensive.

Having sorted out the issue of the stolen roast, June turned her attention to the more pressing matters at hand—one of which was the fact that some shaggy, monstrous-sized, stray dog seemed to have taken up residence on her front lawn, nonchalantly munching on the remnants of his stolen bounty.

The other matter was that she knew she needed to hear this boy out. She couldn't ignore his presence for another minute. Trepidation swelled inside her heart at the prospect.

"Let's sit on the porch and you can tell me why you think we're related, Nicholas."

Nicholas allowed himself to be led to the front porch.

Abandoned books and crooked pots inhabited by various herbs and plants lay scattered amongst old wooden and wicker chairs, partially hidden by brightly coloured cushions. The boy moved some books from one of the big chairs and sank into its depths, sighing wearily.

"So, we'll just call you Nicky, will we? It sounds so much friendlier," said Doc, not for one second assuming that he, too, wasn't

SHAGGY JACK

included in the invitation. "And maybe we could have some lemonade. What do you think, Junie dear?"

"I don't just *think* we're related. I know it," Nicky asserted, when everyone had gathered themselves amongst the hodgepodge of the porch. "But lemonade does sound nice."

"I made some cookies this morning," June hastened to say, before Doc could request anything else. She disappeared into the kitchen, glad to have a task at hand.

"He's a nice dog, isn't he?" Doc remarked when the two were alone, referring to the huge grey animal who had made his way up the few steps and now sat down between them, as if he had done so a million times before.

Doc tapped his hand lightly against his pant leg. The dog inched over to the old man and placed his head on Doc's lap with a gentleness that belied his size. Those hands, which had cared for so many, stroked his shaggy head with great tenderness.

"Kind of a silly-looking dog," Nicholas observed. "I've never seen one that big before."

"Ah, yes, but we're all kind of silly looking in one way or another, don't you think?"

The boy considered this. "Maybe. I guess. But I've seen a lot of dogs and not one like this guy."

"But that just makes him special. What do you think his name could be?"

"I don't know," Nicholas shrugged. "He just started walking beside me a couple of kilometres down that road. We'll probably never see him again after today."

"Oh, we'll see him. He'll stay here."

"How do you know that?"

"Because Junie can't turn anything away, man or beast. Look at me."

"Really?"

"Yup, really. She's the most kind-hearted woman I know."

"She doesn't look it."

"But that means nothing. You can't judge a book by its cover."

"What?"

"It just means that you can't tell what people are like on the inside by looking at their outside."

"Why didn't you just say that then?"

"I think I just did," Doc said, as he scratched the dog's big, floppy ears.

"I hope you're right," he observed.

"Right about what?" Doc looked up, slightly taken aback.

"Right about her not turning her back on anyone."

"Oh, that. Yes, I'm right. Just you wait and see. Are you talking about yourself or this dog?"

"Both."

"I see." Doc nodded thoughtfully. "Well, I hope I'm right too. It would be nice to have some young life around this old place."

The boy appeared unconvinced.

"I'll tell you what, though," Doc said. "She'll be more likely to let this dog stay if we give him a name."

"Why?"

"Oh, because then it'll be a more personal thing. Do you see?"

"I guess so. But maybe he already has a name. He must."

"I've never seen this dog or any dog like this around here. I think he's a runaway." Doc peered over the top of his glasses and down at Nicholas. "Much like yourself."

"I'm not a runaway."

"Are you sure about that?"

The boy nodded. "I'm sure. And how about Jack?"

"How about him?"

"No, I mean for a name."

"Oh, right. For this shaggy fellow." Doc regarded the big, furry beast for a moment before nodding his approval. "Shaggy Jack it is."

June emerged from the house, bearing a large tray with lemonade, sandwiches, and cookies.

"So, this is Shaggy Jack," Doc informed her, placing a kiss on the dog's funny head. Only Doc could do that and make it look like the most natural thing in the world.

June set the tray down on the wicker table in front of Doc and the boy.

"And Nicky is going to tell us the story of how he came to appear at our house on this fine spring day. Right here." He indicated the porch in case there could be any doubt about their whereabouts.

June nodded, taking a glass of lemonade and a sandwich, and sat down heavily on one of the wooden porch chairs. *I should have made myself something stronger than lemonade for this one*, she thought.

"Go on then! Tell us your story," June said, turning to the boy. "Are you a runaway?"

"Not exactly."

"Well, you either are or you aren't. There's no in between."

Nicholas was in the process of wolfing down one sandwich

while already reaching for another. June wondered how long it had been since this child had eaten.

Doc chuckled, biting into his egg salad sandwich with approval. No one made egg salad sandwiches like Junie. "I used to say that to my patients about being pregnant," he remarked. "There's no in-between. You can't be a little bit. You either are or you aren't." After a moment's reflection, he added, "No, wait, maybe that was being dead."

"They're both right, I guess," Nicholas mused. "You can't be a little bit pregnant or a little bit dead. Can you?"

"No, you can't," Doc agreed. "Good point, Nicky." He gave the dog a bite of his sandwich before catching June's disapproving eye.

"Really, Doc?!" She huffed. "That beast just ate Fred Wilson's entire roast beef, and now you're feeding him your sandwich?"

"He's a big dog. He's probably hungry."

"He's bloody massive. And he can just move right along to wherever he came from, like this boy here. I don't know where you two came from, and I don't care. You're not my responsibility."

Dismay flooded the boy's face at the harshness of her words.

Doc remained unruffled and unfailingly cheerful. "Aw, Junie dear, you don't mean that. Please, let's just listen to Nicky's story."

"I'd love to, if you guys would stop talking about being dead and pregnant and feeding my egg salad sandwiches to this horse of a dog."

"Fair point," Doc acquiesced. "Okay, Nicky, you go ahead and tell us your story and how you got here. Take your time."

Nicholas gulped, seeming to make a supreme effort to begin his tale. "I want to tell you about June Howard being my aunt," he began.

"I forgot about that part," Doc cried. "That's the best part."

SHAGGY JACK

June shot him a look that would have crushed a lesser man—or a more lucid one.

But Doc, unperturbed, crossed his long, lean legs, secured another sandwich, and turned to give Nicholas his undivided attention.

Now that all eyes were fixated on him, the boy seemed reluctant to speak.

"Okay," Doc told him. "We're all ears. Tell us who you are and where you're from."

"So, my name is Nicholas Benton." He paused, allowing his listeners to absorb this revelation.

"That settles the matter," June said. "I'm not familiar with that surname. I've never even known anyone named Benton." She rose to her feet, determined to send this urchin on his way.

"You said I could tell you my story."

"I know I did," June said, not unkindly. "But—"

"People can be related and have different last names," Doc interrupted.

"Yes, Doc, I'm well aware of that."

"My mother was your little sister. You were almost twelve when she was born, and you were like a mom to her because your dad was gone and your mom got really depressed and stayed in bed a lot."

June lowered her bulk back down, very slowly and deliberately, to regard him with a new, keen interest.

"Postpartum depression," Doc told them brightly. "It's a very real thing, especially for older mothers. It can be quite overwhelming having a baby as you age. It changes so much of your life."

"Yes, thank you for that, Doc."

"You are most welcome, Junie dear."

June sighed, sarcasm clearly lost on the old man. She turned to the boy. "Anyone in Laventra could have told you that. It is quite common knowledge around here that I raised my little sister. You could have heard that anywhere."

"But I didn't. I heard it from my own mom."

"Listen, Nicky," June continued, making a superhuman attempt at self-control. "My sister fell in with the wrong crowd when she was a teenager. I tried really hard to give her a good home and keep her in school, but she turned her back on me. On the whole town. She left here on her nineteenth birthday with a friend, and I never saw her again. Not once. Then, a few years later, I received word from her friend that she had died in a bus crash out in Alberta. The driver lost control on some ice, the bus fell over a cliff, and it caught fire. So they couldn't identify anyone, but they knew she'd bought a ticket and gotten on the bus."

"She couldn't have gotten on that bus."

"But she did. She must have. And she never tried to contact me after she left. I know if she was alive, she would have come home. She just would have."

"Maybe she lost her way home. She just lost her way."

June narrowed her eyes, regarding the boy steadily. "What do you mean by that?" She hadn't intended the words to come out so severely, but they fell into the spring afternoon like hard stones.

"Maybe she lost her way. Even though you tried to keep her on the right one."

June sat rigid as a statue, staring at this strange boy.

In a considered movement, Nicholas Benton thrust his hand

beneath his stained, ragged T-shirt. He produced a tarnished, silver pendant hanging from an old chain, clutched in his thin, brown fingers.

June recognized it as soon as she saw it. "St. Christopher!" she gasped.

"I know him," Doc cried in delight, pleased to contribute to this peculiar conversation. "He's the patron saint of travellers. You give these charms to people you love who are travelling."

"Yes," Nicky said, his eyes fixed on June. "So they won't—"

"Lose their way," June finished in a whisper. She rose, approaching the boy, reaching out in wonder to touch the pendant. "Chrissy Bear!"

"Yes," Nicky nodded. "You used to call her Chrissy Bear, and she called you June Bug. She told me all about that."

June plunked herself back into the chair. "How could you know that, child? How can this be?"

"I told you. She was my mom."

"But why didn't she ever try to contact me?"

Nicky's face fell.

"She died. Did I say that?"

"No, you did not."

"A few months ago. We were in this shelter place, and she got pneumonia. She wouldn't let me call an ambulance, and when I finally did, she was very sick. They took her to the hospital, but she died. I went to live with a foster family for a while, but I felt like I was just in the way there. They had a shitload of kids and no room. I told them I had an aunt I could live with, and I just left on my own. I've been making my way to Laventra since then."

"From where?"

"BC."

"My God, that's the other side of the country."

"I know. It took forever."

"But you're just a kid. How could you travel so far on your own?"

Nicky shrugged. "I just did. I told all kinds of stories, and people believed me. Gave me rides and stuff."

"Are you telling a story now, Nicky? I won't be cross at you if you are. Just please tell me the truth."

"That is the truth," Nicky insisted. "I promise, Auntie June Bug." He grinned at her, a grin that lit up his scrawny features.

"I've waited so long to call you that."

June gulped, swallowing a lump that had taken up residence inside her throat.

"Hey, I like that, Junie," Doc declared. "June Bug. Didn't your little sister used to—"

"Yes, Doc," June affirmed. "Chrissy always called me June Bug."

"I remember that," Doc proclaimed proudly. "And now, if I'm following this correctly—and I think that I am—Nicky here is Chrissy's son."

Nicky nodded, beaming.

"Well, that is just delightful. I could tell Nicky here belonged to us."

"Doc—"

"Aw, Junie dear, just look at him. Doesn't he look like he belongs here?"

Nicky smiled, raising his palms in a shrug of humility.

"It's not quite that simple, Doc."

"And Chrissy now, where did you say she was, son?"

"She died."

"Oh dear, I didn't even know she was sick."

For some reason, this struck everyone as funny. A gale of laughter erupted, filling the porch with unexpected mirth.

"I'm so sorry, Nicky boy," Doc said, turning to the boy, still grinning. "I meant no disrespect."

"I didn't think you did, Doc. I've had a lot of disrespect from people, so I can tell when I'm getting it."

He sounded considerably older than his young years.

"Chrissy died in a bus crash, Doc."

"No. No, Auntie June Bug," Nicky said firmly. "I told you. She only died three months ago. She was fifty years old."

June shook her head. She couldn't imagine Chrissy at age fifty. To June, she would always be the capricious, headstrong girl of nineteen who thought she knew everything about everything. How could she possibly have produced this delicate reed of a boy perched on her front porch, as if conjured out of nowhere?

"Aw, fifty seems very young to me these days," Doc remarked. "Not enough time to be in this old world."

"It isn't," June sighed, pleased to agree with someone about something. "Did she ever tell you why she called me June Bug?"

"Because you rock!"

"She said that?"

"Oh yeah, she always told me how amazing you were. And beautiful."

June harrumphed. "Chrissy would never have said that."

"But she did," Nicky asserted. "Lots of times."

"Look at me," June indicated her squat body and unruly hair. "Do I look beautiful to you?"

The two males considered, then bobbed their heads up and down in unison.

"Come on," June scoffed. "You're just being silly now."

"Beauty is in the eye of the beholder," Doc pronounced firmly.

"I don't know what that means, but you look beautiful to me. I thought that as soon as I saw you. Anyway, Doc told me not to judge a book by its cover."

"Oh, he did, did he?"

Doc looked askance. He wasn't sure, but it did sound like something he might have said.

"She said she called you June Bug because June bugs are from the beetle family, and beetles rock!"

June's heart tripped over its own rhythm at this long-ago memory.

"She didn't mean beetles that are bugs. She meant The Beatles, like the singing group."

"I know that. She explained it to me. Ringo and Paul and George and one more."

"John Lennon," Doc boomed triumphantly. "He was shot to death in New York in 1980, poor guy."

"Yes," Nicky said. "She always liked that band. The Beatles. Because they rock!"

"Like Junie here."

"Exactly."

Nobody could argue with that one.

Everyone knew the Beatles rocked.

Chapter Three

THE afternoon light of this strange day faded, seeping into velvety dusk. And still everyone remained, sprawled in various stages of repose, on the porch of the old boarding house.

June surveyed them, having absolutely no idea what on earth she should do with these new vagabonds, dog and boy alike.

The dog had consumed the last remnants of Fred's roast, so she felt no compunction toward him. She'd never seen a dog so massive, so shaggy. He was the size of a small horse and lay now, draped across her porch, content with his lot, full to the brim with his ill-gotten gains.

But the boy worried her. What on earth was she to do with him? Was he truly Chrissy's son? She could not wrap her head around this utterly foreign idea. For over thirty years, she had believed her sister was dead and gone. She had never, in her wildest dreams, thought that Chrissy could have survived that bus crash. How could she have just gone on living, never contacting her? The mere thought of this felt like a dagger to June's heart. And to have a son, June didn't even know existed!

She gazed at him now, sitting on the porch, stroking the dog's huge head.

"Now that's a nice sight, isn't it?" Doc observed.

"Is it, Doc? Is it really? What are we to do with these two vagrants?"

"Well, give them a home, of course," Doc said, as if it were the most natural thing in the world. Which it was to him. He didn't deal in the practicalities that ruled June's daily life.

"It's not that easy, Doc."

"I don't see why not. I can help. I know, of course I know, that I get muddled up, Junie dear, but I can do more than I've been doing. I can help out. I've been meaning to talk to you about that."

She raised an eyebrow. "You have, have you?"

"Yes indeed. And I think we should count our lucky stars that these two have arrived. We should be celebrating."

"You guys know I can hear you, right?" the boy asked, without taking his eyes off the dog. "And what's a vagrant?"

"*You* are. And that atrocity of a dog."

"He has a name. It's Shaggy Jack," Doc interjected. "And a vagrant is a wanderer, someone who moves around and doesn't really have a fixed address."

"Well, that's us then," the boy admitted, with a sigh.

"Yes, but now you have a home," Doc told him, reassuringly.

Nicky turned and looked squarely at June, his face brimming with hope. "Do I?"

She, in turn, glared at Doc because this was his fault, after all. "It's not that easy," she repeated.

"I don't see why not." Doc shrugged. "The boy is your nephew."

"And how do we know that for sure? Oh right! We don't."

"Like I said, you guys, I can hear you." The boy pulled his attention away from the dog. "And anyway, I can prove I'm her son. I have my birth certificate."

"Well, that settles it then," Doc smiled with relief. "We're all set."

Nicky stood up, moving Shaggy Jack's head from his lap to the wooden floor of the porch. June tried not to notice how gentle he was with the animal. She did not want to get attached to him. She did not want to love him. Everyone she'd ever loved had left her or died. She was having no more of that.

The dog stretched out his long legs and let out a deep, contented sigh.

Of course, he was content, June thought resentfully. He'd just eaten a roast that would have fed all of them and then some. My God, he must weigh as much as a grown person. Huge beast of a dog. Bloody thief, to boot.

Nicky had retrieved an old backpack from beneath the birch trees at the side of the house. The bag appeared to be on its last legs, like everything else about the boy. "I threw it there before I came to meet you," he explained. "I didn't want you to think I had anything dangerous in it. I didn't want to scare you."

"You don't look very scary." June probably outweighed this child by well over fifty pounds.

"We appreciate that," Doc told him solemnly. "You never know these days."

Nicky nodded and searched the meagre contents of his bag.

"How long did you say you've been with Jack?" Doc asked.

"He's only walked with me the last little bit before I got here. But honestly, I had no idea he was going to steal that roast. I guess he was getting hungry."

"He's a big dog. I'm sure he was."

"I guess he's my friend now," Nicky said.

"Dogs are man's best friends. Always have been. Lucky for you that your aunt is by way of having lots of room for dogs here. She used to run a kennel of sorts. When people went on holiday, they'd bring their dogs here for her to watch. She still does it, just not as much. But there's lots of room for Jack."

"Wait a gall-darn minute there, Doc—"

"Wait, what kind of minute?"

"It's an expression, Nicky dear. Your auntie here just means 'hold on while I think about things.'"

"I don't need to think about things. This dog can't stay here. He'd be a fortune in dog food."

"Jack has to stay. I wouldn't feel right staying without him."

"Wouldn't that be a bloody shame?" June muttered. But no one seemed to be paying the least bit of attention to her.

"Here it is!" Nicky unearthed a crumpled piece of paper from the depths of his bag, waving it triumphantly in the air. "See? My birth certificate! That's how I know I belong to you, Auntie June Bug. It says right here. Mother's maiden name."

"Christine Howard," June read slowly, forming the words aloud in wonder. She felt tears sting her eyes at the sight of this name, so beloved to her, and so very lost for all these years. But she absolutely refused to let them fall, not after holding them back for so long. If she started crying now, she might never stop.

"Then you can go to school. A birth certificate is all you need," Doc beamed. "I can take you on Monday. I know the principal. I used to look after his family."

School? Auntie June Bug? It was all happening much too fast. "I have a few misgivings," she said. In truth, June was full to the brim, almost overflowing, with misgivings. So many that she had no idea how to start verbalizing them.

Doc paid no mind to her. He was focused on the boy. "Do you

have any way to prove that you've had your vaccinations? You'll need them to start school."

June stared at Doc in amazement.

"I know what you're thinking, Junie. But I do remember some things, you know."

"I know you do, Doc. It's not that. It's just that—"

"Here it is!" Nicky had exhumed another grubby paper from his backpack. "I made sure to get these when my mom died. She always carried them in a little pouch."

He handed it to Doc, who studied it.

"Yes indeed," he affirmed. "Tetanus, diphtheria, pertussis, and polio. That's the Tdap-IPV vaccine. And measles, mumps, rubella, chickenpox. That's the MMRV vaccine. That's it, my boy. You're all set! I'll take you up to Laventra Public School first thing Monday morning. That gives us a whole two days to get you organized."

June marvelled at the mind of this man. Some days, she had to help him get his shirt buttons aligned with the buttonholes, and yet here he was, rhyming off the mandatory childhood vaccines without a second thought.

Doc and the boy observed June now, waiting for an answer. It was her move.

She still could not believe that this scruffy boy belonged to her sister. She couldn't fathom the thought that Chrissy had been alive, sharing this world with her, right up until three months ago. It seemed so surreal. Shouldn't she have known, or somehow felt her presence in the universe? Knowing that Chrissy had made a conscious choice to simply never come back home to her was what hurt the most.

And now, how on earth was she to turn this scrap of a child away into the cold, heartless world? The sensible thing to do would be to march him down to the police station and let the foster care system take over. But June Howard could no more do that than she could have flown to the moon.

And Doc seemed to have made these decisions for all of them, which included letting the huge, roast-stealing thief of a dog stay.

She rose to her feet and opened the door to the house. It smelled suspiciously like something wonderful was cooking in the kitchen.

She stood there, indicating for them to enter.

"Get in here, you two," she said, sighing in resignation. "You can stay the night. That's all, mind you, just one night. Just long enough to get things sorted out."

"Jack, too?"

"Yes, all right, fine. He can come in, but just for a while," she said grudgingly. She averted her eyes from Nicky and the stark longing that sprang into his weary face.

Doc clapped his hands with glee. "Welcome home!"

Chapter Four

JUNE'S world was spiralling out of control. Her mind whirled about, working itself into a state of chaos.

"Nicky can take the blue room, just down the hall from me," Doc offered helpfully after they had eaten supper. "That's a nice room for a boy."

"Oh, yes, and Jack will like that one, too," Nicky piped up eagerly.

"Jack?"

"Yes, Auntie June Bug. Shaggy Jack here. You met him outside."

"Of course, I know who he is. If you recall, I said he could come in for a little while. He can spend the night outside. It's warm enough now. And I still have no idea how I'm going to make it up to Fred Wilson about this roast situation."

"I'll get a job and pay him for it," Nicky volunteered. "There must be some place around here where I can work."

"Yes indeed," Doc said eagerly. "There are a few places looking for help from a fine young man such as yourself. I know lots of people I can talk to about that. Don't you worry, Nicky boy."

"I won't."

"But I will," June intervened. "Nicky, you're only thirteen—"

"I'm almost fourteen!"

"That's how it goes!" Doc interjected cheerfully.

"Doc, you are *not* helping. It's not just about the roast. It's everything. This child just drifts onto our front lawn one fine day, and you want him to take up residence here, start school, and now look for a job!"

"And Jack," Nicky said, nodding his head along with these words. "Don't forget Jack."

"Oh, yes, and this fine fellow here," Doc conceded.

June looked at the two of them, shaking her head in disbelief. "Things don't just work like that."

"Why not?" The question came simultaneously from the mouths of both the boy and the old man. They promptly hooked pinkie fingers.

It took a superhuman effort for June to remain calm. "Because they just don't, that's all." She organized and reorganized the tea towels. "Come on, Doc. You know we can't just take in every stray that comes to the door."

Nicky scowled from the doorway. He was no stray.

Good, June thought, resolutely. *Take offense and take that beast and leave.* She was perfectly happy to have the boy go back to BC and leave her alone. She had already done her good deed when she took in Doc. She didn't need to extend any more charity to anyone else.

She tried to ignore the small, persistent inkling of some unknown emotion that simply would not allow her to turn her back on this boy. Not if there was any chance he could be her Chrissy's son.

Doc knew this, of course. He turned to look out the back window, viewing the series of kennels and sheds residing there.

"How many critters have you got back there just now, Junie dear?"

"Only three, Doc. And they're all paying customers."

"So you have a bit of extra room, I guess."

"Doc, I know where this is going. I can see right through you. These are animals whose owners pay me. I don't even have a kennel big enough to put this beast in, and I'd never be able to afford to feed him. I don't even think he's really a dog."

"He *must* be a dog," Nicky exclaimed. "What else could he be? Because dogs are man's best friend. Even Doc said so."

"That settles it, then, I guess." Her sarcasm floated over the heads of Nicky and Doc alike.

"He is quite the biggest dog I've ever seen," Doc said. "I'll tell you what, Nicky, I'll get out my iPad, and we can Google the biggest dog breeds in the world. Maybe our shaggy friend here will pop right up at us."

"It's not going to make any difference. He can't stay—not for good."

Doc left in search of his device with Nicky close behind, paying no attention.

Exasperated, June fussed about in the kitchen, eventually returning some time later with a delicious-looking Bundt cake and three plates. Doc and the boy were in the living room by now, having an animated conversation about dog breeds. Nicky waited politely until she handed him a huge slab of cake, and waited for the others to take their first bites before he dove in. June tried not to notice the famished manner in which he devoured it and how hungry he must have been. She tried to ignore the growing feelings of sadness and sympathy within her.

"What did you find out?" She couldn't resist asking, after they had made short work of the sticky treat.

"Well, we think we found some breeds that look like Jack," Doc said.

Nicky showed her images and explained, "That one is a Leonberger. And look at this one. It's an Irish wolfhound!"

"That looks more like him. Monstrosity of a dog. He probably weighs as much or more than you do, Doc."

"Oh, quite right. They can weigh up to 180 pounds. That's what it says here. This one is a St. Bernard."

"He looks like all of them. He's probably just a big, old mutt."

"It says here that wolfhounds are 'gentle giants.'"

Everyone's gaze turned to the dog who lay sprawled across the braided rug, seemingly without a care in the world.

"Jack is very sweet. I never felt afraid of him when he joined me, even though he's so big. And he just stayed by my side, like he wanted to come here too."

"No doubt. Other people were probably afraid he'd eat them up," June replied, but somehow her words held no sting.

"Look at him, Junie dear. He doesn't have a vicious bone in his body."

June stood up and let out a deep sigh that seemed to originate from the bottom of her toes. She gave a terse nod of her grizzled head.

"Oh, for God's sake, Doc! Just take him to the blue room. But only for tonight. One night, that's all."

Tears sprang to the boy's eyes. He swiftly dashed them away.

She wanted to tell him to bathe. She wanted to tell him so many things. But they could all wait.

Jack lifted his enormous head and proceeded to follow the two up the stairs. Almost stumbling with fatigue, Nicky turned and ran back, throwing his arms around June's plump shoulders.

She sat stock still, unused to and undesiring of any displays of affection.

Doc just waited patiently on the stairs. Doc had always been wise about matters of the heart.

It didn't take very long before she reached her arms up and around the boy, clutching his too-thin body close to hers. A sweetness, hitherto unknown, flowed through her like a warm burst of summer sunshine.

"Now, go on with you!" she muttered, thrusting him toward the waiting dog and man. "Before I change my mind."

And that was that.

Nicky and Shaggy Jack took up residence in the blue room. Not just for one night but for good. Doc had known this would be the case, but he also knew June, and he knew she had to come to terms with things in her own good time and in her own way.

June had never realized how easy it was to run away. She actually couldn't quite believe it. She remembered feeling so trapped when she was a teenager. Tied down with school and helping her grandparents at the boarding house, trying to keep her mother from lying in bed all day, trying to keep Chrissy on the straight and narrow—*a lot of good that had done*. June was quite sure that she would have been hunted down and brought back home if she'd tried to escape for more than a few extra hours.

Yet this reckless, carefree lad had just traipsed all across the country, literally, for three or four thousand kilometers and seemed quite unscathed, even picking up a dog of massive proportions along the way. June didn't know if this made her sad or envious. Certainly, her teenage self would have been envious. She remembered wanting to leave most days at that age.

But, alas, she had just stayed here, right here, in a vain attempt to keep everything going while her sister buggered off on her next big adventure. Like this son of hers.

And now he had come full circle. To the old boarding house. With the weirdest-looking, biggest, shaggiest dog June had ever seen.

Doc, true to his word, walked Nicky to school the following Monday. June, full of so many qualms she couldn't even begin to name them all, waved them off from the old porch. The dog walked beside Nicky, almost as tall as the boy's shoulders. It was quite a comical-looking trio.

June had fed the boy almost constantly over the weekend, taken him shopping for clothes that fit and were in one piece, not hanging together for dear life by a few lucky threads. June ran the bath twice a day for him to wash. The worst of the grime had been scrubbed away from his body, revealing sun-kissed, golden-brown skin beneath, tanned even in these early spring days.

June entertained countless worries about keeping this child, sending him to school, and arranging his life for him. Every time there came a rap at the kitchen door, she thought someone was there to take Nicholas Benton—his name according to his birth certificate—back from whence he'd come.

And she had no idea if that thought made her very relieved or very sad.

Doc arrived back, dog in tow, after a couple of hours during which a myriad of horrific scenarios had traipsed through June's worried brain.

"I made it!" he announced.

"Did you have any trouble?" They both knew what she was referring to.

"No, no, Junie dear. It was only that one time I had trouble and forgot the way home. Think about all the times I didn't forget."

She did not say that various people from the village had mentioned to her, on different occasions, that they had assisted Doc or given him directions when he'd seemed a little vague.

"I introduced Nicky to the principal and gave her his papers."

"She accepted them, with no problem?"

"She seemed to. Anyway, Nicky said he could walk home himself tonight. I told him I didn't mind going to get him."

The blind leading the blind, June thought to herself, stifling a giggle.

"I know what you're thinking."

"Oh no, Doc, you *really* don't."

Chapter Five

LIFE fell into a funny sort of pattern. School days, by virtue of their necessary routine, always seemed to fly by with a will of their own.

Nicky set off each morning, Shaggy Jack by his side. At the end of the side road, the dog would turn and saunter back to the boarding house.

June felt her added responsibilities weighing heavily on her shoulders. A teenager and a big dog, on top of the business of running the kennels.

And Doc, of course. Doc was a joy but also a worry in some ways.

He still possessed a valid driver's license. This fact, in itself, was enough to make June's blood pressure complain.

One day, soon after Doc had moved to the boarding house, she had stood at the end of her lane, watching his rusty old truck disappear in a cloud of smoke and dust. Fred Wilson had happened upon her, out for his daily walk.

"He shouldn't be driving," she'd lamented to him. "He really shouldn't."

Fred had merely shrugged.

"I'm not sure how you can go about stopping him. Can you talk to him about it?"

"Doc is the sweetest man in the world, but he isn't realistic about his condition. He knows that he has memory problems, but he says he'll never forget how to drive Mr. Clatterbox any more than he'd forget how to breathe."

Mr. Clatterbox was what Doc had named his Dodge Ram truck.

SHAGGY JACK

"But he's okay most of the time, isn't he?"

June sighed. "Yes, Fred, but it's a fine line."

"Well, at least he's living with you now. People were starting to get worried about him when he was living alone."

"Yes, he thought living here was a great idea. Said he'd always liked this old boarding house. But driving is a different story." Doc not only knew her house well, but he had also known June's grandparents and delivered her sister and her. Doc was almost like family, which was just another reason to worry.

"I suppose it's his last bit of independence." Fred sighed. "And he seems to manage all right. At least whenever Martha and I see him."

"Yes, he manages," she admitted, "but sometimes he forgets things. They just leave his mind. He's well aware of that. He says his mind goes blank like a big, empty screen, and he can't get anything back. He just has to wait. What if that happens while he's behind the wheel?"

"Well, at least he doesn't go too far. Just into the village."

"You can still have an accident. And he would just die if he thought he was responsible for someone's injury."

"True. Well, it's not like you can go to his family doctor to get a medical note for the MTO."

"That's just it," June agreed. "There's no doctor around but him. He'd have to go to Dalton to see Dr. Sheridan."

They'd shared a laugh over the irony.

Doc was happy living at the boarding house, but he wanted the newcomers to stay. He loved having them there, boy and dog alike.

Doc had taken to getting Jack to come and sit shotgun with him in Mr. Clatterbox. Jack overflowed the passenger seat, his head scrunched under the roof, so it usually hung out the truck window. Then they headed to town, windows open, country music blaring, looking for all the world like they should be driving through the scene of an old Western movie.

Doc told June that, even without Nicky, Jack sat there just as good as gold while Doc did his errands. People would stop and talk to him, fascinated by his size, and Jack always welcomed this attention.

Doc invariably returned with huge bags of dog food and various treats for Nicky.

"You don't have to do that, Doc," June scolded him gently. "You pay me more than enough for room and board. We don't even know if they will be able to stay."

"Why on earth wouldn't they stay?" Doc cried, stricken. "Nicky and Jack belong here."

"We don't know that, Doc. We don't know for sure he's even Chrissy's son."

"Of course he is. Just look at him."

"I do, Doc. I look at him every day and wonder. He's been here two weeks, and I feel like he's been here forever."

"But that's a good feeling."

"Is it? I don't know. You get attached to things and then they get snatched away."

"Junie dear, who on earth is going to snatch this boy away? You saw the look of him when he arrived. He hadn't been cared for in a long time."

"I just worry about it all. I wish I knew beyond a shadow of a doubt that he was my nephew."

SHAGGY JACK

"But you care about him already."

She didn't say anything to that.

"Don't you, Junie dear?" Doc prodded gently.

"Yes, I guess so." That was as much as she was willing to admit.

"Then what difference does it make?"

The shrill ringing of the landline echoed through the confines of the old boarding house. The caller ID read "Laventra Public School."

June, who had been anticipating problems for over two weeks, answered with great apprehension, heart pounding.

"Hello?"

"Hello, is that June Howard?" a woman's voice asked.

"Speaking."

"Hi, I'm here at the school with your Nicky; I was just wondering if you were home and maybe I could come over and have a little chat with you."

"Yeeees?" June answered hesitantly. "Is everything alright?"

"Oh yes, right as rain. We'll be there shortly, then. I'm going to walk home with him. He's been telling me about Shaggy Jack, who meets him on the road every day, and I'm so excited to meet him. See you soon!"

The caller rang off before June could reply. She was far too cheerful for June's liking. And what was school coming to, anyway? Since when did teachers walk students home unless something was very much amiss?

She knew they were getting close when Jack gathered his big body up and headed down the road.

He returned shortly, Nicky laughing and running beside him,

accompanied by a tiny, feminine figure. She didn't look like any teacher June had ever seen.

June rose from her wicker chair on the porch to meet her, feeling bulky and awkward beside this waif-like creature.

As they came closer, June realized that she was older than she'd first appeared, probably close to June's age. Her hair was white and wavy, flowing behind her in the afternoon sunlight. Chestnut brown eyes smiled from a face well-creased with laugh lines.

She stuck out a delicate hand to June. "Edith Moon," she announced. "But people call me Edie. And you're 'Auntie June,' I presume.

June shook the woman's hand. "You presume correctly. Can you tell me what's wrong?"

"Oh, nothing's wrong. Nicky is a wonderful boy."

"Yes, he is," agreed Doc, coming around the corner of the garden. "You got that right."

"Well, you must be Doc," the woman chuckled, a delighted glint in her smile.

"I must be!"

Edie broke into ready laughter.

"If nothing's wrong, why are you here, Ms. Moon?" June queried.

"Oh, please call me Edie."

"Why are you here, Edie?" Doc inquired.

"I wanted to talk about Nicholas, that's all."

"I've never had a teacher come out here before," June remarked warily.

"Oh goodness, I'm not a teacher."

"Then who are you?"

SHAGGY JACK

This time, the words came out in a terse and accusing tone, but June didn't care. She glared at Edie Moon, who continued to smile relentlessly.

Like a bloody Cheshire cat, June thought. *It's not normal.*

"I'm a volunteer at the school. I used to be a nurse, but I'm retired now. I didn't want to be idle after having such a busy career, so I started volunteering. I've been helping students with their reading for, oh, five years now."

June and Doc nodded, each trying, in their own way, to follow along with this woman who refused to get to the point. Nicky and Jack rolled around in the sweet spring grass.

They're the lucky ones, June thought, *not having to endure a visit from little Miss Not-Teacher.*

"Do you want to hear a funny story about my reading students?"

"We would love to!" Doc said, to June's dismay.

"My nephew took me to see that musical 'Bat out of Hell' that was playing down in Toronto, you know?"

"We know where Toronto is," June replied wryly. Her belligerent manner seemed to have no effect whatsoever on this small woman. June was beginning to wonder if she was all there.

"Of course you do. Anyway, Bob, that's my nephew, bought me a shirt and it said 'Bat out of Hell' on the front. I wore it to school one day, and one of my students reamed me out for having a swear word on my shirt. I told him I thought he was in my class because he had trouble reading. He informed me that swear words were no problem to read. I never wore that shirt again."

June gave a perfunctory laugh.

Doc asked, "What's this got to do with our Nicky?"

"You're right, dear Doc. I'm beating around the bush."

"Did I say that?" dear Doc asked, mystified now.

Someone needed to take control of the situation. With hands on her hips, June said, "Come inside and have a cuppa so you can tell us exactly what you came to tell us."

"Oh, good," Doc said with relief, "because I'm lost. *I mean even more than usual.*"

"Oh, we're all a little lost, Doc, don't you think?" Edie asked brightly, allowing herself to be ushered inside to a seat at the table in the cozy kitchen. Once June had put out a plate of cookies and poured each of them a cup of tea (just because she was annoyed didn't mean she was going to ignore proper host etiquette), she took her seat. "Okay, shoot!" she said to Edie. "I mean it. Tell us exactly what you came here to tell us. No talking about Meatloaf and swear words. Just tell us what this visit is about."

Doc's face brightened. "Meatloaf? Are we having meatloaf?"

Edie placed her half-eaten cookie and mug onto the blue gingham tablecloth and cleared her throat.

June shushed him. "I'll explain later."

Edie took a deep breath. "Okay, so as I've told you, I help Nicholas with his reading. And what I've noticed is that, well, he is a little behind in his reading, even though he tries hard."

"That's not surprising," June replied, relieved beyond measure that this annoying woman hadn't been there to share some terrible news about the boy. What a lot of fuss about nothing!

"You're not surprised then?"

"Well, no, not really. I mean, he's been through a lot. We don't even actually know how much he's been through. He's bound to be a little behind." She and Doc could always help the boy with his reading. The whole summer lay ahead of them.

"Well, I was a nurse—"

"And I was a doctor!" Doc shouted in delight.

And I'm going crazy.

"I think . . . no, I'm quite sure that Nicholas needs glasses. Eyeglasses. I think he has astigmatism. And that's why he's behind in his reading."

"That's it?" June exploded. "You think Nicky needs glasses?" Here, June had been having a small heart attack, wondering what awful news this strange woman was there to share about the boy, and in the end, it was a recommendation for a trip to the optometrist? "You could have said that in the first fifteen seconds of your visit out on the lawn. Hell, you could have said that on the phone!"

"But then I wouldn't have tasted your delicious chocolate chip cookies," Edie replied, clearly unruffled by June's outburst.

Chapter Six

Doc and June stood together at the door, watching as Edie Moon walked down the road. June was relieved by her exit and annoyed by the entire visit. Before she was out of sight, Edie turned and waved, calling out a merry goodbye.

Doc returned the sentiment with a vigorous wave of his arm, and June rolled her eyes.

"What a nice, cheerful little person," Doc remarked.

"Far too bloody cheerful for my liking."

"Aw, now, Junie dear, there's nothing wrong with being happy."

"Not *that* happy," June grumped as they returned to the kitchen.

"You could try it sometime," Doc observed.

June ignored him, her mind already racing ahead to all the chores that seemed to be piling up on her plate at record speed.

In addition to caring for four dogs that were boarding with her that week, she was going to have to make an eye appointment for her young charge.

She'd call first thing in the morning. She didn't want another visit from that relentlessly cheerful, bright-eyed not-teacher, who would be sure to be checking to make sure an appointment had been booked.

June muttered words to that effect to Doc, who was setting the plates out on the table as he did every night.

"I just think she cares about our Nicky," Doc replied. "She just wants him to be able to read better."

"That'll be a whole other job for us then. I had no idea he was behind in his reading."

"You're so busy, Junie. I wish I could help a little more, but that's one of the things I have trouble with sometimes," Doc admitted. "Reading is so important. You need it for everything."

June had forgotten momentarily that Doc's "condition" meant he wouldn't be much of a helper when it came to reading. She patted him on the shoulder, her heart swelling with affection. "It's okay, Doc. You did so much, looking after everybody for so long, you've just worn that part of your brain out, is all. We'll figure it out." She hated watching him realize that he was losing parts of himself, one at a time. She wished she could freeze time for him. Or better yet, reverse it for both of them.

The next week found June and Nicky in the optometrist's office, who, after the better part of an hour, confirmed that Nicky did indeed have astigmatism and needed glasses. So Edie Moon had been frustratingly accurate on both accounts.

The optometrist explained Nicky's condition: "Astigmatism is an imperfection in the curvature of the eye. It happens when your cornea or lens has a different shape than normal. The shape makes light bend differently as it enters your eye, causing a refractive error. Sometimes the condition causes blurry vision and headaches, but it's easily fixable with glasses." The eye doctor turned to Nicky. "Don't worry. Your eyes will be as good as new in no time."

June and Nicky spent over an hour choosing glasses for the boy.

He must have tried on every single set of frames in the showroom until June gave in to bribery. "Look, if you choose your glasses in the next five minutes, I'll make you those peanut butter cookies that you love so much."

He had taken a liking to her cooking, especially to her cookie recipes, which had been handed down to her from her grandmother.

Suspiciously, it only took about three seconds for Nicky to find the frames he wanted. "These! I like these ones!" He took a set and gave it to the optometrist proudly. That's when it dawned on June that Nicky had been dawdling just to spend more time with her. She felt a twinge of guilt.

"Come on, Nicky. Let's go home," she sighed. They left the office, drove to the house, and ate so many cookies that it spoiled their supper. And June was fine with that.

A week later, the glasses were ready.

Nicky tried them on and gave a hesitant smile when the technician held up a mirror. "I don't look too bad!"

"I think you look incredibly handsome," the technician said.

"Really?" He brightened like the sun.

"Yes indeed." June nodded her agreement. "They suit you well."

He marvelled at his new vision all the way home. It was a whole new world! "I can see everything! Even where the leaves come out of the branches. They're so clear! I never saw that before."

"Well, reading should be a whole lot easier now," June told him, her lips curled up in a smile she could barely hide. She had to turn her head so he wouldn't notice.

He jumped out of the car the instant it pulled into the lane. Doc was on the lawn, throwing a stick for Jack to fetch.

SHAGGY JACK

Nicky ran to them, flinging his arms around the dog's neck.

"I can see! I can see!" he squealed, half as a joke, and half out of pure excitement.

"You look just wonderful, Nicky," Doc exclaimed. "So intelligent."

"I feel smarter, just because I can see better. Do you think it works like that, Doc?"

"Oh, yes. I'm quite sure it does. How do I look to you?"

"You look amazing! You look like an imaginary friend I had when I was little."

"What?"

"Yeah, I always thought it would be nice to have a grandpa, so I made one up as my imaginary friend. I never told anybody that before."

"Well, just imagine that!" Doc beamed, pleased as punch.

"I did!"

They shared a chuckle.

"Everything looks amazing! I can see so clearly!" Nicky spun around in whirls of excitement. "And Jack looks like the best-looking dog in the whole world."

"He certainly must be the biggest," June said.

"And he's the best, too, Auntie June Bug, the very best."

CHAPTER SEVEN

DURING the course of supper that night, Nicky casually remarked that Edie was planning to come out to the house three nights a week to help him with his reading.

"You call her Edie?" June didn't think children should be on a first-name basis with adults. It just wasn't right.

"She told me to."

"I thought the whole idea was for Edie to provide extra reading help *at school*."

"That's true, but we decided it would be nicer for her to come here."

"Oh, *we* did, did we?"

"Yup," Nicky said and shovelled a huge forkful of lasagna into his mouth. "She said how nice it was here and how she enjoyed her visit. She likes Doc and Jack. And even you, Auntie June Bug."

"Even me? Shocking!"

"I know, that's what I thought," he declared, with an impish grin. "And I said she should come out again. She said she couldn't impose, and I told her it wouldn't be imposing—"

"Slow down there. You *invited* her here for reading help?"

"In a nutshell, yes."

"In a nutshell! Who even says that?"

"Edie."

"Of course she does." June sighed. She did not like the way things were shaping up. Not one little bit. She had too much to do already. She didn't need any extra people hanging around her house. She certainly had no intention of entertaining the woman. Edie could help Nicky and then be on her merry way.

Sure enough, the next afternoon after school, Jack returned from his daily pilgrimage accompanied by two personages—Nicky and Edie.

She was effusive as ever, happy to see everyone. She probably wanted credit for diagnosing Nicky's astigmatism, which June was *not* about to award her.

Under her arm, she held an ancient Scrabble game. "I thought this would help Nicky with his words and spelling. Maybe we can all play."

"Scrabble!" Doc exclaimed with glee.

June muttered some choice words under her breath as she made dinner preparations.

The pair worked away at the kitchen table while she prepared dinner, making it impossible to ignore them.

Even June noticed, begrudgingly, that this Edie woman was very patient and kind with Nicky. And it really would be wonderful if he could get caught up in his schoolwork. She wondered how he had even made it this far if he couldn't see properly. No wonder he was behind in reading. She tried not to think about what kind of life he had endured before showing up on her doorstep. He was so young. And whatever life he'd had was one that he had walked very far to get away from.

"Right, Auntie June Bug?"

Nicky's words broke through her reverie. "Sorry, what's that?"

"Nicky was just telling me how wonderful you and Doc have

been to him. And how happy he is to live here with all this room to run around. And to have Shaggy Jack."

June smiled, in spite of herself.

"I'm glad to hear that. We're happy he's here, too." As the words left her mouth, she realized, with a start of amazement, that she meant them.

"Really, Auntie June Bug?"

"Don't you push it now!"

Edie added, "And how beautiful everything looks now that he can see properly."

Here it comes, June thought. *She'll be wanting accolades for making the diagnosis.*

"Everything *is* beautiful!" Nicky cried. "Everything in the world! Edie and Jack and Doc, and most of all you, Auntie June Bug."

"Don't be ridiculous," June scoffed.

"I'm not ridiculous. You are the most beautiful aunt in the world."

"I'm old and plain and shaped like a cube."

Edie observed her, seeming to consider this remark, but said nothing.

"Anyway, how's the reading going?" June changed the subject.

"Top drawer. Nicky here is doing very well. I'm just so proud of him."

"I am, too," June said, permitting herself a slight, barely noticeable smile at the woman. "So, are you done for the day?"

"We're done with the lesson, yes, but we were hoping to play at least one game of Scrabble."

June stole a look at the clock, which did not escape Edie's notice.

"But it's getting kind of late, isn't it? I should be going."

SHAGGY JACK

The woman could take a hint at least.

"I wish you could stay for a while longer," Nicky told her, throwing a beseeching look in June's direction.

Swallowing her irritation for Nicky's sake, June asked Edie, "Why don't you stay for dinner? Then we can have a game afterwards before it gets too late."

The pair were delighted with this, as was Doc, who had just wandered into the kitchen.

June made a mental note to speak to Nicky afterward. This was not going to happen every time he had a reading lesson.

Everyone ate heartily, declaring the meal a delicious one.

And June had to admit that it was rather fun to gather around the table afterward and play a silly board game. She was winning, too, which was even more enjoyable.

The game was almost finished when Edie used all her remaining tiles to create her last word. "Cube! That's eight points!"

"Cube?" Nicky asked. "Like the shape?"

"Yes indeed," Doc told him.

"My favourite shape," Edie said, looking June full in the face.

June felt the colour rise in her cheeks.

Silly woman! Why would she say that?

Chapter Eight

June's days fell into a comfortable rhythm. Life seemed lighter somehow, brimming with chores and household tasks, but rounds of fun and laughter too.

Some days, June felt as if she should pinch herself, just to be sure that this was really her—this new woman who ruffled a boy's hair in affection, chattered with Doc about anything and everything, and shouted out high-score words in the ensuing games of Scrabble.

She wondered if this was what it felt like to be happy. It had been many years since she'd felt anything even close to this. She voiced these sentiments to Doc one afternoon as they settled on the porch, after cleaning out the kennels.

"It's because of Nicky and Jack," Doc declared over his glass of iced tea.

It was the last day of school, and Jack had trotted off down the lane to meet Nicky. You could set your clock by Jack.

"I suppose."

"You are wonderful to me, Junie dear, but it was dull as dishwater around here before they came along. No offense."

"Oh, none taken," June retorted with a roll of her eyes. Doc took no notice.

"And Miss Edie, of course," he added.

June shrugged. She had gotten used to the woman and had to admit a reluctant affection toward her. It was difficult to stay annoyed with someone like Edie, who was always in such an unfailingly good mood and seemed to genuinely enjoy spending time with them.

SHAGGY JACK

"I don't suppose we'll see much of her now that it's summer holidays," she remarked.

"I don't know. I think you'll find that she'll come around some. She seems to like it here. She's only got a wee room in town. I'm sure it gets pretty cramped in the nice weather. She likes being outside like we do."

At that moment, Nicky and Edie turned the corner of the lane with Jack strolling along between them, like a giant caricature of a dog, shaggy fur in complete disorder as always. Gales of laughter greeted them, drifting on the warm afternoon breeze.

"Looks like you're right, Doc."

"Is that okay with you, Junie?"

"Oh sure. It's pretty hard not to like someone who's been so good to our boy, isn't it?"

Doc nodded his agreement. "Yes indeed. And she's like us. Not too many people are."

June opened her mouth to argue, then promptly shut it.

Because, of course, it was true. They weren't like most people. She and Doc and Nicky, too, were of the same strange tribe. It was difficult to explain, but somehow Edie also belonged there, too.

A kindred spirit, June thought, thinking of *Anne of Green Gables*, a memory from so long ago. After all these years, she had found a kindred spirit. Or, more accurately, a kindred spirit had found her.

Edie Moon was small and sweet, possessing an open heart, shining eyes, and a kind smile. She hugged trees, wished on stars, smiled at sunsets, gazed in awe at the wings of butterflies, kissed animals, and always stopped to tuck a loving finger under a flower petal as she paused to inhale its fragrance.

High spirits prevailed today as they approached the porch.

"School's out!" Nicky cried. "And I got my report card!"

June reached down to accept the proffered paper.

June's eyes scanned the report card, pleased beyond measure as they landed on an abundance of A's. Nicky had worked hard, and it was reflected in the paper she clutched in her hands.

"That's very good, Nicky."

"It's the best one I've ever had," Nicky declared. "And it's all because of you guys. It's like I was meant to come here and be with you."

June stood up and pulled the boy to her in an awkward hug. She couldn't remember the last time she had properly hugged another human being. Tears stung her eyes.

Edie, bold as brass, wormed her way into the hug. Doc, not wanting to be left out, threw his long arms around all three of them.

June, mindful that displaying emotions made her thoroughly uncomfortable, attempted to extricate herself from the unaccustomed group embrace.

But Edie and Nicky held her substantial body firmly.

"Wait, Junie dear," Doc said, in a voice so low it was almost a whisper. "Just wait right here with us. We're having a moment."

"Is *that* what you call it?"

"Yes, a little celebration moment."

"We're quite a motley crew to be sure," June observed.

"The very best kind," Edie pronounced, her brown eyes shining.

"I don't even know what that means," Nicky said.

"Well, Nicky Boy," Doc said, finally allowing June to pull away.

SHAGGY JACK

"It just means that here we are. We were all on our own, and we found our way here. And now we have each other."

Chapter Nine

A whole summer of long, sunny days stretched ahead in all their golden glory, making everyone happy of heart and light of spirit.

June wondered what she'd done before Nicky had come to live with them. He helped with cleaning out the kennels, walking the boarded dogs, and performing all manner of outside chores.

He seemed to have a real knack with the dogs. Even the timid ones responded well to him.

As the summer days tumbled over each other in record speed, Edie Moon became a fixture around the boarding house, a fact encouraged by both Nicky and Doc in equal portions.

One warm afternoon, Edie followed June into the kitchen. She placed her small hands on June's shoulders, turning her around to face her. "Are you a friend of Dorothy?" Edie's face was dead serious as she presented her odd question to a confused June.

"Dorothy? Dorothy who?"

Edie just shook her head. "Oh, that's okay. I just wondered."

"The only Dorothy I ever knew was from the Golden Girls."

Edie laughed a little. "That's fine. Just forget I asked."

"But why—"

Before June could finish her question, Edie flashed a smile and picked up the tray of cookies. "Let me help you take the cookies out to the porch. The fellas will be drooling on the porch by now at the thought of your cookies."

June didn't argue. She followed Edie, bearing a pitcher of

lemonade, happy for the chance to enjoy a rest in the middle of the summer afternoon. There was that word again. *Happy.*

Later, when she and Doc sat down with coffee after supper, she remembered Edie's strange question. "Do you have any idea why Edie would ask me if I was a friend of Dorothy?" She often used him as a sounding board, expecting nothing more than an off-handed laugh. He wasn't usually one to offer a sensible answer, but it was nicer than talking to herself. Doc was unfailingly pleasant but not usually too helpful.

This time, however, he chuckled a little, throwing her a sideways look. "I actually do know what that means."

"You do?"

"Yes. I'm pretty sure I do."

"Like, you know this Dorothy person?"

"I think it's referring to Dorothy Gale from The Wizard of Oz. But don't quote me on that."

"Oh, Doc, I never do."

"Do what?"

"Quote you."

"I'm not sure if that's a compliment or not."

"Me neither, Doc. Don't worry about it. I was just being silly. Do you know why Edie would be asking me about a character in a movie that's over eighty years old?"

"It was a great movie, though, don't you think, Junie dear?"

"Yes," she admitted. "It's timeless, really."

"I agree. One of the best ever. I loved all the characters, but I loved the Tin Woodman best, I think. He only wanted a heart, poor fellow. Didn't realize that life would be much easier without one."

"Would it, do you think?"

"For sure. Then you could make decisions with just your mind and think how much more sensible they'd be."

"I suppose. But then you'd never really know what it's like to love someone."

"Wow, somebody's mellowed in the last little while."

June scoffed. "Maybe a little bit."

"It suits you."

"Okay, Doc, enough of that. You were going to tell me about being a friend of Dorothy."

"Right. I've never heard it referring to a woman before, but I think that term goes back to World War II. And it was a slang word for a gay man."

June was mystified. What on earth was Doc talking about?

He continued, "Because, you see, it was illegal to be a homosexual in those days."

"Okay, Doc, I have no idea what you're talking about. What on earth does being a homosexual have to do with The Wizard of Oz?"

"Judy Garland was supportive of the gay community. In those days, being gay was kept much more secret than it is now."

"Doc, I gotta say, you sound like you know what you're talking about, but I still don't get it."

Doc just looked at her for a moment. "And they say I'm the one who's mixed up," he muttered.

June stared at him until Doc could see the little light bulb sparking in her brain.

"Edie was asking me if I'm gay?" she gasped in amazement.

"I think so. I'm not sure, but I think so."

SHAGGY JACK

A plethora of emotions swept through June—anger, offense, annoyance, confusion . . .

Several full moments passed before she whispered to Doc. "Am I, do you think?"

"Junie dear, you are the only person who can answer that question."

Jack and Nicky bounded up the porch stairs just then, full of energy and laughter.

"You guys look serious. What are you talking about?"

June shook her head. "I truly have no idea."

Nicky threw Doc a quizzical glance, but Doc merely shrugged. He couldn't have said with absolute certainty either.

After the house had settled into the sweet rhythm of the summer evening, June searched her soul. Only the song of crickets and the occasional hoot of an owl broke the stillness of the countryside.

Truth be told, her sexual orientation was something she hadn't considered much in her life, at least not in many years. She just assumed she was asexual. She'd googled it once, discovering that it really was a thing. A person could be asexual, meaning that they felt little or no sexual attraction to others.

When she was younger, several men had asked her out, and she'd gone. It had been pleasant enough. She hadn't hated it, but she hadn't loved it either. She'd certainly never experienced that delirious, head-over-heels attraction depicted in books and movies.

June thought back to when her father left. He hadn't been much of a father to her and Chrissy, never displaying affection or even much attention to his daughters. Yet his leaving had ripped a hole in their world. Her mother, who barely coped with everyday life when their father was there, stopped coping at all after his departure. She simply ceased to function as a parent.

Then her mother started allowing strange men to visit at all hours of the night.

She could still remember them, try as she might to put them out of her mind. Their wandering hands, their roving eyes, their offhand, vulgar remarks. She tried to tell her mother over and over, saying that they made her uncomfortable and that she didn't want them in the house. Her mother pretended to listen, but she had stopped listening by then.

That's when June had washed her hands of men, deciding once and for all that she wanted nothing to do with any of them.

Sometimes at night, when memories drifted back to her on the reaches of darkness, she still cringed at the utter crudeness of those men. Even though she hadn't technically been sexually assaulted by any of them, the threat of it, the possibility of it, hung in the air around her and haunted her for many years, long after her mother had passed away, returning to her in the wee hours of the night as past horrors do.

She'd retreated from close relationships, remaining friendly and pleasant with neighbours and clients, but never desiring intimacy from anyone.

All these things ran through her mind as she lay in her bed, wide awake. A bed that had always been hers and hers alone.

She'd googled the term after everyone had retired for the night

SHAGGY JACK

and had found, to her astonishment, that Doc had been right about the term "friend of Dorothy."

June felt so far behind that she may well have been first.

She thought about Edie Moon, that little will-o'-the-wisp of a woman. She brought to mind her pretty smile, her ready laughter, and her undying interest in everyone, even the dogs at the boarding house.

Had all that interest been feigned because she suspected June was gay? And how on earth would *she* know that, when June herself had no idea? What could she possibly see in a grouchy old maid, with grizzled hair and a lined face, laden down with life's cares and woes?

She didn't know, could never even imagine, the way Edie saw her; the gentleness of June's hands as she stroked the flyaway, tangled hair of Jack, the kindness in her smile as she cared for Nicky, the patience in her voice when Doc was having a bad day, asking the same question over and over again.

And now, June Howard was about to find out about the birds and the bees at the belated age of sixty-three.

Chapter Ten

Doc never mentioned the Dorothy conversation again. That was the great thing about Doc. After the conversation was over, the entire thing flew out of his mind. Sometimes, even *before* the conversation was over. It could be annoying, but in this case, June was grateful for Doc's memory lapses.

When Edie next visited, June decided to take the bull by the horns. She sat down gingerly beside her on the porch, took a deep breath, and began.

"About our conversation the other day."

"Oh, June, just forget it. I was out of line, and I'm sorry. I shouldn't have used that term. We're friends now, and that makes me so happy. Let's just leave it at that."

"That's tempting."

"We'll do that then, June. We'll be good friends. I love all of you, and I love coming here. I don't want anything to jeopardize that."

"I don't either. I like you coming here, too. We've had some good times these last few months."

"Yes indeed."

"I just wanted to say, Edie, that I didn't know what you were talking about the other day when you asked me that."

"It's okay, June. Really."

"But Doc explained it to me."

"Doc??" Edie cried in astonishment. "*Our* Doc?"

June warmed to her words. "Yes, our Doc.".

"Wow, that's surprising."

June sighed. "Doc never ceases to amaze."

"He's a lovely soul. He must have been a wonderful family doctor."

"Oh, he was. Always kind and patient. Much like he is now."

"I guess people don't change their personality too much," Edie observed. "As they get older, I mean."

"And he was always professional as I was growing up, which I appreciated. It's hard enough to be a teenage girl."

"Yeah," Edie agreed. "Puberty's a bitch."

Both women laughed, well aware they were skirting around the main issue.

June confided, "One day, when I was about sixteen, my mom brought me to him for something. I can't even really remember what for, but I must have had some kind of a bug or something because Doc was explaining things in that soothing voice of his. I guess he meant to say 'organism' but instead, he said 'orgasm'."

Edie burst out laughing.

"Poor Doc! What did your mom say?"

"She didn't say anything. She wasn't very interested in much by that time. But I was old enough to know what it meant, and I started laughing. Poor Doc turned as red as a beet. He put his hand on my shoulder and said, 'So sorry, Junie dear—'"

"Wait. He called you that, even then?"

"He did so. Then he told me he'd been up delivering a baby all night and hadn't slept yet. He just got his words mixed up. I managed to control myself and told him it was fine. He recovered, laughed, and declared that it was better to be having an orgasm than a baby or something like that. I don't remember his exact words."

"That's a great story," Edie said.

"Funny, I hadn't thought about that in years. Anyway, speaking of orgasms—"

"Or lack thereof!"

"Exactly. Anyway, I always thought I was asexual."

"Really? Is that actually a thing?"

"It is. I Googled it a while ago."

Edie looked like she was trying to picture June googling sexuality terminology. "And . . . do you still think you are?"

June sighed, burying her head in her hands in frustration and embarrassment. "I don't know, Edie! I really don't!"

"I'm sorry. I didn't mean to make you uncomfortable."

June thought it was absurd to be struggling with such a basic question at her age.

Edie placed her small, slender hands atop June's broad, work-roughened ones. "It doesn't matter. I value your friendship—all of you. I don't want to lose that."

June smiled, touched by these words. Something inside of her heaved a huge sigh of relief. She hadn't realized that she'd been worried about losing Edie's friendship if she admitted to not being of the Wizard of Oz tribe. Or however that went.

"That's good," June said. "I'm glad of that." She took Edie's hand in her own and squeezed, her heart beating out of her chest.

They sat together in silence.

"You know, it's funny," June mused. "I was all by myself here, just running the kennels, looking after other people's dogs. I didn't get too attached to them because they weren't mine. I was alone, but I was content enough. Then Doc was in a bind and couldn't look after himself anymore. The council came to me and asked if he could board here. He wasn't bad enough to go to a nursing home, but he wasn't safe to be at home on his own either. I didn't want to take in an old doctor who was starting to forget things, no matter how nice he was. But I agreed, and he came, and it was okay. Then a runaway tramp of a boy showed up, who is probably my sister's boy. A sister I thought had died many years ago. And he brings a monstrosity of a dog with him, a dog comprising the two largest breeds known to man."

"Which two breeds?"

"Yeah, we're pretty sure we've got it narrowed down. Nicky looked it up. Irish wolfhound and Newfoundlander."

"Wow, sounds like quite the conglomeration."

"That should be Jack's new name."

Both women chuckled softly.

"Anyway," Edie ventured, "you were saying you didn't want any of them. Or me, I suppose. I just kind of came here and kept on coming."

"No, I didn't. I liked my peace, my own space. I didn't want any of you . . ."

Before anyone could ponder that thought, they were interrupted by the sound of Mr. Clatterbox rattling down the lane. Jack's massive grey head hung out the back window, ears and tongue flapping in the breeze. Nicky hung out the passenger window in a similar fashion, holding something in his hands. They could hear the sound of Doc's old country station playing on the ancient radio. All three of the truck's inhabitants howled, quite literally, along to the music.

Nicky and Jack tumbled out of their seats before the truck had even completely stopped.

"Quick! Auntie June Bug! Edie! We got ice cream! You have to eat them quick before they melt!"

The two women took their cones from Nicky. "Doc even got a dilly bar for Jack."

Of course he did.

June turned to Edie, gave her hand a squeeze, and finished her thought.

"I don't know what in hell I'd do without any of you now."

Chapter Eleven

"WHAT the heck? Are you tired, Nicky?"

Nicky, sprawled across the lush summer grass, yawned ostentatiously several times. A long sigh followed each yawn. Jack lay beside him, face to face with the boy.

June took a spot in the grass alongside Nicky, her curiosity piqued. She threw back her head and laughed as Jack proceeded to open his considerable mouth, emitting a yawn of epic proportions.

"You made him yawn," Edie exclaimed.

Nicky rolled over and sat up in his grass-stained shorts.

"It's called a calming signal," he explained. "When you yawn at your dog, they'll yawn back at you. It's like an empathy thing because they want to be like you."

"I didn't know that," Edie said. "But it's kind of the same with people. I mean, if you're with someone who starts to yawn, chances are that you'll yawn too."

Nicky proceeded to crouch beside Edie and yawn in her face. Almost immediately, it was obvious that Edie was now stifling her own yawn.

The two women burst out laughing.

"Good Lord," Doc said, coming around the back corner. "And they say I'm the one who gets mixed up."

"Who says that, Doc?"

"You know. *They*. The Almighty *They*. But I'm not the one lying on the front lawn, yawning at people."

"Nicky is using a calming signal," June explained.

Doc stared at her and asked, "Is it working? Are you two ladies calming down?"

"It's not for us, you silly man," June retorted, throwing a dandelion head at him. "It's for Jack."

"Jack! Well, he's just lying there."

"See how well it worked!"

"I'm trying to find a way to communicate with dogs. Well, with Jack anyway," Nicky explained. "But I might try it out on some of the other dogs that come to the kennels."

"Like a dog whisperer?"

Nicky shrugged, looking a little sheepish. "Maybe. A little. I've always loved animals, and I just think it would be cool if we could communicate with them."

"Like Dr. Doolittle!" Doc exclaimed. "I've always envied that guy. You better watch what you say to the kennel dogs, though, Nicky my boy. They might go home and tell tales to their owners about the goings-on here."

When Doc made remarks like this, it was hard to tell if he was trying to be witty or becoming more demented. June decided she didn't want to know.

"I just think dogs are really smart. They can tell how you're feeling just by your smell."

"Well then, how do I smell?" Doc asked, taking a seat on the grass near the dog.

"I didn't really mean that so much as they can tell a change in how you feel," Nicky explained. "Like if you're happy or scared. Or if you're really sad,"

"Ah, I think that's quite true," Doc opined. "My old dog Sammy always knew how I felt. I never had to yawn in his face, though. I guess that's just your modern dogs. But if I felt really sad, he'd always lick my tears away."

June could hardly bear the thought of Doc crying. He'd wiped away so many tears of others in his long career.

"I can't remember one single thing that I would have cried about now. That's the great thing about being like I am. You can't remember what made you feel sad. Or glad, for that matter. It's all gone, like a big old blank."

"It's a great thing, is it, Doc?" Edie asked, her tone slightly teasing. She smiled warmly at the old man.

Doc merely shrugged.

"It is, you know. There's no use in remembering sad things. It'll just make you sad all over again. It's very nice to be here with you bunch, though. You never make me feel sad. Although I must say it's a little peculiar lying on the grass, yawning in each other's faces, but hey, I'm not judging."

They all laughed, reluctant to leave the soft fragrance of the warm grass.

"See that cloud up there, right above us? Doesn't it look like it's in the shape of Africa?" Edie mused, pointing at a particularly fluffy-looking cloud as it sailed lazily across the soft blue of the summer sky.

"It does, actually," June agreed.

"That's just the sort of cloud I want to land in when I'm all done on this old world," Doc remarked, smiling. "I want a nice, soft landing into a cloud that looks just like that one. I don't care if it looks like Africa or not, though."

"Oh, Doc, that won't be for years and years," Edie chided him gently.

"I hope not. I like it here with you bunch. I'd like to stick around a few more years if I can."

June reached over and patted Doc's forearm. Jack lifted his enormous head and nuzzled the old man's shoulder.

"You're a beautiful soul, Jack," Doc remarked, caressing the long, sprawling, grey ears. "If it weren't for dogs, some people would never be able to understand what unconditional love means. And I think there's a lot to be said for what our Nicky is saying. Our dog whisperer. Dogs are such great companions, aren't they?"

"They can't speak words, though. Wouldn't it be great if they could?" Nicky inquired.

"You could work on that, Nicky boy. You should see if you can get this shaggy old guy here to talk."

June scoffed.

"Doc, don't encourage him."

"Why not? It could happen. Parrots talk."

"In case you haven't noticed, Jack is approximately a thousand times bigger than a parrot."

"True, but you never know. I think if anyone could get Jack to talk, it would be Nicky."

June just shook her head, rolling over to enjoy the warmth of the afternoon sun.

Edie lay beside her, close but not quite touching. It felt very nice.

"Auntie June Bug?"

"Yes, my dear boy?"

"I know a couple of guys from school that I hung with a bit. I saw them yesterday when Doc and I went to the store. They were petting Jack. They'd never seen a dog like him before."

"I can well imagine that."

"Anyway, would it be all right if we got together to hang out?"

"Sure, that's fine. Who are they?"

"Max and Dillon."

"Do they have last names?"

"I guess so. I don't remember."

"I know them," Doc declared. "I can't think of their last names, but the one boy's father had to be institutionalized for—"

"Doc!" June interjected.

"Oh, I'm sorry. Sometimes things just come into my head."

"But you don't always have to say them out loud," she reminded him.

A few weeks before, June and Doc had encountered a middle-aged man from the village and exchanged greetings. As they turned to leave, Doc had made a remark to June regarding the man having had a bad case of gonorrhea in his younger days.

June, aghast, had shushed him and hurried him out of the store. He hadn't realized the magnitude of his error, and just said the first thing that popped into his head. The man had given no indication he'd overheard, for which June was sincerely grateful.

Because, as she told Edie later while reiterating the story, it's unlikely that you would bring the word "gonorrhea" up in casual conversation.

"Doc!" she'd scolded him. "You've lost your filters. You can't just say anything that comes into your head."

"I'm sorry, Junie dear. I'll try to find some of those filters," he'd replied, causing her to wonder if he had the faintest idea what she was trying to tell him.

Running her hand over the grass, June answered Nicky's question: "Sure, they can come here and hang out if you want. We've got lots of room."

"Really? You don't mind?"

"No, of course not. Why would I mind?"

Nicky just smiled and murmured his thanks.

"Maybe you'll all be dog whisperers. Wouldn't that be nice?" Doc exclaimed. "Dogs are smart. They know lots of things. And they're always sure about their own sexual orientation, too."

He directed this last offhand remark at the two middle-aged women on the grass, throwing them a pointed glance.

"Whatever," Nicky shrugged, utterly oblivious.

Edie and June exchanged a sideways glance, then burst out laughing.

"This is the best summer of my life," Nicky exclaimed one evening as he sauntered out of the kitchen to walk the kennel dogs. Only two dogs were boarding that week. He'd placed them on a double leash before proceeding to trot them down the side road. Jack lumbered off-leash beside them, taking long strides. The smaller dogs had to scramble to keep up.

Doc agreed with Nicky's proclamation. It had been the best summer ever. He didn't know how many he had left, or what kind of shape he'd be in when they came, but he certainly appreciated these beautiful days of companionship unfolding at the old boarding house.

"Keep those dogs away from my supper!" Fred Wilson shouted as Nicky set out down the road approaching Fred's house.

Nicky waved cheerfully.

Fred had forgiven Jack for his misdemeanour earlier in the spring, although he had not yet forgotten. Martha had done neither, of course.

This did not bother Nicky. He knew Jack had been ravenous at the time of the barbecue incident and was quite sure he'd never steal anything now. There was no need, since he had a good home and lots of food. And Doc supplied Jack with all kinds of treats, many of which would not impress June if she'd known. Of course, she didn't know, and Nicky never ratted out Doc.

The two boys Nicky had mentioned, Max and Dillon, visited often now, filling the place with their combined boyish energy and laughter.

Doc loved having them around. They helped him with several chores, and after only a few afternoons together, he dubbed them his "Huckleberries."

"What's a huckleberry?" Nicky asked, the first time Doc said it.

"A huckleberry is the exact right person for the job."

"What job?"

"Well, any old job at all. You boys suit me right down to the ground."

The boys shrugged. They'd been called worse.

They were good boys. Max was quite forthright while Dillon was much the shyer of the two. But both boys were pleasant, well-mannered, and treated Doc with respect even when his words were mixed up, or his memory was faulty, or his filters were nonexistent.

"Are you two ladies any further ahead with things?" Doc asked now, entering the kitchen where Edie and June were finishing up the last of the supper dishes.

"What do you mean, Doc?" Edie inquired.

June cringed inwardly. Damn it. Of all the things that slipped freely from Doc's short-term memory, it appeared as if their chat wasn't one of them.

Doc tilted his head and stared at June, who began fussing with a random tea towel as if it were the most important thing in the world. After an excruciating moment of silence, Doc sighed. "I can't remember exactly now. Pay no attention to an old man. I'm going outside to enjoy the last bit of sunshine with Nicky and Jack. The other boys have left to go home."

He gave June a little pat on the shoulder on his way out, causing her to wonder if he really had forgotten. Maybe he was attempting to give her an opening to this sensitive topic of conversation.

June had continued to struggle with the question of her own sexuality during these long summer days. She wished she had someone to talk to about it all, someone totally removed from the situation.

She'd been on her own for so very long. She'd gotten used to being alone and no longer even thought about her situation in life. But things were different now. She missed Edie the days she didn't come to visit. In fact, she missed everything about her—the sound of her laughter throughout the house, the rhythm of their easy banter, the feeling of goosebumps when Edie was nearby.

She took a deep breath and thought about all the words she should say. All that she could muster was, "I miss you when you're not here."

Edie knew what she meant. "I miss you too, June," she responded. "I think you know how I feel about you." She paused and smiled hesitantly at June. "But if you just want to be friends, that is fine with me. I will never mention the other again. I just always want to have you in my life."

June turned to face her, placing her big, rough hands on Edie's small shoulders. Then she drew a deep breath and gave a short, curt nod of assent.

"Are you sure?"

"As sure as I'll ever be," June declared, her voice trembling.

And so it happened that, when Doc and Nicky returned to the house an hour later, the kitchen lay empty in unaccustomed silence.

"Where's Auntie June Bug? And Edie?"

Doc indicated upstairs. Muffled giggling drifted down from the front bedroom. "Something's tickled their fancy," he told the boy.

"What's a fancy?"

"It's a lady thing."

"A lady thing? Doc, what are you talking about?"

Doc turned to the boy, considering. "It's a lady thing. Like a lesbian lady thing. You know what that is, right?"

Nicky nodded. "I know what it means, yeah." Nicky grappled with the idea for a few minutes, visibly confused. "Really?" he asked finally.

"Yes, really."

"Whoa! Who knew?" Nicky gasped, totally taken aback at this new turn of events.

But Doc knew. Of course he did. He'd known all along.

Nicky sent Doc, who seemed quite unconcerned, a quizzical look as he attempted to grasp the situation. "I don't care if they're lesbians, Doc. I mean, it's cool with me."

"It's cool with me, too," Doc said.

"It's just that," Nicky chuckled now, as he asked, "wow, like how long were we gone?"

Chapter Twelve

THE whole dynamics of the boarding house shifted.

June had been mortified, unsure if she could even show her face after that earth-shattering evening. Things had changed for her so completely, her whole perception of everything, including herself. *Especially* herself.

She felt totally awakened for the first time in her life. And to think that it was Edie, wee Edie Moon, small in stature but huge in kindness and goodwill, who had opened her eyes to who she actually was. And had always been, she supposed. She had no idea how these things worked.

Life rolled along without a hitch—the sunshine, the chores, and the beautiful company of Doc, Nicky, and his friends. Nothing had changed, and yet, everything had changed for June.

Sometimes she simply couldn't believe that she—crusty old maid June Howard—possessed the capacity to derive the degree of delirious happiness that she had somehow managed to attain. She wondered how she'd managed to live sixty-three years while oblivious to so much love and joy, not even believing that it could truly exist.

And Edie, sweet, kind, loving Edie, behaved just the same to her. She'd been a little concerned about this. Somehow, she'd always thought that the ultimate sexual act would change everything between two people, make things tense and difficult. But it hadn't. Perhaps she had become a little more outwardly demonstrative, but that was all. And June was gradually learning to accept this.

"So I didn't know that you two were lesbians," Nicky remarked casually over a breakfast of blueberry pancakes. Several days had passed since the evening Doc had dropped the bombshell. June choked on a mouthful of coffee, sputtering across the table.

"You're not the only one," Doc remarked, grinning.

"You didn't know either, Doc?"

"Oh, I did suspect, Nicky, my boy. I was talking about your Auntie June Bug here."

"*She* didn't know?"

Edie, who was generously pouring syrup on her pancakes, elaborated for the boy. "Sometimes, people just have to work different things out for themselves, and sometimes, it takes a while," she told him.

"Oh, okay," he shrugged. "Like lesbianism, I guess."

"Yes," Edie affirmed. "Like lesbianism. Do you mind, Nicky dear, that your aunt and I are more than just friends?"

"No, I don't care. As long as you guys are happy."

"We are. Very much so."

Nicky nodded, then added, "And as long as you both stay here and don't leave me."

"Nicky, that's never going to happen," June said, finding her words at last. "Never."

"Why would anyone mind anyway?" Doc asked. "About the lesbianism, I mean."

He speared a rogue blueberry and rolled it in the maple syrup on his plate, swallowing it with great gusto.

"You'd be surprised, Doc," Edie told him. "Some people still do mind."

"Well, that's up to them, I suppose. But I've always thought that you love who you love in this old world. And if you're lucky enough to find someone who loves you back, then you're pretty darned lucky for sure."

"Very nicely put, Doc," Edie murmured, placing her hand affectionately on the old man's arm.

"I have my moments," he winked.

"Doc doesn't actually remember too much. So you can basically tell him anything you want, and he'll just forget it," Nicky explained to his friends one day. Doc had just disappeared around the bend in Mr. Clatterbox, having made an offhand remark apropos of absolutely nothing at all.

"Isn't that annoying, though?" Dillon asked. "I don't think I'd like that, man."

"It's not annoying. It's awesome," Nicky replied. "Because you can say anything to him, like literally anything, and he doesn't remember. So he never stays mad about anything."

"I think that'd be cool," Max said. "I wish my mom was like that. I do one thing wrong, and she remembers forever. Whenever she gets mad at me, she brings up all the shit I did in the last million years."

"Oh, I wouldn't like that," Nicky said. "Auntie June Bug wouldn't do that. I don't think so anyway. I can't remember if she's ever been mad at me."

"You're lucky, dude. Do you think that's because she's a lesbian?"

"No idea. I've never known any before. At least . . . I don't think

I have. But her and Edie are great to me, so I don't care. Doc says you love who you love."

Both the other boys shrugged. They didn't care either.

"Well, it's great here, that's for sure," Max observed.

"Yeah, and you always get different dogs to walk. Who's here this week? Have you done any more lessons with them?" Dillon inquired.

Nicky rhymed off the list of dogs currently boarding at June's.

"That one dog, the one you just said, Leslie, she's been here before, hasn't she?"

"Yup," Nicky affirmed. "She comes quite a bit because her owner is old and can't walk her. Her daughter comes to visit, but when she does, she just brings Leslie here because she can't be bothered with her, and she doesn't like dogs."

"How can you not like dogs?" Dillon mused. "Leslie's a great dog."

Max shrugged. "Beats me. Leslie's probably got a better personality than the daughter."

The three boys dissolved into laughter.

"Probably." Nicky agreed. "Even Edie said she was unpleasant. The daughter, I mean, not Leslie. That's a lot for Edie. She doesn't usually say anything bad about anybody."

"Maybe you'll end up with Leslie for good," Max mused.

"That'd be all right. She's a nice girl," Nicky said. "But she's getting old. I don't think she sees very good." Leslie was often running right into the back of Jack on their walks, as if she didn't see him there. At first, it was funny and cute. But after a few times, Nicky wondered if it didn't mean something more serious.

"Maybe we could help her with that," Dillon said. "Maybe we

could get some old glasses and tie them to her head and see if she can see any better. We could ask Doc."

"I'm not sure if Doc would know about that," Max said, his voice tinged with uncertainty. "He gets pretty mixed up."

"Yeah, he does, but he still knows lots of things," Nicky said. "He knows all this random stuff."

"Too bad we couldn't just ask Leslie what's the trouble with her eyes," Dillon sighed. "Then we'd know how to help her see better."

"Well, we're working on that," Nicky reminded him.

Edie approached them with a tray of lemonade and cookies, catching the tail end of the boys' conversation. "Is that your summer project?" she asked. "Helping dogs to see?"

"Maybe," Max conceded. "A little."

Edie regarded the trio of youths and smiled. They seemed to be shot through with summer sunshine, blades of grass stuck in their hair, dirt stains on their knobby knees. Boys that age always seemed to be of the same tribe somehow. The outdoorsy ones, anyway. They were the ones Edie liked the best.

"I think it's marvellous," she told them.

"We think Leslie doesn't see so good," Max told her. "Maybe we could get her glasses. That might help."

"Yeah, like you did for me," Nicky told her, pointing at his spectacles that were hanging, as they often were, askew on his thin, young face.

"I'm not sure if it works that way for dogs," Edie pondered, squatting down beside the boys. "I've never seen a dog with glasses before. Wouldn't they just paw at them until they came off? They wouldn't understand that they're there to help them."

The boys thought about this.

"She gets around all right, though," Edie continued, in an effort to console. "I've never noticed her having any trouble. What makes you think she needs help with her vision?"

"I dunno," Nicky finally replied. "I guess I just think she looks like she's having trouble seeing where she's going sometimes."

"Well, she is getting older, that's for sure," Edie agreed. "I wish dogs lived longer. They're such nice animals."

"If you treat them right, they're nice," Max said, turning over to scratch Leslie's long, smooth ears. "If not, they can be mean."

"Well, isn't that true of every creature?" Edie asked.

June stepped out and onto the lawn to join the conversation.

By the time Doc returned in Mr. Clatterbox, who exuded a belch of exhaust fumes before coming to an unceremonious halt, the four of them were no further along in their medical diagnosis. He strode toward them now, grocery bags dangling from his long arms, a huge grin adorning his craggy features.

"Doc, what on earth have you got there? I thought you were just going for milk."

"Well, Junie dear, I did remember the milk."

"I'm glad to hear that because we're all out."

"Yes, you wrote down 'milk' for me and I remembered that, but then I couldn't remember if I was supposed to get anything to go with it. You know, to kind of . . . sweeten it up a bit."

"Sweeten it up?"

"Yes, so I got ice cream and cookies for dessert. They go well with milk, right?" He turned to the boys for approval, who, being boys, nodded their agreement enthusiastically.

"It doesn't have to be for dessert," Nicky told him. "Does it? I mean, can't we have it any time at all?"

"Hear, hear!" cried Doc, as if to pass an official proclamation for anytime-ice-cream. "I like the way you think, young man. Summertime is a great enough reason to have cookies and ice cream."

"Doc, you used to warn people about the dangers of eating things just like that."

"Oh, yes indeed. I did so. But I know better now."

June sighed in defeat.

"Hey, Doc," Max asked, sending the old man a sidelong look. "Was that lady you like working today? At the grocery store?"

Doc's face went completely blank.

"Do I like a lady at the grocery store, Nicky? I think I like them all. They're all good to me. You know when I forget things. As I do sometimes." He added this with the air of someone making a huge revelation.

"Of course they're nice to you, Doc," Edie told him. "You're quite a lovely man, you know."

"Thank you, my dear. I do what I can."

"But there's one Doc likes more than the others," Dillon persisted. "Or . . . let's say, he *admires* her more than the others."

Doc shrugged noncommittally. "Maybe," he replied, clearly not following.

Nicky laughed. "They're just teasing you, Doc, because last week when we went with you to the store, you mentioned something about her, um, legs."

"Her legs? Well, she does have a nice set of stems, if that's the one I'm thinking of. Sorry," he nodded to the women, "I know you're not supposed to say stuff like that anymore, but I was just making an observation." He winked at the boys. "I'm a leg man, you see."

It was hard to take offense at anything Doc said, even if you felt that, morally, you really should.

Max could hold it in no longer. "Doc told us last week that Melanie, that's her name, the one with the legs, has two nice legs that go up and make a perfect ass of themselves."

June groaned theatrically. "Did he at least wait until you'd left the store before making that observation?"

The boys exchanged looks again. "Not sure," Nicky said. "But he said it."

"I don't remember," Doc said.

"Doc, you can't always use that excuse," June told him.

"Sorry, Junie dear, it's the only one I've got. Oh, come on, let's go inside and have some cookies and ice cream before it melts in this heat."

"We'll spoil our appetites for supper," June protested.

"Oh, good. That's what summer's for," Doc declared.

"You just want to go back and get some more so you can see Melanie's perfect legs," June muttered.

"It's her ass that's perfect," Max corrected her, giggling.

"I think me and the Huckleberries need a summer project," Doc declared one August morning after weeding the same front garden for what felt like the hundredth time that week.

SHAGGY JACK

"If you say so, Doc," June said, wondering what on earth he would come up with next. "Did you have a specific summer project in mind?"

Doc looked puzzled. "What's that, dear?"

"You said you and the lads were thinking of a summer project."

"I did, didn't I? Did I say what it was?"

June sighed. "Why don't you come sit down and have a cup of tea? Maybe it'll come back to you."

Or maybe it wouldn't, with any luck at all. June was already exhausted with all the changes in her life and in her boarding house. Things were moving fast. It was almost unbelievable to acknowledge how much had changed in just a few months.

Nicky ran into the kitchen. As always, Shaggy Jack trotted alongside him. "Hey, Doc, did you ask Auntie Bug about the cobblestones?" Somewhere along the way of the summer, Nicky had dropped the "June" from "Junebug."

"Cobblestones!" Doc cried in jubilation. "I knew it would come to me."

June and Nicky exchanged indulgent smiles.

"Don't you think a cobblestone path would look nice coming up from the driveway?" Doc asked her now.

June considered the idea. Right now, the closest thing to a "pathway" she had was a worn path running haphazardly through the grass from the driveway to the front porch. Cobblestone would certainly look better than that, but how much would it cost for so much stone? Certainly too much.

"I have a bit of money and I want to use it on cobblestones." Doc continued, as if reading her mind. "The boys and I can design it and lay it all out ourselves."

"You don't have to pay for it, Doc. It's not the money," June protested. But, of course, it was. June knew it, and she knew Doc knew it. June didn't have any room in the budget for such things. Money was tight. It always had been.

"I've already got some picked out down at the store."

"Did Miss Melanie help you?"

"Of course not," Doc scoffed. "Don't be silly. These stones are at the hardware store. I think they would look good and it would be nice, really nice, for me to do something to help around here."

"You do lots."

"All I do is lay the table and take out the trash and little bits here and there."

"You supply comic relief," Edie declared, entering the kitchen.

"I'm not sure that's such a great thing," Doc said.

"It's a most wonderful thing," Edie assured him.

"But the boys and I still want to lay down that cobblestone path," he insisted.

"We do," Nicky nodded. "It'll be great." No matter how many activities and chores he did throughout the day, Nicky somehow managed to have more energy to burn. Nicky liked being a part of things at the house. It made him feel like he belonged there.

June nodded, giving up the fight.

That afternoon, Nicky, Doc, and Jack set off in Mr. Clatterbox to investigate the ins and outs of cobblestones.

"God only knows what they'll come home with," June sighed.

"Oh, they'll be all right. Nicky will keep him focused."

"I'm not so sure either one of them is focused," June retorted.

But when the noisy old truck returned, its box was indeed

loaded down with so much stone it almost appeared as if the truck bed were sitting right on top of the tires.

"We're starting work tomorrow," Doc told her, jumping down from his driver's seat. "The Huckleberries are coming over first thing."

June thought about the chaos that would surely come with Dillon, Max, and God-only-knows-how-much stone and tools they'd have spread out all over her driveway.

Again, as if knowing her every worry, Doc said, "You'll be surprised at how fast we'll work and how great it will look."

"I'll be surprised, all right," she said dryly.

And so the undertaking began. June entertained serious doubts that the pile of jagged rocks residing in Mr. Clatterbox's truck bed would morph into anything resembling a presentable path. She voiced these thoughts only to Edie, who waved them away, saying that she had complete and utter faith in Doc and the Huckleberries. June wished she could feel the same.

She tried to stay positive and stop herself from fretting, she really did, during the weeks that followed. But, try as she might, her patience wore thin as the project persisted. The summer days were long and dry and hot. Dust filled the sun-baked air as stones were banged from truck to wheelbarrow to path. It took everything in June not to cringe at the clatter and ever-present noise.

"What is all that unholy racket coming from your place, June Howard?"

June and Edie startled at the dissatisfied voice breaking through the roasting afternoon. They turned to face Martha Wilson, standing in their driveway, hands on substantial hips, a sour expression on her face.

Had she been fonder of Martha, June would have tended to commiserate with her. But she was not fond of Martha (negative, constantly complaining Martha) and could feel her shackles rising at the woman's words.

Sensing this, Edie rushed in. "Doc and the boys are putting together a cobblestone path. See what they've done here so far? It's going to run from the driveway right up to the porch. I think it will be beautiful."

Martha sniffed. "Beautiful, really?"

"Well, of course it's nowhere near done yet," Edie admitted. "And it is hot, dusty work."

"I can see that. Bloody noisy too. I can hear those rocks clanging around inside the wheelbarrow from over at my house. Not a minute's peace for days on end now. Not to mention all the yelling and caterwauling that comes from here."

"That would be the boys and Doc singing. Sometimes the dogs join in," Edie explained, smiling sweetly.

"Singing? That's what you call it, do you?"

"We do," June interjected, her tone as dry as the summer air.

"Look at the muscles these boys are building," Edie said, indicating the three youths who did, indeed, seem to be growing, biceps expanding. "Doc mainly supervises and directs them, but he's been pitching in with some of the work too. It's a wonderful thing to observe."

Martha looked at her as if she might have three heads. With

a disdainful "Harrumph!" she turned on her heel to return from whence she'd come.

Doc approached the two women.

"What was Martha doing over here? Come to admire our work of art, did she?"

"Something like that, Doc."

"Well, it's still a work in progress," Doc told them.

Both women nodded. That was a bit of an understatement.

A full two weeks passed before Nicky ran into the kitchen, dust and sweat pouring from his slim shoulders in equal portions. Edie and June had been chopping vegetables for a salad as an ancient fan clanged about, mainly just moving hot air around in the kitchen. It was too hot to use the oven, so salad and grilled cheese would have to suffice for their evening meal.

"Auntie Bug! Edie! Come outside. Doc wants you to be there when we put the last cobblestone in."

All three scurried outside. June had tried not to observe her front lawn in too great detail for quite some time now, secretly dreading the outcome of all the bustle and noise. She'd delivered countless gallons of water and lemonade but had averted her eyes as best she could, lest she be bitterly disappointed at the progress they were making. Or lack thereof.

"Ta-da!" Doc swept his arm to indicate the pathway that commenced at the driveway, curving across the lawn to encircle June's flower garden and coming to rest in a beautiful conclusion at the doorstep to the porch.

The women gasped at the sight. June was surprised at how well the odd assortment of smooth stones and rocks had morphed into quite a presentable pathway.

"It's amazing," Edie proclaimed. "It really is."

June wasn't sure if she was getting sentimental in her old age, or if it was the fact that anyone would put in so much time and effort into something just for her and this old house, but the sight of the finished project brought tears to her eyes.

"It looks just wonderful," she pronounced, quickly blinking lest anyone think that she was growing soft. "You did a great job. All of you."

"Here, Junie dear," Doc held out the last piece of stone. "You put the last one in. Right there, see?"

June threw her arms around Doc in an uncharacteristic display of emotion before taking the rock and placing it, with great reverence, in its proffered spot.

Edie, in true Edie style, thrilled to the sight of the cobblestone pathway. Extolling its beauty, she laughed and danced up and down the length of it. She looked like a little fairy, clicking her heels and waving her arms to the summer sunshine. You couldn't help but smile at the very sight of her, at her energy and all-encompassing happiness.

"Joie de vivre," Doc murmured, having no trouble recalling the perfect French phrase at the perfect moment.

"What's that, Doc?" asked one of the boys.

"It means 'joy of life,'" he explained.

Doc indicated Edie with a nod of his head. "*She* has it, don't you think?"

"Yes, I suppose she does," June responded.

SHAGGY JACK

"I always think it's a wonderful thing to have, you know."

"You have it, too, Doc."

The old man smiled.

"So do you, Junie dear. It's in you, too, you know."

For decades, the true joy of anything seemed to have eluded June. She had settled for routine and contentment instead. Chores, kennel dogs, cooking, cleaning, repeat, almost always followed by retiring to the porch with Doc to eat cookies and contemplate the world. This had been her daily life for the last few years, and, for her, it had been enough. But now there were times when she thought that maybe she really could have more, that she could find her own 'joie de vivre' right there in her own soul.

"I thought you were going to make some obscure reference to the Wizard of Oz," she told him.

"What's that, dear?"

"Oh, never mind. I was just being silly. You know about Dorothy and the yellow brick road."

"Some of the bricks are yellow, but I thought the different colours made it more interesting. I hope you like the colours," he added, a little worriedly.

"I love them, Doc."

June laid a reassuring hand on the old man's arm. He had clearly forgotten the "Dorothy" reference. That is, until it popped back into his head.

Edie, finishing her little dance with a flourish and a bow, approached them, praising them for a project well done. The boys beamed at her words. They all stood back, admiring the fruits of their labour.

"I know a joke about a cobblestone path," Doc chortled. "I just remembered it now."

"Oh, yes, Doc, can you tell us?"

"I think I can."

"I mean," June said pointedly, "is it fit for young ears?"

"I think so," he repeated. "Now just give me a minute."

They dutifully waited, as June wondered if he had the mental capacity to remember a joke in its entirety.

"I've got it! Okay, there were two nuns, and they were riding their bikes down a path to get to town. The one nun says to the other, 'I've never come this way before.' The older nun turns and looks at her, very serious she was too, and says, 'Oh, it's the cobblestones.'"

Edie burst out laughing as June turned, aghast, hoping the boys hadn't grasped the meaning of the joke. She watched comprehension dawn on Max's young face, who quickly relayed it to the others. All three dissolved into gales of laughter.

June groaned.

"Just for future reference, Doc," she glared her disapproval at him, "that joke is *not* appropriate for young boys."

"Oh, they'll probably forget all about it in a few minutes," Edie soothed her.

"Fat chance of that," June retorted, observing the giggling youths.

She was right, of course.

Chapter Thirteen

"As my old dad used to say, 'If you're looking for sympathy, you know where to find it, eh? It's right there in the dictionary between sex and syphilis.'"

All hands were on deck for cleaning out the kennels before the next batch of dogs arrived for the week. June welcomed Doc's comic relief, taking her mind off the drudgery of the task at hand.

"Who's looking for sympathy?" Edie asked.

June rolled her eyes.

"Oh, I don't know. Somebody Junie dear and I were talking about. It seemed appropriate at the time."

"*Did it*, Doc?" June asked, hands on hips. "Did it *really?*"

"Don't worry about us," Max proclaimed with a grown-up air. "We took all about that stuff in health class last year."

"Well, yes, that's wise. You boys should know all about these things before you go into high school," Doc said, nodding his head gravely.

"What things, Doc?" Edie asked, a mischievous twinkle in her eye. "Where to find sympathy?"

"Oh yes, and other things too, of course."

"The person who was looking for sympathy was Leslie's owner," June said, wanting to interject before Doc could start on the myriad of "other things." She had not yet recovered from the cobblestone joke.

"The old lady? Mrs. Maxwell? I hope she's okay," Edie said. "She's such a sweet old dear."

"She is," June agreed. "But no, not her. Well, I guess in a roundabout way. Her health is failing, and she's going to have to go into Green Acres." Green Acres was the local nursing home.

"That's too bad."

"It is. But it will be better for her because she keeps falling, and she's getting a little mixed up. It's a nice place."

"It is a nice place, as far as these places go," Doc said. "I mean, it happens, right? If I hadn't had Junie dear, I would have been there already."

"Oh, Doc, you won't have to go there for a long, long time. If ever," June assured him.

"I don't mind, you know. But I just like it here so much. I've always loved the country. It's in my blood. As long as I can drive my old friend, Mr. Clatterbox, to town and back once in a while, then I'm happy."

"How long will you be able to drive, Doc?" Dillon asked.

"Wait. Who decides when you can't?" Nicky asked.

"Typically, the family doctor decides. So I guess that's me!" Doc replied cheerfully.

He met June's level gaze, adding, "You'll have to let me know if you think I'm not safe anymore." The look in his eyes broke June's heart a little. She could only manage a curt nod. "Sometimes I do forget the way, but then people steer me in the right direction and I'm alright."

Edie walked over to Doc and gave him a loving squeeze. "That's the great thing about you, Doc," she said. "You know everyone, and everyone knows you, so there's always someone around who knows what direction to steer you in."

"What about Leslie?" Nicky said pointedly. After spending so much time with Leslie, working on her training and taking care of her, he'd become quite attached. Even Shaggy Jack seemed reluctant to ever leave Leslie's side. "Is she going to be able to stay with us? Or is the daughter taking her? What's her name again?" He had chosen not to remember her name.

"Sharon," said June.

"Sharon!" Doc exclaimed, perking up at the mention of a name he recognized. "Sharon Maxwell. She's the one who was looking for sympathy. A most unpleasant woman."

"She certainly is." Edie nodded. "Poor Mrs. Maxwell, worrying about Leslie when she has to go to a nursing home."

"But can't Leslie stay here, Auntie Bug? I mean, she's here quite a bit anyway, and she likes it here."

"Leslie's one of the dogs we've been using calming signals on," Dillon said. "And she's Jack's friend."

June thought about the ramifications of another mouth to feed, or another creature to take care of.

As if on cue, Jack and Leslie trotted around the corner of the boarding house, looking like a parody of Mutt and Jeff. Leslie, a mini schnauzer, white and pristine, drew a stark contrast to Jack's huge, scraggly, grey disarray.

They look as mismatched as Edie and me, June thought, chuckling inwardly. She'd have to share that observation with Edie later. How very lovely it was to have someone to store up things to tell at the end of the day. Edie had started staying over now. Not every night, but often.

"So, what do you do?" June asked aloud. "With your calming signals."

"Well, we've only tried them on Jack and Leslie so far," Nicky admitted. "But we've been studying this calming exercise to keep the dogs grounded."

The adults nodded their encouragement, so Nicky continued.

"You take both your hands and run them down the sides of the dog's face." He demonstrated with Leslie as he explained. "Like, you start at their nose, then down their face and shoulders, and then down each leg. Then you just hold your hands there and try to think about being calm, and that makes the dogs feel calm."

"That's wonderful," Edie exclaimed. "Do you boys all do that?"

All three nodded.

"I'm impressed," she said to them.

"So it'd be nice to keep Leslie, don't you think, Auntie Bug?"

June sighed. "I don't think that we have much of a choice. Sharon doesn't want her, and Mrs. Maxwell is worried sick about her."

"And she's a sweet little thing," Edie said, looking at the dog that couldn't possibly weigh more than fifteen pounds.

"She is," Doc replied. "It's too bad she has to go to the nursing home."

"I meant Leslie, Doc."

"Oh, right. Well, she's sweet, too. I'm glad she's staying."

After Max and Dillon had departed on their bikes into the glow of the sunset, June decreed that Nicky go inside to run a bath as they all needed the summer day scrubbed off their hides before retiring to bed.

It hadn't rained in weeks now, and June was a little nervous about the state of her well. She remembered in years past when the boarding house had been running at full capacity and the well had run almost dry several times during the hot summer months. Attempting to avoid this, she instructed Nicky and Doc to try to use the same bathwater, adding a little more as they finished washing. She would have a wash when they were done.

They had been managing as such through the dry summer.

She waved Edie goodbye and sank back into her chair on the porch. She watched the sun fade into dusk as she waited for the tub to be available. It felt good to be tired and happy at the end of the day.

Nicky emerged, Jack by his side, hair clean, skin gleaming. They sat in companionable silence.

Doc soon appeared, patting his white hair with a towel.

"Always feels good to be nice and clean, doesn't it?" he declared.

June rose. "I guess I'd better wash up too. You left the water in, right?"

Nicky shifted uneasily in his chair.

"What? Did you leave the water in?"

"Yup."

"Okay, good. I just don't want to tax the well too much until we get some rain."

"But, um, Auntie Bug?"

"Yes, my dear. What is it?"

"I might have peed in the water. I didn't mean to, it just happened. I'm sorry."

"Nicky! Really?"

"Sorry, Auntie Bug."

"Ah, Junie dear?"

"Yes, Doc?"

"I, ah, I might have peed in there too."

"Oh, come on, you two! Honestly!"

Doc hung his head.

"Well, did you, or didn't you?"

Doc nodded ruefully. "I did."

Humidity hung in the house like a formidable presence. The heat had continued without one drop of rain for so many days now that June had lost track. Nor did she want to know, she decided as she descended the stairs after another hot, restless night.

She felt hot and grumpy and dishevelled. She had been making do with washing mainly in the big kitchen sink, having lost any faith in the males that inhabited her house to keep the bathtub presentable for her. The long, dry days of summer were starting to seriously worry her. How much longer could this go on?

She paused on the last step before the kitchen, her ears perking up at the sound of Edie's voice on the porch. It sounded like shouting, but she'd never heard Edie shout.

She hurried outside to the sight of Edie, still in her cotton, eyelet nightgown, standing on the lawn, waving her arms about and crying, "Pula! Pula!" to the sky.

"Edie! Have you taken leave of your senses? Has the heat finally gotten to you? Edie!"

Edie turned, laughing, to throw her arms around June.

"Look up, June! Look up at the sky! It's going to rain!"

No sooner had the words escaped her lips than the heavens

opened and buckets of nature's tears fell down, not gently or softly, but in great torrents of water.

June laughed, lifting her face to welcome the raindrops.

"We need it so bad," she cried. "I was so worried."

"I know, my love, I know, but it's all good now. Those clouds look like they're full to the brim."

They drew apart to run, holding hands like children, to the porch for cover.

"What were you shouting to the sky when I came out, Edie?"

"Pula. It means 'rain' in Setswana."

"Okay, I still don't know what that means."

"Setswana is a language they speak in Botswana. In Africa. 'Pula' means 'rain,' but it also means 'blessing.' When it rains, the people there shout 'Pula.' They see it as a life-giving force."

"Well, I'm appreciating it today, that's for sure. But, Edie, how do you know all this about Africa?"

"I went there on a mission three times, with some of the doctors and nurses I used to work with. We set up clinics near the Kalahari Desert. Once, when we were there, it was just at the end of a drought, and it started to rain. The African people were overwhelmed with gratitude and called to the skies. I loved it there. I loved the people. They love 'pula' so much that their currency is called that."

"I didn't know that about you," June gazed at her in wonder. "How could I not have known that? You never cease to amaze me, Edie Moon."

Edie smiled modestly. "It was a while ago now, but I have good memories of being there."

"Edie?" June drew a deep, sharp breath, then paused.

"What is it, my love? Is something wrong?"

"Oh, no." June shook her head decisively. "Nothing is wrong. Everything is just right. I wondered—"

Silence ensued until finally Edie prompted, "What did you wonder, June?"

"I wondered if you'd come here to live. Give up your place in town and move in here."

"Here, in this place, with this menagerie of assorted oddballs?"

"Yup."

"I'd love to," grinned Edie. "I'd just love to."

June sighed. "I've never asked that of anyone in my whole life."

"Well, I'm very happy to be the first," Edie declared.

They stood in contented silence, drinking in the sight and sound of the blessings the rain delivered to the world.

"We can have a proper shower now," Edie observed. "At least, if this keeps up, we should be able to. No more whore's baths for us."

"Edie!" June turned in shock to regard her companion. "Is this because I told you the men peed in the tub?"

Edie laughed. "No, no. Of course not. Sorry, I don't know what's gotten into me this morning. I'm drunk at the sight of all this rain. It's just a slang term used to describe a wash you take in the bathroom sink when you can't completely bathe. You know, just washing the essentials, so to speak."

"It must be a nurse's expression," June observed, unconvinced.

"It's raining!" Doc's voice boomed into the morning, full of glee. "Yay!"

He entered the porch, laden with a tray bearing three large mugs of coffee.

"Doc, you're a lifesaver," June told him, not yet completely recovered from the latest revelation. "Yes, it's a good, steady downpour, too. Our well needs it so badly."

"It does so, Junie dear."

Doc settled himself back under the porch roof, crossing his long legs, savouring his coffee as he smiled at the cloud-covered skies.

"You girls can have a proper shower now. You know, like ladies and not ladies of the night."

The women exchanged glances.

"Did you hear that last conversation, Doc?" Edie ventured.

"I'll just say this," he chuckled. "I know lots of terms that nurses used to use when they were caught between shifts and so on. Even though I am sadly lacking in some of my faculties, I still have impeccable hearing."

June hastened to change the subject before Doc took it and ran with it, as he was wont to do. And not usually in the most conventional of directions.

"Well, this is a great day," she said. "We are so in need of this rain. Also, Doc, big news to share—Edie is moving in here. For good."

Doc lifted his cup to his lips, beaming.

"All I can say is, it's about time, my dears, it's about time."

Chapter Fourteen

SUMMER days are the best days. Every Canadian knows that. How could we ever find the strength to endure the bitter cold and endless grey of winter, the mud and rain of spring, were it not for the promise of clear blue skies and warm summer sunshine?

When you're young, just verging on the edge of high school, yet still enough of a child to frolic with an open heart, summer days are priceless.

June felt herself infused with new life by the very presence of Nicky and his two friends. She'd forgotten how it felt to be so completely alive and full of hope and energy. If she'd ever really known.

It was a busy time for June; many of the kennels were full most of the time, and the boys' help was invaluable. Plus, the burden of work in the house had increased since Max and Dillon—especially Dillon, who was not always in a hurry to return home—often stayed for at least one meal a day. But Edie helped with groceries and cooking and made life wonderful.

Edie had given notice to her landlord. She and June were taking a leap of faith. It didn't feel like that, though. It felt absolutely right.

I guess this is the way it's supposed to feel, June would think to herself at regular intervals. *Too bad it took sixty-three bloody years to figure it out.*

One hot afternoon in late August, Mr. Clatterbox rattled up the road from a return trip to town. Boys and dogs respectively tumbled out from the seats and flatbed, each bearing bags overflowing with groceries. The boys did anyway, not the dogs.

Whenever Doc made a pilgrimage to town, he returned with lots of groceries. Sometimes he couldn't remember what he'd bought the day before, so June's kitchen contained many duplicates.

Today, he approached the house cradling a guitar reverently in his arms. "Just look at this beautiful gal. My old guitar. Cracklin' Rosie, I used to call her."

"That's your guitar, Doc?"

"Oh yes indeed. My dear old friend, Rosie, for short."

"Where on earth did you get it?"

"We were at the grocery store—"

"Admiring Mel's legs," Nicky interjected.

"Admiring Mel's—hey now!"

"Sorry, Doc," Nicky laughed.

"Where was I?"

"We were checking out." Dillon, always the more serious, picked up the thread of the story. "And Mrs. Hill said they'd been cleaning out some stuff from Doc's old office and they found his guitar and asked if he wanted it."

"And of course I did. So we stopped by and got it. And here she is. My Cracklin' Rosie girl."

"That's quite a name for a guitar," Edie observed, smiling at the old man's enthusiasm.

"It really is, isn't it? I'm going to see if I can get her back into working order. Then we can play a few tunes tonight."

"I didn't know you played the guitar, Doc," June said. How had this not come up before? They spent hours each day talking and sipping tea on that porch, and yet she had no idea that the old man played guitar. He probably didn't remember himself until he laid eyes on the guitar.

"Ah, I'm an enigma, aren't I now?" he responded gleefully. He held the old instrument close to his chest lovingly, admiring the strings.

Edie and June exchanged grins. A more transparent man than Doc would be hard to find.

But later, when supper was over and the dogs had been walked and "calmed," they all gathered together—June, Edie, Nicky, Max, Dillon—on the porch in anticipation that Doc would play them a song.

June wondered how he would even remember how to play as Doc folded his long, lean form into a wicker chair and appeared to tune Rosie.

"What shall I play?" Doc inquired grandly. "Any requests?"

"Something by the Beatles?" Nicky suggested. "Because Auntie Bug is a beetle."

"And the Beatles rock!" the boys yelled in unison, grinning at June.

"Do you know any of their songs, Doc?" asked Edie.

"Now, just let me think."

Doc pulled out an old red pick, seemingly from behind his ear, and started strumming softly on Rosie's six nylon strings.

"Scrambled eggs," he sang. "All my troubles seemed so far away."

"Yesterday?" June mouthed to Edie, who shrugged. She didn't know either, although the tune seemed to fit.

"Doc," she ventured quizzically. "Is that a Beatles song?"

"Yes indeed. You know the one Paul McCartney sang. I think it was him. He wrote it anyway."

SHAGGY JACK

"Why are you singing 'Scrambled eggs'?"

"Isn't that how it goes?"

"I think it goes, 'Yesterday. All my troubles seem so far away . . .'" Edie sang for him. Her voice was soft and sweet.

Doc nodded happily. "That's it! Of course! I don't know where I got that idea from."

"Actually," Dillon said, holding out his phone, "it says here that the song 'Yesterday' was originally called 'Scrambled Eggs.'"

"No way!"

"Yep. It says when Paul McCartney wrote the song that he didn't have the exact words he wanted yet, so he filled it in with 'Scrambled eggs' because it had the right number of syllables."

"That's why it fits in there, I guess," Edie mused. "Well, who knew?"

"Doc knew," Max said.

"And I didn't even know I knew," Doc declared, delighted with himself.

So they all sang "Yesterday," getting most of the words right and to the proper tune. At the end, they all sang, as of one accord, "I believe in scrambled eggs."

"It does fit," June laughed. "I'll never be able to hear that song again without thinking those words in my head."

"Maybe that's how Paul McCartney feels," Doc laughed.

"Can we sing Moon River?" Edie requested. "I like the part about the huckleberry friend."

The boys had never heard that song, but they grinned as the three adults sang to the music, swaying in time to its beautiful melody.

"Did you always like that song, Edie?" Nicky asked her.

"I did," she said. "But I like it even more now. I never knew what a huckleberry friend was. And I sure never thought I'd be lucky enough to have so many of them."

"Me neither," Doc grinned. "We're doing all right, the bunch of us. But hey, we've got to finish with 'Cracklin' Rosie.' In honour of my friend here."

He patted his guitar affectionately. They stumbled through a rendition of the Neil Diamond song, humming whenever they didn't know the words. Mostly it was Doc who, in a surprisingly mellow baritone, completed the lyrics. Edie made a valiant attempt to sing along.

"Oh, it's getting late," June sighed, rising to her feet, as the echo of the last chord faded away.

"Yes, I better go before it gets too dark," Max agreed. "My folks don't want me out too late, even though I have a light on my bike."

Nicky turned to June, coughed a little, and said tentatively, "Auntie Bug?"

"Yes, my dear."

June stifled a yawn.

"Is it okay if Dillon stays over tonight? There's nobody home at his house."

"Well, of course. He can stay in the end room beside yours."

"Thank you so much, Auntie Bug," Dillon murmured.

Because they all called her that now. Of course they did.

Later, when everyone had retired, June and Edie lay side by side, hashing over the day's events.

"I'm not so sure that Dillon is happy at home," Edie whispered.

She thought about his nature in comparison to the other boys.

SHAGGY JACK

"I have wondered that, too . . . He's timid, isn't he? I mean not just shy but quite timid."

"Yes, he really is for a boy his age. He seems to like it here, though."

"I'm glad. I like having him around."

"Me too."

They lay in a companionable silence, breathing together to the beautiful rhythm of the summer night and their beating hearts.

"June, for God's sake, girl, take off your underwear."

"I always sleep with my underwear on. You know that."

"Take 'em off, June, my love. It's healthier for you, especially in the summer."

"Healthier?"

"Yes, it has to breathe, you know."

"Edie!"

"It does, June. It just does."

Chapter Fifteen

"Hey, when you were a little girl, did you ever have those days of the week underwear?" Edie asked the question softly the next morning, as the two women made their way stealthily down the stairs, so as not to awaken the sleeping youths.

"What is it with you and underwear lately, Edie? Or lack of it, I should say."

Edie giggled. "I was just thinking that they'd be useful now. At our age. You know, you'd always know what day it was."

June gave her a playful push, and they tumbled into the kitchen only to realize they weren't alone. The ladies startled to a halt at the sight of Dillon sitting at the kitchen table. He didn't appear to have heard their conversation, which was just as well as far as June was concerned. But the sight of him tugged at her heart a little.

Of all three boys, Dillon was the quiet one, the serious one. But this morning he looked almost despondent, a solitary figure. Shaggy Jack's enormous head rested on the tabletop (because he was big enough to do that) beside the boy. Dillon brushed the grey fur absentmindedly.

"Dillon," Edie approached him, laying a gentle hand on his slim shoulder. "Are you alright?"

The boy gave the two women a long look, as if trying to decide what to say. Finally, he just nodded.

"Are you sure?" June asked. "How come you're up so early? Did Jack wake you?"

"I think I might've woke *him*. I just couldn't sleep, so I got up,

SHAGGY JACK

and Jack came to keep me company, I guess. He's such a good guy, aren't you, Jack?"

"He is that," June agreed. "Well, if you're sure you're okay—"

"I'm fine." The words came out louder now.

"We were just about to make blueberry pancakes," Edie told him. She started to pull out eggs, flour, and sugar as June measured coffee into the coffee maker.

"I'll take Jack out for a little walk down the road," Dillon offered, rising.

"Well, they'll be ready when you get back, so bring your appetite," Edie said. "Doc picked these blueberries down Towbridge Road yesterday and they're sure to be sweet."

"I will," Dillon called back, closing the door behind them.

"That boy's not a real happy one," declared Doc, entering the back door, where he had been sitting, drinking in the beauty of the new day.

"You're right about that, Doc," June agreed, placing a steaming cup of coffee in front of him.

"It's a shame, isn't it? When you're young, you shouldn't have a care in the world, but so often that's not how it goes."

"Do I smell pancakes?!" Nicky thundered down the stairs and burst into the kitchen, following his nose, as adolescent boys do.

"Yes indeed," Edie told him cheerfully. "You're just in time!" She poured him a glass of juice as June placed the first round of pancakes on the table.

Before any of them could take a bite, Dillon burst into the kitchen, Shaggy Jack at his side. He was visibly upset, his hand clutching something to his chest.

"What's the matter, Dill?" Nicky asked. "Sit down, man."

"I'm okay," Dillon said, his voice shaking, expression grave. "I'm fine."

The two women paused to regard the youth with concern.

"What's in your hand, honey?" Edie asked him. "Did you find something?"

Dillon shook his head. "No, it's my necklace. Jack and I were horsing around, and the chain snapped."

"I didn't know you wore a necklace," Nicky said. "I guess I never noticed."

"It's my Star of David. My mom gave it to me before she left."

"Wait—what? Your mom left?" Nicky gasped. "Why didn't you tell us?"

Dillon shrugged. "I don't know. I guess I just wanted to pretend it never happened."

"I get that," Nicky said. He reached under his T-shirt and produced his own chain. "My mom gave me this one. It's St. Christopher."

"Nice," Dillon nodded. "This is a real old one. It used to belong to my grandpa, and Mom said I could have it and wear it, and it would protect me. Then she said she was leaving, and I had to be brave."

Tears welled in his eyes at these words. They spilled over, trailing down his boyish cheeks. He dashed them angrily away with his free hand.

Edie led him to a chair and opened his hands with her dainty ones.

"It's beautiful, dear. So delicate. I'm sure the chain can be fixed."

Dillon shook his head.

"My dad won't get it fixed. He just won't."

"Let me see that." Doc reached for the chain, studying it. "You know, Dillon, we can solder this. I have all the tools out in the shed. We can do this in no time. You boys can help me just to keep me on the straight and narrow."

"Oh, Doc, when have you ever been on the straight and narrow?" Edie laughed.

"Can you really do that?" Dillon asked.

"I can."

"We'll look it up on YouTube and see if we can get some pointers," Nicky suggested.

"My what?"

"YouTube. Have you heard of that, Doc?"

"Can't say as I have, but I'm sure we can figure something out. Here, Junie dear, you hold onto this star part. Me and the Huckleberries will get the chain fixed."

"I'll put it up on top of the sideboard where it'll be safe," June told him. "It's beautiful, Dillon. I love the Star of David."

"My middle name is David," Dillon told them softly.

"A very good name," Doc declared. "It means 'beloved.'"

It took a Herculean effort on Dillon's part not to cry yet again, but no one appeared to notice, and the moment passed.

After several rounds of blueberry pancakes had been consumed, Edie stretched out a hand to Dillon, asking gently, "Who's there at home with you now that your mom's gone?"

"My dad. But he's not doing so great."

"No?" Edie asked.

"No," Dillon sighed deeply. "He-he gets drunk a lot. Well, pretty much every night, really."

"That's too bad."

"It is. It hurts to see your dad like that."

"I can only imagine you're right, my dear."

"Sorry, guys, sorry. I didn't mean to get into all that stuff."

"It's quite alright," June told him solemnly. "I hope you feel safe enough here that you can tell us things."

"I'm okay. I just really don't want to lose my necklace. It makes me feel closer to my mom when I have it on."

"We will solder it up so well that it will never break again," Doc professed. "Don't you worry, Dillon. We'll get a hold of this tube, whoever's it turns out to be."

"Tube?"

"I think he means YouTube," June said.

"That's it! Now let's all brighten up. Everyone's looking so serious. We'll get this all fixed up, so we will. Smile, Junie dear, you're so pretty when you smile."

June scoffed at the man. "Oh, Doc, you're being ridiculous. There's not much to be done with this old face with its lines and jowls."

"What are jowls?" Nicky asked, leaning over to scrutinize his aunt's face.

"These things," she pointed. "These sagging things on the sides of my mouth."

He observed them so intently and for so long that June began to laugh.

"Auntie Bug," Nicky grinned. "You don't even have them when you smile. You should just smile all the time if you don't like them."

"I can't smile all the time. I'd look like a bloody Cheshire cat."

"Well, I guess it's better than looking like a constipated bulldog," Doc offered.

"What? Who said I looked like that?"

Doc shrugged. "I think it might've been me. But I wasn't talking about you. I was talking about someone who never smiled. I think so, anyway. I have no idea."

He grinned at her sheepishly, only receiving a scowl for his efforts.

Doc and the boys had gotten into the habit of picking up stray articles from the side of the road. A habit that June found immensely annoying.

"Doc!" she protested, time and time again. "People put stuff out because it has outlived its usefulness."

"But maybe not for everyone," he would say. "After all, one man's trash is another man's treasure."

"Not always."

Doc thought that everything could be put to some use by himself or one of the boys.

One day, they arrived home with several half-empty cans of paint in the back of the truck.

"But we don't need anything painted!" June protested.

"The boys and I are going to paint our names on the side of Mr. Clatterbox," Doc proclaimed, unloading various cans and brushes.

"Paint what? And there's all different colours."

"Yes, all the colours of the rainbow, so you and Edie will be represented. Get it?"

"Yes, Doc, I do get it, thank you."

Someone had told Doc that the rainbow was a symbol of gay pride. This information had taken root in his brain, and he traipsed it out at regular intervals.

Shaking her head, June returned to the house to finish her chores, leaving the males to their project.

Several hours later, Edie, arriving home from town, dragged her from the kitchen to survey the finished result.

Doc and his Huckleberries

And Shaggy Jack.

The words adorned both the driver and the passenger doors and were displayed in, as promised, every colour of the rainbow.

"Doc says the rainbow colours are in honour of us," Edie whispered. "Bless his heart for remembering the significance of them."

June just groaned and shook her head, wishing he'd remembered something else, maybe something of value.

Several days later, the whole crew, depicted on the truck doors, went to town for dog food, returning with a chiminea lying askew in the bed of Mr. Clatterbox.

The boys hauled it carefully from the back of the truck, depositing it on the ground. Doc stepped back, regarding it with great pleasure.

"Now just look at that, Junie dear," he told her. "We can have little fires in the evenings. It's perfectly safe, and think how much fun it will be."

Edie clapped her hands in delight. "I think we've got some marshmallows. We can have a fire tonight. It's in pretty good shape. Where did you get it, Doc?"

"Oh, back of the fifth line there. Someone had it out to be taken away. Imagine! It's still got lots of life left in it."

"Like you, Doc," Nicky teased him.

"Just like me, is right."

"The man who lived there came out to talk to us. He knew Doc," Max said.

"Of course he does. Everybody knows Doc," Edie said.

"I think I might have delivered one of their babies or something," Doc said vaguely.

"The guy said you were with his mom when she died," Dillon clarified.

"Oh, wrong end," Doc said cheerfully, then, seeing the curious glances directed his way, added, "Wrong end of life. You know it's all connected, the circle of life and all that."

"He said you were kind to his mom when she was dying. He said you were just great."

Doc sighed. "I guess I used to be great. But that doesn't matter now."

"Of course it matters," Edie protested. "It matters a lot. Or what's the use of being great at all?"

"What indeed?" Doc mused. "I don't know. I can't remember. They could tell me anything."

"I'm sure they wouldn't say you were great if you weren't."

"*Anyway,*" June interrupted pointedly. "Where are we going to put this thing, oh Great One?"

"Over there," Doc pointed toward the middle of the lawn. "We can get those deck chairs out of the shed, and we can sit around with Cracklin' Rosie and sing."

The chiminea worked perfectly and turned out to be quite a success. Doc withdrew an old pipe from under his jacket and, stuffing tobacco inside its archaic depths, proceeded to light it.

"I didn't know you smoked, Doc," June observed.

"I don't. Well, not really. That's the great thing about getting old. You forget that you once craved a little bit of pipe tobacco."

"Just be careful, Doc," June pleaded. "Please."

"You bet, my Junie dear. I can't even remember the last time I fired up old Smokey here. I just keep him around for the odd, rare occasion. But don't worry, I never do it by myself. Wouldn't trust myself for that."

"I do love the smell of a pipe," June smiled. "Makes me think of my grandpa."

"On top of Old Smokey," Edie started to sing, as Nicky produced the marshmallows. The woodsy odour of campfire logs and Doc's pipe drifted into the summer evening.

"Let's tell ghost stories!" Max suggested, rubbing his hands together after the marshmallows had been dutifully roasted to golden brown perfection.

"Yeah!" Nicky agreed.

"We could just each tell a story," Edie said, noting Dillon's lack of enthusiasm at the idea. "You know, take turns."

"Sounds good to me. Edie, why don't you go first?" Doc suggested.

SHAGGY JACK

"I don't have one right in my mind just now. Does it have to be true?"

"Doesn't matter. Anything."

Silence prevailed for several minutes, as everyone tried to think of a story.

Then Max piped up. "I heard a story last week when I was at the grain store with my dad."

"Yay! You go first, Max," Doc encouraged him. "Tell us the story."

"Well, my dad was talking to Chuck and another guy who works there, and they were talking about Mike Churchill. You know he lives down past the post office there before you get to the road going out of town."

The little group nodded.

"Well, the story was about Mike's sister. I forget her name. Susan or Sharon, I can't remember."

"Sandra!" Doc chimed in.

"Yeah, Sandra, that's it."

"I remember because she had a history of—"

"Doc!" June warned.

"Oh, right. Sorry. Sandra Churchill. Right."

"Well, apparently she kind of lost her mind—"

"Not surprising," murmured Doc. "Due to her history, I mean. Sorry. Go on."

June sighed.

"She went crazy and she just started walking along down the road going into town."

"Okay," Nicky looked at his friend quizzically. "Like that's the whole story?"

"No, no, I was pausing for effect. You know, what do you call that?"

"I think you might mean dramatic effect," Edie suggested.

"Yeah, that's it. Anyway, here's the best part. She was naked!"

The other two boys gasped.

"Naked? Are you sure?"

"Yup, Chuck saw her with his own two eyes. Anyway, my dad says to Chuck 'Oh God, you saw her?' and Chuck said that yeah, he saw her before they came and got her and took her to the funny farm."

"Max!" Edie reprimanded.

"I'm sorry, Edie. I didn't say that myself. I was just like quoting the moment when Chuck said that 'cause you can do that when you're telling a story, right?"

"Yes, you can," Doc agreed heartily.

"Okay, well, Chuck said he sure as hell did see her, and my dad asked if she looked like Mike, and Chuck said—" Max doubled over with laughter now, the infectious kind that makes everyone else want to laugh too. "Chuck says, 'I don't know, man, I wasn't looking at her face.'"

Nicky and Dillon exploded into laughter, too.

"Poor Sandra," Doc said, shaking his head a little. "She's had a rough time of it."

"What will they do to her at the funny farm?" Max inquired. Edie shot him a look. "I mean the psych place."

Doc shook his head.

"I don't know. I only remember bits and pieces of things like that. Treatments, I mean." He looked despondent. "I do remember something about her, though," he said, perking up. The upside to his unravelling memory was that Doc was never glum for very long.

SHAGGY JACK

"Tell us," Nicky urged. "Your turn now, Doc."

Good Lord. That was a recipe for disaster, June thought. "Doc, please remember that young ears are listening."

Doc considered. "I don't think my story is any worse than the one about her face. It's just a different part of her anatomy, is all."

"Doc!"

"It's just a remark, really. Not even a story. She came into the office one day because she was sick with a cough. She had a bug of some kind."

June caught Edie's eye at this.

Doc fell into deep thought, furrowing his eyebrows. "I think it was Sandra, but mind you, it might have been one of the Smith girls. I'm just not a hundred percent sure right now . . ."

"—Is it important to the story?" June asked, growing impatient.

"No, not all," Doc said brightly. "And it's not even a story, really. Just a little slip of the tongue on my part."

"What did you say, Doc?" Dillon asked eagerly.

"Well, as I said, she presented with cold-like symptoms, so I got my stethoscope out and was listening to her chest, and I meant to say 'big breaths' but it came out—"

"Big breasts!" all three boys yelled, jumping the gun on Doc. They could see where this story was going and proceeded to roll around on the grass, laughing.

Doc smiled at their boyish silliness.

"I tried to cover up my mistake, but she started giggling and I knew she'd caught it. She didn't take any offense, though. Thank God."

"And did she?" Max dared to ask in a whisper.

"Did she what?"

"Have big . . . you know . . ."

"Oh, I don't even remember."

"Yeah, and besides," Nicky said, his face full of mischief, "we all know Doc is a leg man."

That was all it took. The three boys dissolved into laughter so hard they were gasping for air.

Chapter Sixteen

"Nicky, I swear it must be you who's attracting these oddball dogs. I never used to get any before you came along," June told the boy one morning.

He was wolfing down a plate of eggs and toast, absentmindedly singing "scrambled eggs" between bites.

"Are we getting another oddball dog?" Doc inquired, eyes meeting hers over his coffee cup. "Or just another oddball? I don't mind. I'm just asking."

"We've got enough oddball people around here already, don't you think?" she asked, smiling indulgently at him.

"Is there ever too many? I don't know. Is there a quota?"

"Anyway, what's the oddball dog?" Nicky asked, reaching out to tousle Jack's grey ears, never too far from the boy's reach.

"And you're not an oddball dog, Jack," he continued in a stage whisper. "She's not talking about you."

June laughed, replying, "He's the very oddest of all oddballs."

Nicky was a firm believer that dogs could understand what people said. "Jack can't help how he looks. You're unique, aren't you, Jack? What's that?"

He bent over as Jack emitted an indistinguishable noise.

"Aw, I love you too, buddy."

"Isn't it wonderful how Nicky taught Jack how to communicate with him?" Doc asked.

June turned from her post at the stove to observe the man,

unsure if he was just being incredibly supportive, incredibly inane, or a little of both.

"He says he loves you too, Auntie Bug," Nicky told her. "And what kind of new dog are we getting? What kind of oddball? They're more fun than normal ones, anyway."

"We're getting a deaf dog. For six weeks. His owners are going on a six-week vacation all over South America. I don't know why we don't just get ordinary dogs anymore," she reiterated. "We have Leslie, who's almost blind, and Jack, who is the size of a small horse, and now one who's deaf."

"Is it a Dalmatian dog?" Nicky asked.

"Well, yes, actually it is, but how on earth did you know that?" June asked.

"Because there's a high percentage of Dalmatians that go deaf. And almost all deaf dogs are white."

"Nicky! You're a fountain of information!" Doc exclaimed, amazed.

"It's the special cells that make the dog's hair colour, and without that layer of cells, the dogs can't make the special layer of hearing cells." He shook his head now, a little frustrated with himself. "Or something like that. I can't remember exactly."

"I'm impressed," Doc said. "Have you been reading up on that kind of stuff?"

"A little bit. I've been looking up information about communicating with dogs. I always thought it would be cool to be a vet, even when I was just little. Not that it'll ever happen," he added sheepishly.

"Why on earth not?" Edie demanded. "There's no reason you couldn't do anything you put your mind to. Look how well you did in your classes once you got your eyesight figured out."

"Thanks to you!"

"Yes, well, now you're passing that help on to the dogs. I think it's great," Edie declared with a big smile. "I'll bet you know how to communicate with a deaf dog already."

"Brilliant! And you didn't even know we were getting a deaf dog!" Doc exclaimed. "Oh, and I know ALS."

Observing the puzzled looks, he recanted his words, saying, "Sorry, I know ASL. That's what I know."

"I still don't know what that is," June said.

"American Sign Language," Edie said. "Right?"

"Right!" Doc and Nicky responded in unison.

"But will that even work on a dog?" June asked. "A Canadian dog?"

"Ha ha, look who's funny now," Edie groaned. "And I don't know. Our Nicky here seems to be the expert."

"Actually, when a dog's deaf, it doesn't change their ability to learn, just how they receive the information."

"I could try my sign language on him," Doc suggested hopefully. "Although I may be a little rusty. I know what you're thinking, Junie dear."

"And what's that? What am I thinking?"

"That I sometimes don't get the spoken word right, let alone a whole bunch of sign words."

"I wasn't thinking that. I was impressed that you know sign language."

"There used to be a family that lived in Laventra, and the mother was deaf. That's when I learned it. I wanted to be able to communicate with her. She had five little kids. She was a remarkable woman. Very pleasant most of the time, but boy, she had a temper too."

"If I had five little ones running around, I might lose my temper, too," June laughed. "Did she ever get mad at you?"

"Just once. Because, you know, you can mix up words when you're signing too."

"I'm sure you can."

"Once I made the sign for, well, 'f-u-c-k you'"— Doc spelled the profanity out, blushing —"instead of 'thank you.' 'Thank you' is this."

Doc put his hand on his lips, then moved the hand forward and down a little.

"What's f—I mean the other one?" Nicky asked.

Doc put his hand under his chin, moving it in much the same way.

Everyone laughed.

"You can bet I never mixed them up again. That mother reamed me out but good, deaf or not. She was signing so fast I couldn't follow half of what she was saying, but I sure got the gist of it. It took a while for me to convince her that it had been an honest mistake and I'd meant no offense. Funny, I hadn't thought about that in years."

"Maybe you don't forget everything you think you do, Doc. Maybe you just have to be reminded," Nicky suggested hopefully.

"Ah, Nicky, you're a great boy. If only that were true."

"Anyway, I think this dog has his own hand signals that his owners use with him. She's going to come over a couple of times before they leave so she can show us."

"That's a good idea," Nicky said.

"And if we get those signals mixed up, at least this Dalmatian won't be cross at us," Doc said.

SHAGGY JACK

"That's why I love animals so much," Nicky said. "They don't take offense at stupid stuff like humans do."

"Oh, Nicky, what a wonderful vet you will be someday," Doc declared, grinning from ear to ear.

"I'm just dreaming, Doc. I'll probably never get there. What do you call that kind of dream, that probably won't ever happen?"

"Like a pipe dream?" Max suggested. "Isn't that what you call that?"

"Yes, a pipe dream," Edie confirmed.

"Best kind of dream, Nicky dear, best kind. Just ask Old Smokey."

The deaf dog arrived. His name was Nelson. He was a regal-looking Dalmatian standing almost two feet tall. He actually looked like quite a big dog, until Jack wandered nonchalantly onto the front lawn.

Nelson's owner, Mrs. Prewett, gasped at the size of him. "I have never seen a dog so big or so shaggy in my life!" she exclaimed.

Much was made about Nelson's deafness, and a series of signs were outlined for June and the boys. Edie recorded them for all to learn. Nicky was familiar with most of the signs already.

"These are easier than the human ones," Doc declared. "I think I can remember most of these."

"That's because dogs are easier all around. You only have to know 'walk, down, eat, go pee, quiet, no, all done, stay.' They're just common sense."

June was relieved that this wasn't going to be a monumental task. Nelson was probably going to be less trouble than any other dog.

"He's very gentle," Dillon remarked. "Even Leslie gets along with him." Of all the dogs, Leslie was the most finicky about the company she kept.

"Yes, maybe it's like the blind leading the blind. Or you know, the deaf," Doc chuckled. "I'm glad to know these deaf signals. And you can't mix them up really. They're pretty straightforward."

"And if you did, nobody's going to accuse you of using swear words," Max added.

"True, very true. Just look at that bunch," Doc pointed to Shaggy Jack sauntering down the lane, Leslie and Nelson respectively trotting behind him. They did pose an impressive sight, enough to make anyone do a double take.

The summer days flew by now, tumbling over each other, filled with boys and dogs and sunshine.

Some summers just seemed too difficult to surrender, but September crept up on them anyway, whether they were ready for it or not. It was the beginning of a new school year, and that changed the rhythm of the house considerably. Nick continued his work with Nelson whenever he could, which was usually after school and on weekends.

One warm afternoon after school, Nick and June lay side by side on the lawn looking up at the clouds when Nick asked her, "You know what I love most about Nelson, Auntie Bug?"

"What would that be, dear boy?"

Nick sat up, regarding his aunt earnestly. "Well, he's almost completely deaf, but I guess he used to have some hearing. If he were a human, he'd be all bitter and sad about losing his hearing, but Nelson is just happy being Nelson."

SHAGGY JACK

"He is, is he? You mean he doesn't mind being deaf?"

"I don't think so. I mean, look at him," he gestured toward the dog who was looking at Nick expectantly, tail wagging. "He's just smiling, happy with his own little world. He doesn't know he can't hear, and he doesn't care. He's a great guy, aren't you, boy?"

Nick leaned over and kissed the top of Nelson's black and white head.

"You have to be careful you don't startle him because then he gets scared, but when I'm just here with him, he's fine."

"His owners left a whistle when they brought him," June remembered. "I wondered about that at the time. What's the use of a whistle if Nelson is deaf?"

"Dogs have so much better hearing than people that they can hear high frequency sounds we can't. I think Nelson must have a little bit of hearing because he sometimes reacts when he hears it. It's like 35,000 Hertz."

"I don't know what you're talking about now, Nick," June said.

"I'm just learning, Auntie Bug, but Hertz measures the number of cycles in a minute. So we can't hear it. We can only hear 20,000 Hertz, so we can't even detect the whistle; they're so high-pitched. But dogs can hear it."

"My goodness, you've really researched this, haven't you? Good for you." June liked how much Nick's face lit up when he talked about animals.

"It's interesting. Nelson's owners have trained him really well, and they helped me learn the commands. But he's getting close to me now, too, I think. Aren't you, boy?"

Nick rolled over on his back and ever so gently stroked Nelson's head. The dog nuzzled into his hands.

"Yes, I'd say you and he are doing all right," June observed with a smile.

The customary roar that accompanied the arrival of Mr. Clatterbox broke the afternoon silence.

"It's hard to believe that Nelson can somehow hear a whistle that I can't detect, but he can't hear that old rattletrap coming up the driveway," June observed dryly.

Doc strode down the path calling out a cheerful greeting to the group. Then he knelt and softly laid his hand on Nelson's round, floppy ears.

"What's all the lollygagging about?" he inquired.

Nick rolled his eyes. "I don't know where you get some of these words, Doc. I never heard that one before."

"It's a word, right, Junie dear?"

Doc turned to June, who confirmed that it was, indeed, a word, albeit one that was rarely spoken now.

"Nick was just explaining to me all about dogs and their hearing. He's been working hard with Nelson here," June told him.

"He sure has," Doc agreed. "Dr. Nicholas Benton, veterinarian extraordinaire, here you come."

Nick blushed, casting his eyes down to the grass.

"I don't know about that, Doc," he mumbled. "I don't know if I've got what it takes for that."

"Of course you do. I have great faith in you. Mark my words, Nicky boy, you are going to be a most wise and wonderful vet. And we'll all be there to celebrate."

And wouldn't it be a wonderful world if everyone had faith in life as Doc did, reflected June. She did not. She knew that. But Doc . . . well, he had the faith of a child.

SHAGGY JACK

She smiled at the old man.

"Have you always been this optimistic, Doc? This relentlessly optimistic?" she asked him.

Doc shrugged.

"I guess so. I like to look ahead and see a bright future. Or it wouldn't be so great to look ahead, would it? I can just imagine shaking the hand of this fine young fellow when he graduates. What a happy day that will be!"

Doc rose to his feet and headed up the porch. Nick and June exchanged smiles.

"I tell you," June remarked. "Optimistic is an understatement. Here I am hoping that I'll be around to see that, and Doc's got it all planned out."

"You gotta love that guy," Nick agreed.

With autumn settling in on the land, so did the brilliant colours, blazing maples, and cooler breezes. The chiminea was lit in the evenings for warmth now, not just atmosphere. No one could quite bear the thought of putting it away for the year, just yet.

Without the boys there all day, the workload increased, but so did the time that Edie and June had to spend together.

It didn't take too many uninterrupted days for them to discover that they could now share an intimate escape into the golden hush of the long afternoons—another hitherto unheard-of pleasure.

Jack had taken to accompanying Doc as he accomplished

the outside tasks. Both vastly preferred to be out of doors whenever possible.

They both burst into the kitchen one sunny fall day as the women were finishing up the kitchen chores after lunch. Doc was humming a tune that caused Edie to tilt her head in his direction.

"What's that song you're humming, Doc?"

Doc beamed at the two, his face a cheery grin.

"Oh, it's just an old song from the '70s, I think. It's a funny thing. There are so many things I don't remember, but the old songs I can remember every word."

June nodded. "That's true, Doc. You are great at remembering songs. And your voice is still good."

But Edie continued to regard him with a little smile.

"Well, you must remember the name of that song then, I guess?"

"Yup. It's called Afternoon Delight. I forget who sang it, though."

June shook her head. "I don't recognize it."

"Oh, I do," Edie persisted.

"I imagine you do, Edie dear. I worked with lots of nurses who had to do night shifts. This could have been their song, so to speak."

June felt perplexed.

"I'll explain later," Edie whispered.

"Anyway." Doc continued. "I just came in to tell you ladies that Jack and I are going to town. I want to get some of those lovely fall mums they have at the hardware store, and maybe we'll take a wander around the grocery store. So you girls just take your time, whatever you're doing. I won't be back for a couple of hours. Anything you want me to pick up?"

"No. I think we're good, thanks," June replied, still oblivious.

SHAGGY JACK

"Alright then. Come on, Jack."

The two of them departed as Doc sang, "Gonna find my baby, gonna hold her tight. Gonna grab some afternoon delight."

Light dawned on June's comprehension, just as Edie grabbed her hand and they ran giggling up the stairs for their own afternoon delight.

Some days they simply enjoyed the beautiful warmth and splendid colours of the season, sitting on the porch, sipping tea and discussing every topic under the sun.

But there were days, too, when June missed the presence and noise, the very life, that the boys brought to her home. Without fail, her heart leapt at the sight of Nick striding up the cobblestones at the end of his day, making her world a complete and happy place to be.

Nicky had to take a bus now that he attended high school but still had to walk to the side road to catch it. Jack accompanied him to the bus stop every morning and strolled back down to meet him every afternoon.

"My Huckleberries are growing like bad weeds," Doc observed, watching them gather twigs for the fire one late Saturday afternoon. "Feels like only yesterday that they arrived."

"It's true," mused Edie, "once they get to high school, they grow up way too fast."

"It's so nice having them here, Junie dear. The boys. And the dogs. So much nicer than when it was just you and me, eh?"

June regarded him, an unreadable look on her face.

"I'm not sure that was a compliment, Doc."

"Oh, don't go getting offended on me. It doesn't suit you. You know what I mean."

"Do I?"

"You do, Junie dear. It's just nice having the Huckleberries around, that's all."

"Oh, I know, Doc. Dillon might as well live here now, too."

"It's been good for him," Edie said. "He's opened up, hasn't he? And he's doing well in school."

"I don't think he sees his father much," June observed. "Even when he goes there after school, he usually manages to find his way back here before too long. He told me he wants to get a job so he can pay me for his upkeep. I told him not to worry, that there was plenty of time for that down the road. And his friendship is a great thing for Nicky."

"You, Junie dear, are a wonderful woman."

June scoffed, waving the compliment away.

"You've got that right, Doc," Edie smiled, reaching for June's hand. June didn't pull her hand away as she once would have. The Huckleberries weren't the only ones who had evolved.

"This might be our last chiminea night," Doc observed later that evening. A decided chill had penetrated the air. "It's supposed to get really cold next week, maybe snow."

Everyone sighed. Canadian summers were short. Always too short.

"Well, I have a story for tonight," Max announced. "I haven't written it down or anything, but I'm going to because there's a short story competition happening at school and I might enter it."

"Oh, the Maple Leaf Competition," Edie nodded.

Edie still helped out with the reading programme in Laventra.

SHAGGY JACK

If something related to literature occurred in the village, she knew about it.

"Yeah, that one," Max agreed. "I probably don't have a chance of winning, but I thought I'd try anyway."

"Don't say that, dear," Edie chided him gently. "Don't even think it. Just think that you're going to win. Put those positive thoughts for your story out there."

"Exactly!" Doc agreed. "What Edie said! Now, just a minute . . . let me get out Old Smokey and light her up. She's going to have to hibernate for the winter soon, so I want to enjoy her once more."

He pulled out the ancient, brown pipe and lit it. The pungent smoke lingered on the evening air, unfolding into the semi-darkness, evoking a sense of warmth and nostalgia.

After inhaling a deep, profoundly satisfying breath, he said, "There. Perfect. Now tell us your story, Max," he said and rubbed his hands together in gleeful anticipation. "I do love a good story."

"Well, I can't tell you exactly because it's all just in my mind right now. But it's about an older couple, one was really cheerful but the other one could be grouchy. Not exactly grouchy but just a little more negative."

"Were they a lesbian couple?" Doc asked. "Anybody we know?"

"Doc!"

"Sorry, I didn't mean anything bad. Never mind, Max. Go on. Go on."

Max went on. "No, they weren't lesbians. They were just a normal couple. Oh shit, that didn't come out right."

Edie grinned.

"It's okay, just continue. There was a couple, older, man and wife, right?"

"Yup." Max nodded his head, relieved. "And they had this mouse in their house. They tried to catch it, but they never could. It was quiet during the day, mostly. Sometimes they'd catch sight of just the tail end of it, scurrying around. Like literally the tail end. Get it?"

The others laughed dutifully.

"Anyway, they kept hearing this mouse at night, scratching at the walls, and they found some mouse turds in the cupboards. Sometimes their cardboard boxes had been chewed through. Is there a better way to say 'mouse turds'?" he inquired of Edie.

Edie considered this.

"You could say 'evidence of mice' in the cupboards. That might sound a little better, I think."

"Okay, do you think the judges will know what that means?"

"Oh, I think they will," Edie assured him.

"Well then, sometimes the old couple found evidence of mice mixed in with chewed-up cardboard bits in the cupboards. So they knew for sure the mouse had been there. They tried traps, but the mouse was really smart. The old woman said the mouse was smarter than they were, which pissed off the old man. Anyway, one morning she fried him up an egg and it had a little mouse turd right in it. Okay, I gotta work on that. I might need your help with the wording."

The boys and Doc giggled at the prospect of finding mouse poop in their morning fried egg.

"Anyway, I'll get this bit all worked out, but the climax of the story—"

"Climax?" Doc interrupted.

"Yes, you know, like the turning point," Edie told him.

"What are you, twelve?" June asked Doc disapprovingly.

He shrugged.

"The turning point," Max continued, "like, I think this is going to be my ending, is when the old woman gets up one night, after trying to find the mouse for many days, and she hears a weird sound. She walks down to the kitchen, and there's the Roomba going around on the floor."

"What's a Roomba?" Doc asked.

"One of those robot vacuum cleaners," June explained. "It looks like a big, round disc, and it goes all over your floors so you don't have to vacuum manually."

"Well, can you believe that? So this robot thing was vacuuming the floors in the middle of the night?"

"Yup. And guess who was riding around on it?"

"The mouse!" everyone shouted in unison.

"Well, now, how on earth is anyone going to top that story?" Edie posited. "If that's not a winner, I don't know what is. Look out, Maple Leaf Competition."

"Thanks, Edie. I've been writing things down for a while now, like little stories and stuff like that. I think I might want to be a journalist some day."

"That's a wonderful idea, Max. I think you'd be a great journalist."

"I don't know. Sometimes when I'm riding my bike home, ideas pop into my head. I told my mom, and she said I should write them down. She's the one who told me I should write a story for the competition."

"Excellent!"

"Anyway, Auntie Bug," Max continued. "I thought you said you knew a story for tonight."

June laughed. "It's not a story; it's just something I was thinking about the other day. I hadn't thought about it in years."

"Tell us," Edie prodded encouragingly. "Like a memory?"

"Kind of like that. I was looking at that row of spruces at the back there."

She gestured behind the boarding house, before the kennels. A line of tall spruce trees had stood there for many years now, spreading their lacy green branches up in an attempt to touch the sky.

Everyone turned and nodded. They knew the spruces.

"Well, my grandma told me a story about them one day when I was sitting on the back porch with her. She told me those trees were really old and to be valued because they took so long to get that big. All trees do, of course. But then she asked me if I knew why there was that big space in the middle of them. I had no idea. I just thought they grew that way, but she told me that her mom had planted them. She thought they would provide a nice space for her family to sit under as the trees grew. A few days later, her dad got annoyed about something and marched over and ripped two of them right out of the ground."

"That wasn't very nice," Edie remarked.

"No, that's what I said, but Grandma said she thought her mom was a little afraid of his temper. Anyway, Grandma asked her why she didn't just replant them, and Grandma said that she left a space there so she could go and sit in the space and remember to be patient."

"How did that make her patient?"

"I'm not sure. I didn't ask. I was just a kid. But I remember she said when she was annoyed at him, she'd go out there and sit in that space."

"Maybe it reminded her of what happens when you let your temper get the best of you. Or maybe it was an attempt to make something good from a bad situation," suggested Edie.

"Maybe," June considered this. "I don't know. I just know that I often found her out there in that spot, resting from the afternoon sun."

"Some people do teach us how not to be," Edie said. "By showing us behaviour we don't want to have ourselves."

"That's how I feel about my dad when he drinks too much," Dillon said softly. "Which is every night. Literally."

"That's too bad, man," Max murmured.

" It just hurts, that's all."

"That's how I felt about Garth," Nicky said, unexpectedly.

"Garth? Who's that?" June asked. "Is somebody giving you a hard time now that you're in high school?'

Nicky gave a brief laugh.

"You don't have to worry about that, Auntie Bug. Anyway, look at me."

Nicky stood up, pointing his thumbs back at himself.

"I'm taller than all those other grade 9 shrimps."

"It's true," Max agreed. "Nick's the tallest one in our class. Nobody would take him on."

"Well then, who's this Garth?"

"Oh, just somebody my mom lived with off and on."

"Really?"

June's face clouded. She didn't like to think about her sister living with less-than-desirable men. But Chrissy had been lost to her for so very long that she really had no idea regarding her lifestyle.

"Was he your . . . your dad?"

"Oh no. Just some random dude that kept coming in and out of our lives. But I hated the way he talked to me and my mom. Or anybody, really. And I decided that I didn't want to be the kind of man that he was."

Uneasiness seeped inside June, like the cold clutches of an icy hand.

"Does he know where you are?"

"No, and I'm keeping it that way, Auntie Bug. I like it here with all of you. And this big old goon."

Nicky reached over to run his hands through Jack's unruly fur.

"I like the way those spruces look," he continued, clearly finished with the subject. "Sometimes I look out my bedroom window at night, and they look like the shapes of witches back there. Just the way the branches are growing."

"That's where Edie and Junie have their coven meetings," Doc teased, an irrepressible glint in his eye.

"You say witch like it's a bad thing," Edie said. "Did you know that the word 'witch' comes from the old English word 'wicce,' meaning 'wise woman'?"

"Well, you two lovely ladies are definitely that," Doc conceded graciously. "So if you did have coven meetings, they would actually be wise women meetings. Me and the Huckleberries would be left out."

"Not wise enough," Max agreed.

"Will you just look at that beautiful moon?" Edie said. "It's lighting up the whole world, so it is."

SHAGGY JACK

"The moon is my very oldest friend," Doc declared. "Many a night it guided me home from a house call when I was too tired to even see the road."

"That's a nice thought, Doc. Max could write a story about that," Edie smiled.

"Ah, yes, these Huckleberries of ours are going to be amazing. And in not very long, a few years from now, Max will be a journalist and Nicky here will be a veterinarian. And you, Dillon? What will you be? Do you know yet?"

"I'd like to work with animals too. But I wouldn't want to be a vet—maybe a vet tech or something."

"Great. I hope I live long enough to see you all do what you want. Or at least I hope I don't lose my mind. What's left of it, anyway," he added cheerfully.

Silence fell on the little group, a sweet, beautiful silence, in appreciation of the sacred darkness and the silver, glowing moon. It seemed a shame to have to go indoors and sleep on such a glorious night.

Doc broke the quietude with an excited cry.

"I know what would add to your story, Max. Maybe that pesky mouse could be munching on a big piece of cheese when he scooted by on the robot machine. He could wave at the lady of the house with his free hand as he soared by her!"

Chapter Seventeen

"Those maple trees in the front yard make me glad that I live in Canada," Edie remarked one October morning. "And couldn't you just cut your heart on the blue of that sky?"

"The days are sure flying by," June sniffed, not usually given to such flights of fancy. "It's hard to believe that Nelson's owners will be back on the weekend."

They had enjoyed keeping Nelson. Nicky had done well with the hand signs and now felt qualified to look after other deaf dogs.

"I don't know any other deaf dogs, Nicky. You can teach any dog hand signals, I guess. It's not as if they can talk back."

At this, Nicky had called Jack over, telling him "I love you" over and over in a low, monotone voice.

A low croon emitted from the dog's big mouth.

Nicky grinned triumphantly.

"See! See! Doesn't it sound like 'I love you'? I mean, if Jack could actually say words."

June shrugged.

"I don't know, Nicky. Maybe."

"I think it does," Edie piped up. "And Jack does love you."

"He brought me here," Nicky mused. "Remember?"

June swatted the back of his head playfully with her tea towel. "As if I'm likely to forget the sight of the two of you standing on my front lawn, looking like you'd been dropped out of a clear, blue sky. It's funny how no one ever came looking for him."

SHAGGY JACK

No one had come looking for Nicky either, but June refrained from mentioning this.

"Well, they can't come now," Nicky said cheerfully, tousling Jack's shaggy head and ears. "Because he belongs here with us."

"He does," June agreed, with a firm nod of her head. She couldn't imagine life without any of them. And Nicky did have a point about Jack, though she wouldn't have admitted it aloud. Jack did seem almost human at times. He would tilt his head when you spoke to him as if truly considering the merit of your words. June had known grown-ups who had not possessed this degree of consideration.

"And he saved someone's life yesterday." Nicky continued. " Did you know that, Auntie Bug?"

"Who saved someone's life?" Doc turned, almost knocking the coffee pot over.

June silently retrieved the pot, shaking her head. "I didn't know anyone's life was in need of saving," she remarked wryly.

"Well, I don't know if it was for sure. But he said it was."

"Who did?"

"Dick."

"Dick who? Start at the beginning, Nicky."

Nicky sighed.

"All right. I think I forgot to tell you because when I got home, Leslie had gotten out and we all went to find her and by the time we got all the dogs sorted out, it was late and—"

"That's okay," June waved away his explanation. "It doesn't matter. But whose life was at stake?"

"I don't know if it was really at stake or if he just said it was at stake."

"Who?"

"Dick. I told you."

"Go on."

"He was standing up on that bridge, the big one on the way into town. On the highest ledge that leads up to the very top. Jack and I were walking by and I yelled, 'Hey man, be careful you don't fall.' And he said he wanted to fall. I told him that was silly that he'd hurt himself, and he said he didn't want to live anymore. And I said, 'Don't be a dick, man.' And he said he was a dick. I said he probably wasn't, and he yelled at me and said he was; that was his name. Not short for Richard, but just plain Dick. So he was allowed to be a Dick."

Doc roared with laughter.

"You just can't make this stuff up, can you? Was that really his name?"

"I guess so. I mean, why would he lie about it?"

Edie shrugged.

"So what did you do?" she asked. "That seems pretty intense."

"It kind of was. I told him my name was Nick, so not that far off. By the way," he continued, "I think I'd like to be called Nick from now on."

The women nodded, assuring him they'd try to remember.

"Nicky," Doc reflected. "Just in the nick of time."

"For what?"

"For Dick!"

"That's lame, Doc, even for you. Continue, Nicky—Nick."

"Well, the rest was down to Jack. I told you he can feel things.

SHAGGY JACK

He could see this guy was in distress. He went to the bridge and got up on his back legs and started pawing at the ledge."

"Oh wow! Did it scare the guy?" Edie asked. "I mean, Jack is pretty tall when he's on his hind legs."

June nodded.

"I imagine he's close to seven or eight feet, wouldn't you think, Doc?"

"Yup. Easily."

"Well, Dick had never seen a dog that tall. He was afraid Jack was going to hurt him, but I told him that he just wanted to help. He ended up sitting down with his legs swinging, and Jack nudged his head around in his lap, you know, like he does. He sat there for quite a while, didn't say much, just that he was having a rough time."

"How old was he?"

"I don't know. I've seen him at the school. I think he's in grade 12 or something."

"That sure can be a rough time," Edie acknowledged.

"Suicide is a permanent solution to a temporary problem," Max said softly.

"That's very astute," Edie observed.

"And very true," June agreed. "Where did you hear that?"

"Oh, I don't know. I read it somewhere."

"Okay, so this Dick is sitting on the bridge and Jack is snuggling up to him and what do you say then, Nicky boy?"

"I just told him that Jack and I would stay with him and listen to him if he wanted to talk. He said, 'For how long?' and I said, 'For as long as it takes until you feel like getting down.'"

"That was a good answer, Nicky," Dillon said approvingly. "How long *did* it take?"

"I don't honestly know. Mostly, he just asked about Jack and why he was so big. He told me he'd seen ponies smaller than Jack. But he really liked Jack. You could tell because he kept stroking him and once, he even kissed his head, but I pretended not to notice."

"Good job, buddy," Dillon commented.

"Anyway, eventually he said he felt better and he should get home."

"Did you ever find out what the matter was?"

"No, but I think it might have had something to do with his dad. He said, 'Just imagine if one dad was different, how all the next dads would be different, and then the whole world would be different.' I just said I didn't know because I'd never known my dad, and he said there's things worse than that."

Dillon nodded, averting his eyes.

Edie sighed.

"How sad to be so young and feel so hopeless. I'm glad you and Jack were there that day. Is he okay now, do you think?"

"I saw him in the halls today, so he's still living," Nick replied cheerfully. "He nodded at me, but we didn't talk, and that's fine with me."

"Well, that's a relief anyway. There are so many broken people in this world," Edie sighed. "I guess we're all broken in some way or another."

"At least we're lucky enough to have our Junie to put all the pieces back together for us," Doc declared, raising his coffee cup.

SHAGGY JACK

"It's a tough job, but somebody has to do it," June laughed. "Anyway, good job, Nick. See, I remembered."

"Remembered what?" Doc inquired. "Did I miss something?"

"It's okay, Doc," Nick told him. "I just wondered if you'd call me Nick now instead of Nicky. Since I'm getting older."

"I'll try, my huckleberry friend. I'll try. Sometimes I'll remember in the nick of time, no doubt. Maybe I should call you 'Nick of Time.'"

"Don't be a dick, Doc."

Chapter Eighteen

Evenings nestled in early around the boarding house, wrapping it soundly and sweetly in velvet dusk. The chiminea was carefully stored away in the shed until next summer. Doc placed Old Smokey inside it, bidding him farewell for another year. Doc would not allow himself to smoke on his own. "Too forgetful," he decreed of his own self.

It was one afternoon, a few weeks later, when Max came flying through the kitchen door, waving a sheet of paper over his head, panting for breath.

"Max! Are you okay?" Edie cried.

June bolted to the kitchen window, her heart in her throat. "Is everything all right?"

"Everything's fine," he gasped. "I ran . . . all the way . . . from the bus stop because . . . I've got something to tell you guys!" He had an ear-to-ear grin, clearly enjoying the dramatic effect he had created.

"Good news, then?" Doc prompted. "Is it good news, Max?"

"Yes!" the boy yelled, throwing the paper up into the air. "I won! I won the Maple Leaf Competition! Out of the whole high school."

Cheers and whoops of joy filled the kitchen.

"That competition is a big deal, Max," Edie remarked, beaming. "You should be very proud of yourself."

"We're all proud of you, too," June pronounced.

"Did you use my ending?" Doc asked, after being reminded of the story's plot. "The mouse skedaddling around with a piece of cheese."

SHAGGY JACK

"N-no," Max said, uncertainly. "I'm not sure that's even a real word, Doc. Would the judges have known what it meant?"

"Sure, they would. It's a great word."

"Well, I just said 'cruising around' on the Roomba, waving a piece of cheese. And the judges said that was their favourite part. The ending. The ending you suggested, Doc."

"Just imagine that, will you?" Doc declared, pleased as punch.

One afternoon, Dillon's father fell down his stairs. He was found by a neighbour who had come to the door with a package that had been delivered to their house by mistake. The neighbour heard yelling and cursing from inside the door and looked through the window, only to see the man lying at the bottom of the steps. An ambulance was summoned, and Dillon's father was taken to the hospital.

The women were grateful that Dillon had been spared this traumatic scene, having been at school.

Radiology revealed a fractured pelvis, thus requiring a lengthy hospitalization.

"I'm going to come and stay in the end room till my dad gets out," Dillon told Nick brightly, dragging his backpack up the stairs. "Auntie Bug said I could stay here as long as I want."

Nick wasn't surprised. His aunt acted all tough and stuff, but he couldn't imagine her turning someone away when they were in need.

Dillon's face became serious for a moment as he turned to Nick: "Is it wrong that I feel more at home here than I do in my own house?"

"No, man. It's okay."

"I used to not mind being home when Mom was there . . ." Dillon reached under his hoodie, clutching his Star of David. "But it's not the same now. I mean, I love my dad and everything, but it's hard to find the real him when he's drunk all the time. He's not a bad guy. He never hit me or anything."

"A dad should do more than just not hit you," Nick said. "I know that, and I've never met my real dad. Anyway, maybe he'll get all sober in the hospital."

"Maybe," Dillon shrugged, but his voice held a world of doubt.

"Well, I'm glad you're here," said Nick. "And I think supper's ready."

They both heard the sound of Doc's voice wafting up the stairs, singing, *"Heeeeey, good lookin'! Whaaaaaat you got cookin'?"*

Both boys laughed. "He knows the weirdest songs," Dillon said.

The boys scurried down the stairs, Jack at their heels.

"You boys will never guess what's cookin' tonight," Doc chortled as the three halted to a screeching stop, almost running into each other.

"What's cookin'?" Dillon asked, glancing around the kitchen. Edie and June stood beside the stove, their faces full of some indiscernible emotion. Excitement? Apprehension?

"Beef stew," June replied flatly. "Wash up and sit down."

"That's not all!" Doc declared, barely able to contain himself.

"Doc, you're worse than a kid," June admonished.

Edie thought Doc's child-like nature was part of what made him so endearing. He didn't care about rules and regulations or the proper way of going about things. He marvelled in the simple joys of life as they came to him, day by day.

Edie now gazed at the bunch of hopeless, hapless males sitting around the table and announced quietly, "June and I have made a decision."

Nicky and Dillon froze. "A decision?"

Identical expressions of misgiving passed over the boy's faces.

"Oh, don't look like that," Edie smiled. "It's good news. For all of us."

"Edie and I have decided to get married."

June approached the table, placing her hands gently on Edie's shoulders.

"We know it's quite soon," Edie continued. "But we're very sure."

"And you're old enough to know your own minds," Doc said approvingly. "I know, boys, it's a shock. But think how much fun it will be to have a wedding."

"Is it going to be *here*?" gasped Nick in excitement.

"Well, we were just planning on going to the Justice of the Peace," June pronounced. "No fuss or anything. And not until the spring. That will make it a year that we've been together."

"Oh, Junie dear, you should get married here," Doc proclaimed. "That's a great idea, Nicky. We can decorate the place and make it look nice. You can get married in The Patience Spot."

Ever since the tale about the spruce trees, the boarding house residents had dubbed that spot "The Patience Spot." When one or the other of them made their way to The Patience Spot, there was an unspoken agreement that they must be left alone to mull things over and perhaps regain their patience. Or at least that was the intention.

"You wouldn't need an arbour because the spruces would lend

you their branches for that, and the Huckleberries and I could pound together a little platform. Oh, it would be so nice."

June shook her head, laughing.

"Doc, you are incorrigible," she said.

"It would be all right, you know, June," Edie said, a little tentatively. "Doc paints a nice image."

"Just imagine how much fun it will be. And that gives us lots of time to prepare."

"Will it be legal? I mean, can two women get married?" Dillon wondered out loud.

"Yes, they can," June proclaimed. "Since 2003."

"Yes, lesbian ladies can get married, and it's all legal. I was thinking about the topless ones," said Doc.

An outburst erupted in the little kitchen.

"Sorry, sorry. I was thinking about the law that women could go topless in Ontario. That was earlier. I got them mixed up," Doc explained.

"Wait—What?" Nick asked. "I still don't get it. Women can go topless, and it's not against the law?"

Edie and June both nodded sagely at his skeptical look.

"Yup," Edie affirmed. "They can. I think it was passed in the late 1990s."

"Well, that's a rip-off!" Nick snorted. "I've never seen any topless women around town."

"That's how I felt when the law was first passed," Doc told them. "I thought I'd see lots of topless ladies walking about, but alas, it never happened."

"The woman who initiated it was just making a point anyway.

SHAGGY JACK

I don't remember the details exactly, but it was a sweltering hot day, and men were taking their tops off, so she thought women should be allowed to as well. But she got charged. Not enough support."

June glanced around the table, waiting for her little joke to sink in.

"Very funny," Doc said, grinning. "Anyway, I'm sorry. I got lesbian ladies' marriages and topless ladies on hot days muddled up a little. Both are legal, so all is well."

"It will be nice to have a wedding here," Edie declared. "And we've got lots of time to get ready. As long as we want."

"It will be nice to have something to look forward to," June agreed.

Canadian winters are good for hibernating, for throwing snowballs at loved ones, and for rehabilitating dogs.

"It's not enough we board these guys, but now we're a bloody rehab centre," June grumbled.

"We're expanding!" Nick declared. "It's great."

"I need to bring my dad here," Dillon remarked. "He could use some rehab."

"I think it'd be easier to rehabilitate a dog than a human," Doc observed.

"I think you're right, Doc. Anyway, my dad sure doesn't want to be rehabilitated. At least I don't think so. Because if he did, he would have stopped drinking by now."

"Aw, my Huckleberry friend," Doc sighed. "If only it was that easy. I've never been a drinking man myself, but I know once it gets a hold on you, it can be really hard to escape its grasp."

"If anyone had a reason to get better, it's your dad, Dillon," said Edie. "But we are very glad you're here with us."

Dillon's dad had been discharged from the hospital and was home now, but Dillon still spent much of his time at the boarding house. No one asked outright, but it seemed that weeks in the hospital had not rid the man of his alcohol addiction.

"Anyway, which dog are we rehabilitating?" Doc asked now. "And why? Got into the whiskey, did he?"

Dillon threw the old man a perplexed look, uncertain if he was goofing around or not.

"No, Doc, he had surgery. He had a broken pelvis after being hit by a car."

"That is like your dad, Dillon. Maybe he was drunk."

"My dad wasn't hit by a car, Doc. He fell down the stairs."

"But he was drunk and fractured his pelvis, right?"

"Yes, but—"

"Never mind, Doc." June snapped. "I never knew anyone to get as off-topic as you do!"

"We were talking about BJ."

"BJ? Okay, I *am* lost," Doc conceded. "I know what you're all thinking."

"Really? What are we thinking?"

"You're thinking I should have that written on my shirt. The lost bit."

"No one was thinking that, Doc," Edie reassured him.

"It's a good point, though," June muttered.

SHAGGY JACK

"I *was* thinking it," Nicky chirped. "Or written on the side of Mr. Clatterbox."

"In rainbow letters!" Doc chortled.

"When is BJ coming?" Dillon inquired.

"Okay, who's BJ again? I forget," Doc asked humbly.

"It's all right, Doc. I don't think we said," commented Edie. "BJ is the dog who got hit by a car and fractured his pelvis. They put in a screw somewhere and attached it to his sacrum. That's all I know."

"Aw, poor little BJ," Doc murmured sympathetically.

"He's not little," June said. "I wish he was. He's a big, black labradoodle."

"Now that's a funny name. A doodle. Do they doodle when they walk? You know, with their tails or whatever. It's kind of a silly name, don't you think? They used to have only regular dogs in my day. These doodles are something new."

"It refers to the poodle, Doc. They are part poodle and part Labrador. BJ is a pretty big dog, actually," explained June.

"Oh, I see!" Doc nodded his head. "Interbreeding. I used to know a family like that out at the back of the quarry road. They were doodling around with their own breed, though."

"Doc!"

"Is he as big as Jack?" Dillon asked.

"I don't think there's a dog alive as big as Jack," June said, glancing at the enormous canine draped across her kitchen floor.

Everyone nodded. Shaggy Jack was in a class of his own.

"Well, it will be interesting to meet Mr. Doodle," Doc mused.

"BJ. His name is BJ. It's short for Blue Jays. He's a nice dog.

I've met him. He just needs rehab, and his owners can't provide it right now. They're both working very long work weeks," said June.

"He is a nice dog," Edie agreed. "Very quiet and friendly."

"Well, he would be, with a broken pelvis," Doc observed. "He's probably stoned."

"Stoned?" Nick and Dillon gasped together.

"On dog meds. I imagine they have to give dogs something for pain, like humans. A fractured pelvis is very painful. Poor, little, doodling thing."

BJ turned out to be a pleasant dog, in spite of his size. He was quiet and obedient, better behaved than the boys, as June pointed out.

Doc loved BJ at first sight.

"It's rather sweet to see Doc with him," Edie observed one evening, as she and June lingered at the dinner table. "He has a healing gift, don't you think? I mean, he's always kind with the dogs, but he's so very gentle with BJ and his injuries."

"Yes, he's a born healer, that's for sure. Although he still thinks BJ is either stoned or an inbred."

"Or both!" The women shared a laugh.

At this point, Doc and the boys burst into the kitchen.

"Did you know that BJ was named for the Blue Jays?" Doc asked, full of excitement.

"Yes, Doc, we told you that when he first came and you asked what his initials stood for."

"Oh," Doc appeared a little crestfallen. "I didn't remember that."

"That's okay, Doc," Nick assured him, "you know now."

"No wonder he's such a great dog. He's a baseball fan!" declared Doc.

"Or his owners are," Dillon said.

"True," Doc acknowledged. "Well, he's the first doodle I ever knew, and he's named after the Blue Jays. I feel like this is noteworthy."

"*And* he's the first dog we've ever had in our rehab program," Nicky remarked, throwing his aunt a sideways look."

"We don't have a 'rehab program,' Nick," June reminded him. "I only took in BJ because his owners really needed help."

"But I'm sure there's more dogs that need it," Nick said. "I mean, there must be."

"Nick, a person can only do so much," June told him wryly.

"Exactly!" Nick pounced on the statement. "A person can. But Auntie Bug, you've got so much more than just one person now. Right? You've got us. We can all help."

"Yes, you do all help," June conceded. "And I'm grateful. I really am."

"Just think, Auntie Bug," Nick grinned. "We've got the room and the help. We could expand and open a rehab centre for dogs."

"Yes, we could!" Doc exclaimed with glee.

June's days were filled to overflowing with chores and activities.

"I might not want to be quite this busy," she grumbled. "It'd be nice to have a little bit of peace and quiet, once in a while."

"Ah, but that would be dull now, wouldn't it?" Edie smiled at her. "You wouldn't want life to be dull."

"Wouldn't I?"

As if on cue, the rumble of Mr. Clatterbox sounded outside.

"I swear that damned truck gets noisier every day," June pronounced. "It's going to just disintegrate one of these days and leave a pile of rust on the cobblestones."

Edie laughed. "With some rainbow letters scattered among the rust particles. I wonder why Doc drives such an old relic," she mused. "Do you think it's a question of money?"

"I don't know," June replied. "I mean, he always pays for his room and board on time, most months ahead of time. Sometimes, he's even tried to pay me twice for the same month because he's so afraid that he'll forget to pay."

"And he's very generous with groceries or anything that's needed at the house," Edie added.

"He's always been like that," June said. "He never spends money on himself. When he needs new clothes or anything, he just gives me the cash and asks me to pick them up. Says he doesn't trust himself anymore to get the right things. But I think he could afford a new vehicle, if he wanted one."

"Oh, he probably doesn't want one," Edie laughed. "You know, Doc, he gets so attached to things. Like Mr. Clatterbox."

"I *am* attached to Mr. Clatterbox," Doc affirmed, coming through the door on the tail end of the conversation, Jack and the boys at his heels. "That truck has more personality than some people I know. *Used* to know," he corrected himself, gazing around the room. "Everybody I know *now* has lots of personality."

June turned and scoffed but secretly took the statement as a compliment. Better to have personality than be boring.

SHAGGY JACK

"Max is writing poetry now," Nicky announced. "You gotta listen to this. He wrote a poem about the dogs."

"Max, you are on your way to becoming a full-fledged writer," Edie beamed at him.

The boy blushed.

"I was just fiddling around with some rhymes because we're supposed to write a poem in English."

"Let's hear it!" Doc commanded, gratefully accepting a steaming mug of coffee from June.

"Doc, you heard it in the truck."

"Yes, but I don't remember it exactly," Doc admitted sheepishly. "Anyway, I was thinking that the women might like to hear it too. I can't always hear too well in Mr. Clatterbox. I don't like to say anything when we're riding in him because I don't want to hurt his feelings, but he can be a little noisy at times."

"We've noticed," Max grinned.

"Oh good, it's not just me then."

"No, Doc, dogs in Europe could hear that rattly old thing," June told him.

"Really?"

"No, of course not. Here, sit down, you bunch. Edie just made peanut butter cookies."

"My favourite kind!" Doc declared.

"You said that about my chocolate chip ones last week," Edie teased him.

"And I meant it at the time," Doc informed her, with great dignity.

"Well, have a cookie and then let's hear this masterpiece."

"What masterpiece?" asked Doc.

"Max's poem."

"Yes, of course."

"It's not a masterpiece," Max protested, the pinkish hue returning to his boyish face. "I was just fooling around."

"Okay, well let's hear it!"

Max cleared his throat, qualifying with, "It's not done yet. I have to work on it."

"Tell us what you have written so far."

"Okay, here goes," he said, and read his poem.

> *"There are oodles and oodles*
> *Of dogs who are doodles*
> *With legs that are poodles*
> *We like them a lot.*
> *Leslie is blind*
> *Nelson is deaf*
> *BJ is in rehab*
> *We like them all too.*
> *Our Jack is quite shaggy*
> *His tail is all waggy*
> *He's big as a pony*
> *And we love him the best."*

"I love it!" Doc said. "Even the second time."

"Max, you are very talented," Edie smiled.

"I'm not done yet. *Obviously*," Max affirmed, self-consciously.

"No, but it's a very good start."

"Well, maybe I'll have more dogs to write about if you get more dogs for rehab," Max said, looking around at the other boys, seemingly for support.

"More dogs?" June asked.

"Okay, Auntie Bug," Nick jumped in. "I mentioned it before, but will you just hear me out?"

"I always do."

"That is true," Doc nodded, happily munching his fourth or fifth peanut butter cookie. No one was counting, least of all Doc.

"Well, Kevin Young has this dog. It's a Bernedoodle."

"Another doodle!" Doc cried. "These doodles are doodling around all over the place."

"You just like to say doodle, Doc," Edie winked at the old man.

"That's true," he admitted.

"Anyway," Nick continued. "He's a very good-natured dog. At least he always was. But then on Saturday night, Kevin's dad got drunk and kicked him."

"Bastard!" Doc exclaimed uncharacteristically.

Everyone looked at him in shock.

"Sorry about that," he muttered.

"I have to agree," June said. "It's a whole other level of low to kick an innocent creature of any kind."

"Right?" Nick regarded his aunt. "I knew you'd think that, Auntie Bug. Anyway, this dog, his name's Bernie, he's had a bit of a personality change."

"Bernie for Bernedoodle," Doc observed with delight, dropping his anger as fast as he'd picked it up.

"What do you mean by personality change?" June asked.

"Well, since Kevin's dad kicked him, he just seems off, and Kevin can't get him to eat very much. He's really worried about him."

"That's a shame," June agreed. "He doesn't sound like a very nice man. I hope he doesn't kick Kevin."

"I said the same thing," Dillon remarked.

"What did Kevin say?"

"He said he didn't because Kevin could run faster than him. He said his dad is too short and fat to run."

"Auntie Bug," Nick continued, his voice pleading now, "we were thinking that maybe Bernie needed some rehab. You know . . . because we're kind of open to that sort of thing now . . ."

June cocked an eyebrow. "I wasn't aware that we were."

"Well, we have BJ in rehab."

"Yes, but that is completely different than what you're talking about, dear boy."

"Rehab can be for the mind or the body," Nick pointed out.

"Yes, well, that's true for people. I'm not sure where it stands for dogs."

"Could we at least have a look at Bernie? Please, Auntie Bug?"

"I suppose it wouldn't hurt to have a look at him sometime," she conceded.

"Oh good," Nick cried, hopping to his feet. "Because he's waiting in the truck."

Chapter Nineteen

"I wish I could just snuggle up here in bed with you and send my body out to have a run on its own," groaned June, one particularly bitter cold January morning.

"Like a disembodiment," Edie giggled. "No wait, the disembodied bit would be here in bed with me."

June swung her legs around to perch on the side of the bed. The warm, cozy bed.

Darkness still held the world in its foreboding embrace.

"Anyway, I thought you decided against taking up running. I really don't think you should be running, June."

"Why not?" June asked crossly. "Because of my age or because of my size?"

"Neither. Because we only get so many joints, that's why."

"I can't really run on these icy roads anyway," June sighed. "So I just walk fast. I don't know how much weight I'm going to lose that way. I've been moving non-stop since Nick came with his entourage of boys and dogs, and it hasn't made any difference at all. Mind you, it's been round and round in circles, but I'm still moving."

"Yes, you sure are. You're busy every day. Which is why you should stay here and rest instead of going out into the cold."

"I'll never lose any weight that way. And I want to look good for our wedding."

"Junie, you will look amazing, like you always do. I don't care what you weigh, and you know it."

"But *I* do," June replied firmly, exiting the room.

Sometime later, she hobbled back into the country kitchen where Edie and Doc were having their morning coffee. Daylight had just begun to seep into the frigid world. June sank heavily into a kitchen chair, exuding a deep moan of pain.

"Oh, June," cried Edie. "What on earth did you do to yourself?" She rushed to her side, looking for signs of injury.

June looked down at her leg with a scowl, as if it had betrayed her. "I twisted my damned ankle going around the corner to the side road."

"I don't doubt it," Edie said. "It's glare ice."

"Why were you out there so early?" Doc asked. "It's barely daylight! I said I'd get up and feed the dogs. I didn't forget."

"Oh, Doc, I know that. There's no one more reliable than you, even with—"

"I know," Doc finished for her. "Even with half a brain."

"I was *not* going to say that," June objected.

"Oh, I know, Junie dear. But that doesn't mean it's not true. Anyway, lift your snow pants and let me look at your ankle."

June winced as Doc examined her appendage with skilled, gentle fingers.

"You've done a number on it, for sure. I don't think it's broken, but it's badly sprained. You're going to have to rest for a few days until the swelling goes down. Elevate it and put ice on it, that's the best thing."

"I can't," she protested. "There's too much to do."

"You can and you will," Edie's words were kind but firm. "We will all pitch in and help."

June groaned but allowed herself to be led, limping, to the couch where Doc hoisted her leg up and slid a pillow underneath it.

Edie retrieved two acetaminophen pills. June swallowed them before lying back and closing her eyes in despair.

"Well, that was certainly the most nonproductive morning I've had in quite some time," she complained.

"Yes, it sure was," Edie said sternly. "And for no reason at all."

"What was the reason?" Doc inquired. "Did I miss that?"

"Oh, June has some hair-brained idea of losing weight for the wedding,"

"What wedding? Oh, the lesbian wedding!" Doc lit up, then caught himself. "I mean *your* wedding."

"Which *is*, in fact, a lesbian wedding," June said. "But no need to define it as such every time you mention it. It's just a wedding of two people who love each other."

"Exactly," Doc nodded. "I agree. So why do you want to lose weight? You have to have something to come and go on, after all."

"I don't even know what that means," June retorted crossly.

"It just means that you want to have some meat on your bones, in case you get sick or something."

"Oh, Doc," June moaned. "You don't understand."

"I don't understand lots of things anymore. You're right about that, Junie dear."

"That's not what I meant. You don't understand about wanting to look different. I want to look nice for my wedding."

"But why would you want to look different? Edie might think she's marrying another lesbian lady," he said before catching himself again. "I mean another lady."

"I agree. I don't want her to look any different," Edie interjected.

"This has nothing to do with me. I'd like to make that fact crystal clear."

"That's because you're both skinny. You don't know how I feel. I've always been a square shape. Like a cube. The boys at school used to say, 'Here comes the Cube.'"

"They used to call me Stringbean," Doc shrugged.

"Exactly!" June shouted, pointing an accusing finger at him. "You've always been skinny."

"But I didn't like being called Stringbean any more than you liked being called the Cube. Kids used to say things like, 'Doesn't your mama feed you, Stringbean?' Well, of course she did. I couldn't help how I looked."

June exhaled a deep, frustrated sigh.

"You just don't understand. Neither one of you."

"I think," Edie said gently, "that Doc is trying to say that we just are who we are."

"That *is* what I am trying to say, Edie. Thank you. You're going to look so beautiful at this wedding. I can't wait. I'm going to get The Patience Spot all ready as soon as the snow melts. I'm going to plant some sunflowers all around the front of it. I've always loved sunflowers. They're just so cheerful, aren't they? Maybe we should take you out and deposit you there now until you get some patience back. It's a thought," he said, flashing June a mischievous smile. "You, Junie dear," he continued, "are going to be the best-looking lady to ever be married there."

"I don't think anyone has ever *been* married there, Doc."

"Exactly!"

SHAGGY JACK

"I'm going to read a little poem I found on the internet today," Edie announced.

The winter winds were chasing each other around the house, causing snow to twirl and dance in front of the windows like ghosts pirouetting in a peculiar, wraithlike fashion. Everyone was pleased to be snuggled under blankets in front of the living room's wood stove.

Doc had done a great job stoking it. Now it roared, sending a companionable warmth into the crevices of the old boarding house where the cold seemed to creep in and linger. Max had stayed after school, and the three boys lay on the ground, giggling about something they'd found on their phones. Something June decided she didn't want to know about. If she didn't know, she didn't have to worry about it.

Jack was draped behind the boys like a huge, grey rug. Nick's head rested near the dog. Every once in a while, Nick's hand found its way to the sprawling ears, scratching them gently.

"Okay, boys, listen. Edie says she has a poem she'd like to read to us."

"Usually, Max is the reader of poems," Doc observed. "I've never heard one of Edie's before."

"Oh, I didn't write it, Doc," Edie explained. "Erin Hansen wrote it."

"And who's that now?" Doc asked. "Do I know him?"

"No, Doc, it's a poem I came across on the internet. But I wondered if you'd mind if I read it."

"Look at us, being so literary," Doc said approvingly. "I hope I understand the poem."

"Oh, you will, Doc, and you'll understand why I thought this would be a good time to read it."

"Proceed, my dear. We are all ears."

Edie began.

> *"You are not your age, nor the size of the clothes you wear,*
> *You are not a weight, or the colour of your hair.*
> *You are not your name, or the dimples in your cheeks.*
> *You are all the books you've read, and all the words you speak.*
> *You are your croaky morning voice and the smiles you try to hide,*
> *You're the sweetness in your laughter, and every tear you've cried.*
> *You're the songs you sing so loudly when you know you're all alone.*
> *You're the places that you've been to and the one that you call home.*
> *You're the things that you believe in, and the people that you love.*
> *You're the photos in your bedroom, and the future you dream of.*
> *You're made of so much beauty, but it seems that you forgot.*
> *When you decided that you were defined by all the things you're not."*

Doc started clapping and declared, "That's a great poem, Edie, even if you didn't write it. And I know why you read it now."

"Yes, it's quite obvious to me too," June said, sarcasm dripping from her voice. "I'm pretty sure the message was directed at me."

"Of course it was," Doc agreed. "Even I got that bit."

"What was the message?" Nick asked.

SHAGGY JACK

Max made a gesture with his hand, sweeping across the top of Nick's head. "Went right over your head, did it, buddy?"

"I get it. I just don't know what it's got to do with Auntie Bug."

"Oh, I was just trying to get in a little better shape before the wedding, if you must know," June said sullenly. "I didn't want to make a big thing about it."

"But now it *is* a big thing, because you've hurt your ankle," Edie told her, her voice gentle.

Dillon's brow wrinkled. "Better shape?"

"Yes, like another shape but a cube shape," Doc said helpfully.

"Doc!" Dillon gasped.

"I'm only quoting," Doc explained. "That's what Junie said, not me."

"He's right," June sighed. "I did say that. That's why Edie read that poem."

"To make you see that you're more than your perception of your shape," Edie agreed. "So much more."

"That is very true," Doc nodded. "You're a wonderful human being, Junie dear. Look at all of us. None of us would be here if it wasn't for you. Why, I'd probably be buried underneath a big mountain of snow because I would have forgotten my way home and no one would be out looking for me."

"And I'd be somewhere lost in the prairies with no place to go, stuck wandering around all those grain fields. And who knows where Jack would have ended up? Someone might have shot him for making a buffet dinner of their barbecue grill."

"I'm very glad to be here, Auntie Bug," Dillon said softly. "I don't care what shape you're in."

June laughed. "You're all just being ridiculous."

"No, actually, we're not," Edie declared. "You have no idea what this has meant to us to be able to live here. I'd just escaped a very unhappy marriage."

"To a man?" Doc asked inquisitively.

"Yes, Doc, to a man."

"Before you jumped ship, I guess."

"Precisely."

"Jumped ship?" Max inquired.

"I just meant jumping from marriage to lesbianism," Doc explained. "I've never done either, so I was just curious, is all."

A particularly strong gust of wind ripped around the house, causing the windows to shudder in protest, momentarily blinding them in a veil of white.

"Auntie Bug?"

"Yes, Nick."

"I was thinking."

"Yes."

"I was thinking that it must be awful cold out in the kennels tonight."

"Nick, the kennels are sheltered and there's lots of straw, and each one has an enclosure so the dogs can go and lie in there. I mean, they're not out in the elements. Not by a long shot," June replied.

"That's true," Nick admitted. "I know that."

A long pause ensued before Nick gulped audibly, then continued. "But they might be scared. The winds are awful loud tonight. And Leslie's blind and Bernie's already traumatized and BJ's—"

"Nick, I did not ask for all these screwed up dogs. You're the one who talked me into having such a mishmash of creatures. It's not all that cold out, only windy. And they *are* sheltered."

"I know. I know. It was just a thought."

Everyone's eyes turned expectantly in June's direction. She tried to ignore them, feeling that she had been quite clear on this issue.

"Why don't I get Cracklin' Rosie, and we could maybe sing a couple of tunes?" Doc suggested. "It's so cozy and warm in here with that fire on."

"That would be great, Doc," June nodded. "Yes, it is nice and warm. Thanks for getting the wood split and the fire going. I feel very lucky to be able to recuperate in such a nice spot."

"It's lovely and warm in here, that's for sure," Edie agreed.

"Oh, for God's sake," June sighed in exasperation. "Why don't you boys go out and bring those bloody dogs in here, so I don't have to look at your woebegone faces."

"I didn't say anything," Nick protested.

"You didn't have to. I know how you think."

"There's only three of them," Dillon said. "They won't take up too much room."

"Plus Jack," June said. "He takes up enough room for five normal-sized dogs."

The boys had scrambled to their feet.

"You sure, Auntie Bug?" Nick asked.

"Hurry up! And don't leave the door open too long. It's bloody cold out there!"

Chapter Twenty

June's ankle improved with time and rest, just as Doc had predicted.

Dogs continued to come and go. Some just came and stayed. Like Leslie and Bernie.

Since the night of the storm, Leslie had remained indoors at night. Or "wormed his way inside," as June put it.

He had somehow become Dillon's dog. The first time June had discovered Leslie on top of the bed with Dillon, both deep in slumber, she had merely sighed in resignation.

"I suppose they both need the comfort," June remarked one night, after peeking in on the boys. "They look pretty content tucked up there together. Who am I to ruin that?"

"See? This is why I love her so much," Edie turned to Doc, smiling.

"Yup," Doc nodded. "She's not half as hard-hearted as she wants us all to think."

"Something like that."

"I can hear you two, you know. And I don't want you to think I'm hard-hearted."

"Well, that's good," Doc said. "Because we don't."

"Well, somebody has to enforce some rules around here. Since we seem to be running a home for wayward dogs *and* boys."

"We do, don't we?" Doc agreed. "Isn't it great?"

"There's only Leslie and Jack inside," Edie pointed out reasonably. "BJ's gone home now."

"All fixed up, waiting to cheer on the Blue Jays," Doc declared.

"I suppose. What about Bernie? Do you think he'll be going home soon? Surely he's over the trauma of being kicked by now."

"I feel sad that ever happened," Edie said. "Bernie's such a nice dog. And Kevin says he's very happy here."

"Kevin is happy here, too," Doc said. "He's a nice lad."

"If I turn my back, you'll have Kevin and Bernie living here," June grumbled.

"Well, we do have room," Doc observed.

"Doc, I can't take everyone in. I just can't."

Doc only shrugged. He didn't see why not.

"Maybe Kevin's dad needs to learn that dogs respond better to kindness than being kicked," Edie said.

"And boys do too," Doc added.

"You're right, of course, Doc," June conceded.

"Who have we got lined up for the kennels this week?" Edie asked. "Besides the usual suspects."

"I think the word seems to have gotten out that we take special needs dogs," June said dryly. "Someone called yesterday and asked if we took in dogs that are paralyzed and if we have any of those wheels you can get for dogs with back leg problems."

"What did you say?" Doc inquired eagerly.

"I said no, of course. We've got enough to do without having dogs like that."

"We could manage, though," Doc suggested, warming to the idea. "We could hook them up in their little carts, and Jack could pull them around the yard. They could race to see who has the best time around. That would be great."

"Oh, Doc, that's just not practical. Anyway, I said no."

"Maybe you could reconsider."

"No!"

"Too bad. I can picture it already in my mind. Maybe Max could write a story about it."

"So, do you have any other dogs lined up, June?" Edie asked. "Dogs that have use of all four legs, I mean."

"There's two coming this week and three the next. You'll like this, Doc." She turned to the old man, who was trying not to feel too disappointed about the racing cart dog idea being so unequivocally squashed.

"What will I like?"

"The one that's coming this week is called 'Fivemiles.'"

"Five miles?"

"Fivemiles. All one word."

"That's a funny name," Edie observed.

"The owner said he called him that because he liked to tell people that he walked five miles every day."

"I do like that," Doc nodded. "Max could write a story about that, for sure."

"That would be a better topic," June agreed.

"Maybe you should write stories, Doc," Edie suggested. "You're good at seeing opportunities for Max to write stories all the time."

"Because he's such a good little writer, even at his age. I just like being on the lookout for ideas."

"He is. But you must know lots of stories from all your experience as a country doctor. Whenever you tell them to us, they're always interesting. You could write some of them down."

"We'd have to censor them first," June observed wryly, "to make sure no one is mentioned that has any sexually transmitted diseases or babies from someone other than their husband." She threw a stern look in Doc's direction. He had been known to mention both of those things in passing.

"Yes," he sighed, "it's true. I've lost the way to say things appropriately. That's why I'm so lucky to have you girls to tell me when to shut up."

"We've never told you that, Doc," Edie gasped. "Never."

"Junie did one day."

"I'm sure she didn't mean it like that."

"I did, actually," June affirmed. "He started to tell a story about a person with an STD *and* an illegitimate child. A person that the boys knew quite well."

"Oh, right! Max's mother, that must have been."

"Yes, Doc, but teenage boys don't need to know about these things. Especially regarding their mothers."

"Junie dear, you are absolutely right, as always."

June just shook her head. It wouldn't stop Doc from spouting out the next unsuitable thing that popped into his head when the opportunity arose.

"That's why Max should do the writing," Doc concluded triumphantly. "And I'll just keep on gathering up ideas for him. What was the one I just had?"

"Fivemiles," Edie reminded him.

"Ah, that was it."

The whole story had to be related to the boys at the end of the school day—about the new dogs and the unusual name and joke attached to it. Doc advised Max to write a story about it.

"It's sure to be another winner," he pronounced. Doc always added this to any mention of Max's writing, ever since he won the story competition.

Leslie crept down the stairs, sidling up to Dillon's side. Dillon squatted to envelop the little schnauzer in his arms.

"Oh, and we were talking about dogs with those little wheels for their back legs . . . You know, for dogs that are paralyzed and can't walk," Doc continued.

"We were?" Excitement thrummed through Nick's voice. "That's awesome! I was also thinking that we could set up a centre for dogs in need. Could we do that, do you think? They could learn to press an emergency button."

"Really?" Doc exclaimed. "You could teach them to do that, Nicky?"

"We could try. You know how we taught Nelson to sign because he's deaf? Maybe something like that would work. I'd have to look into it."

"Wait a minute," June raised her hand. "Just wait a minute. We are *not* going to have dogs with little wheelchairs here. We never said we were."

"Doc just said you were talking about it," Nick replied defensively.

"Just talking about how we weren't going to do it."

"Well, maybe some other time we can think again about the little wheelchairs." He turned to his dear Huckleberry friends, adding excitedly in a stage whisper: "I was thinking we could have races with them."

Chapter Twenty-One

Spring arrived like a sweet benediction after the harsh starkness of winter. The days grew longer as the sun stretched its warmth across the blessed earth, awakening life from its frigid slumber. Buds began to curl open, their delicate blossoms painting the landscape with soft, welcome colour. The air grew fragrant with the scent of their blooms, and the gentle hum of bees and chirping of birds filled each new morning with melody.

"Just when a person is ready to slit their throat at the thought of one more grey, overcast day, finally the sun decides to shine," June remarked one such May morning.

"Oh dear," Edie said, taken aback. "That seems a little extreme."

June sighed and plopped down into one of the porch chairs. "You're right. I guess I got kind of down this winter, what with not being able to get around. And then when my ankle did improve, I was afraid to walk too far because the bloody roads were so icy."

"Fair enough. But we're on the downside of all that bad weather now."

"I'm going to have to do something about these chairs soon," June said, feeling the wicker sagging underneath her. "These are from my grandparents' time. They're getting pretty worn."

"Well, will you look at that!" Edie crooned. "Talk about serendipity."

June turned to the sight of Mr. Clatterbox rumbling into the yard, its truck bed overflowing with porch furniture. Jack and the boys hung out the windows. It drew up close to the house, clunking up and down on the cobblestones.

"Now I know what that nun meant," Nick sang out, laughing.

"Nun?" June shot Edie an inquisitive look.

"I think he's talking about Doc's old joke."

"Joke?"

"About the nuns riding their bikes on the cobblestones."

"Oh, for God's sake! I forgot about that. Bloody boys forget what I tell them, even if I say it a million times, and yet they remember some stupid joke about nuns getting off from riding over the cobblestones."

Edie dissolved into giggles, and before long, so did June, despite all efforts to the contrary.

"They're teenage boys," Edie said. "What do you expect?"

The furniture perched precariously in the truck, fastened with an elaborate pattern of knots and twisted rope, which Doc and the boys proceeded to disentangle.

"Voila!" Doc turned and bowed to the women seated on the porch, as if unveiling a magic trick.

"We got some new porch furniture," Nick announced.

"I see that. I didn't know you were going to do that."

"I didn't either," Doc mused. "I picked my Huckleberries up because they were going to help me get some plants to decorate The Patience Spot. You know, for the lesbian wedding."

"Doc, remember how we talked about not wanting to define it as a lesbian wedding? Can we just call it the wedding? I might have mentioned this before?"

SHAGGY JACK

"Junie dear, you might have, and I'll try. I just think of it in my mind as the lesbian wedding because I've never been to one before."

June sighed, resigning herself to the inevitable.

"Anyway, we went to look for some flowers. I thought pansies would be nice. They have those cute little purple and yellow faces. I thought they'd be good in The Patience Spot. People would look at them and think they should be patient just because their faces were so darned cute."

"Do you think people will get that connection, Doc?"

"Well, we can hope."

"Fair enough. I don't know if they make me more patient, but I like them too, especially at this time of year. They're nice and bright."

"I agree, Junie dear."

Dillon emerged from the cab of the truck carrying multiple flats of the bright purple and yellow flowers, enough to decorate several Patience Spots.

Doc motioned to the truck bed. "I'm afraid I got waylaid because they had all this new porch furniture at the hardware store and I thought that it would look awful nice on the porch."

June observed the furniture piled in the truck. It gleamed white and pristine in the sunshine, quite a contrast to any furniture ever before seen at the old boarding house. "It's beautiful, Doc," she admitted. "And it looks expensive? I mean, you don't usually buy things like this—things that are brand new."

Doc's usual method of acquiring things was by scouring the back roads for anything people had thrown away. Or "recycled," as he preferred to put it.

"I know you don't totally approve of my methods of acquiring furniture and so on, but this is different, because this is my present to you for the les- . . . for the wedding."

"Doc, you don't need to do that. I'll gladly reimburse you. We needed new furniture. I should have replaced it years ago."

Doc waved her concerns away.

"I won't hear of it, my dear," Doc declared. "It is my pleasure. We drove over to Dalton to see what plants they had—that's what took us so long—and the man there told me all about the new furniture and how much more durable it is. Apparently, it's called resin wicker or something like that and lasts longer than the stuff they used to have. It'll outlast me, anyway. I told him that, and he told me that he knew me. I couldn't remember him, but he said that was okay. It had been kind of an embarrassing problem that he came to me for."

"Shocking!" Edie laughed. "Those are usually the ones you remember the best, Doc."

"I know. That is true, but I didn't remember this guy, so I told him his secret was safe with me, which it is. Anyway, he said he gave me a good deal, but I have no idea if it was or not. We got cushions too. Nice cheerful red ones and other ones with maple leaves on them. For Canada Day. And also to remember Max's big win."

"We'll go in and get a pitcher of lemonade and a tray of cookies," Edie told him. "You guys are going to be hungry and thirsty after all your hard work."

"That sounds wonderful," Doc declared.

"Come on, my Huckleberries, we have a wedding to get ready for!"

Chapter Twenty-Two

THE wedding was set for the second Saturday in June.

"It seems soon," June reflected, lolling on the new porch furniture one sweet spring evening. Peepers sang their beautiful song of freedom from the back swamp, and birds chirped their springtime joy amidst the happy noise of laughing boys and barking dogs.

"Soon for what?" Doc asked. He'd just finished mowing the lawn, and blades of grass clung to his face at precarious angles.

"I love the smell of freshly mown grass," Edie smiled. "There's really nothing like it, especially after this long winter."

"Me too," June nodded, inhaling deeply. "Thanks so much for doing it, Doc. Nick said he would've done it. He said he told you that."

"Oh, he did. But they're busy with school. I like cutting the grass. Always have. I thought it needed it. Did you think it was too soon?"

"No, it was getting long," June said. "I was thinking it was too soon for the wedding."

"Why would it be too soon for the wedding? Isn't any time a good time for a wedding? June is supposed to be the best month to get married. I remember that old wives' tale—something about being married in June and having a lifetime of happiness. My memory's not what it used to be, though."

"We know that, Doc."

"Yes, I suppose everybody in Laventra knows that, come to think of it. But I remember June is a good month to be married. I mean, if you feel so inclined."

"Oh, it's not that. It's just a big change, that's all."

Edie took her hand. "I am very sure that it's going to be perfect. I have no doubts."

Doc grinned. "Me neither," he declared. "Not that I'm getting married. I'm just sure about you two, is all. I think you just feel a little unsure, Junie dear, because you're new to the idea that you're a lesbian."

June laughed. "It's not always about being a lesbian, Doc, although you're right. The idea is quite new to me. It's just that I don't know anything about planning a wedding."

"Oh, there's not much planning involved," Edie assured her airily. "There's only going to be about forty people or so."

"There is?"

"I sent out the invitations, June," she told her gently. "We did talk about it."

"Oh dear, I'm not used to that many people all at once."

"It's only just people in the village. And people we know from boarding their dogs."

"I don't even know what to wear. I know you told me you had a dress, Edie, but you look beautiful in anything. You're so small and dainty."

"You know how you told Doc it's not always about being a lesbian? Well, it's not always about being small either."

"Exactly!" Doc exclaimed.

"But I seriously don't know what to wear," June moaned.

"You haven't even looked yet, have you?"

"No, I don't have time."

SHAGGY JACK

"You'll just have to make time," Edie told her firmly. "I could go with you, but you might not want me to see it before the wedding."

"I could go," Doc volunteered.

The women exchanged dubious glances.

"We could take Nick, too." He looked so eager that June didn't have the heart to decline his offer.

"Oh, all right," she acquiesced, ungraciously. "But I'm driving."

"That's fine. We'll go tomorrow."

"Tomorrow?! I don't know about that."

"The sooner the better," Edie pronounced.

"Then it's all set," Doc told them.

He called to Nick, who was romping with Jack on the newly mowed lawn.

"Nicky, my boy, we're going shopping with your Auntie June tomorrow to get an outfit for the wedding. We'll pick you up after school."

Nick gave a thumbs-up in their direction.

"Bring the Huckleberries if they want to come. We can all help!"

June buried her face in her hands with a long-suffering groan of defeat.

Chapter Twenty-Three

THE wedding day arrived in a burst of brilliant sunshine.

June's eyes popped open before dawn. She lay very still, turning her head to drink in the sight of the small figure sleeping peacefully at her side. Tears filled her eyes, slipping softly and silently onto her white, embroidered pillowcase.

Never in a million years had June Howard imagined her life would, or could, contain so much happiness, so much joy that it seemed to overflow from her, warming her heart like her own beautiful source of sunshine. At almost sixty-five years old, one would think that the best part of your life was well behind you. June knew, with a certainty grounded in her very soul, that the best of hers was yet to come.

Creeping out of their room and down the old wooden stairs, June revelled in the streaks of colour drifting across the glory of the morning sky. She decided to sit on the porch and gather her thoughts for just a little while before beginning all the tasks of the busy day ahead.

She quietly pushed open the kitchen door, thinking she must be imagining the rich aroma of coffee in the air.

"Junie dear, it's your big day!"

June emitted a shriek as the shadowy figure, settled at the kitchen table, took on the lanky shape of Doc. "You scared the life out of me, Doc!"

"I am pretty scary looking, especially first thing in the morning," he agreed, missing the point completely. "I've brewed a nice pot of coffee from those Colombian beans Edie bought in Dalton last week. I thought this would be the perfect day for it."

"You're so right as always, Doc. I was just thinking of taking a cup out onto the porch to drink it. That patio furniture you got is so comfortable."

"It did turn out good, didn't it?" Doc beamed with pleasure. "And that's a fine idea. We can kind of get the day straightened out in our heads. Or you can. My head doesn't do such a great job of that anymore."

"You're doing just fine, Doc," June reassured him. They gathered their mugs and the coffee pot and headed for the porch. "And you're right, it's going to be a busy day. It'll be nice to have the benefit of this great coffee."

As she followed the old man onto the porch, she realized that he was, indeed, doing just fine. His mind seemed to be even a little better, certainly no worse, and this pleased her immensely. The company of the boys and dogs kept him busy and happy.

Doc settled into one of the chairs, throwing his head back to inhale a long breath of pure satisfaction.

"What a beautiful morning. And it's your day, Junie dear. It's your day. Look at that sky, with all the red and pink. Pretty as a picture it is."

"Red sky in morning, sailors take warning. Isn't that what they say? Oh dear, I hope it's not going to rain," worried June. "I don't know what we'll do if it does."

"Ah, now, Junie dear, you just leave all that to me."

"What on earth can you do about it if it rains, Doc? It'll be almost impossible to have all those people in the house if everyone is soaking wet."

"Leave it to me," he repeated. "Don't think about it anymore. Those sailing people have been wrong before, I'm sure."

She decided to take his advice because there really was nothing she could do about the weather any more than Doc could. But he seemed absolutely convinced that everything would go well, in his incurably optimistic way. She would choose to believe him.

After consuming another mug of the delicious coffee, he rose, announcing that he was going to start cutting up the ham and roast beef that he and the boys had cooked the previous day. Then he would round up the Huckleberries and they would proceed to town to buy fresh buns.

"You've done so much, Doc," June told him. "You can take a break sometimes, you know."

"Aw, I like to be busy, Junie dear. I like to earn my keep."

"You do more than that. And you're entertaining too. Life is never dull with you around, Doc."

Doc considered this remark. "Well, that's something, anyway."

The day passed in a whirlwind of activity. Doc and the boys returned from town with the buns and literally a truckload of flowers.

"You can't have a wedding without flowers," Doc announced to Edie and June.

They stood transfixed, observing the hodgepodge of jumbled blooms overflowing from the cargo bed of Mr. Clatterbox.

"Where on earth did you get all these, Doc?" Edie asked.

"Oh, different people," Doc replied airily.

Dillon attempted an explanation. "Doc told everyone that it was going to be a special wedding, especially for him because it was his first—"

"Don't tell me," June groaned. "His first lesbian wedding."

"Exactly!" Doc beamed. "I can't wait. And Edie . . . I got a nice bouquet of sunflowers for you to carry, if you want."

"Oh, Doc, I hadn't even thought about a bouquet. They're beautiful. Thank you."

"You are most welcome," Doc said with a small bow. "Sunflowers are my favourite flower because they're so cheerful, don't you think?"

"I thought you liked pansies with their little smiling faces," June teased him.

"I like them both. But sunflowers have always been my favourite. Come on, my Huckleberries, let's get this place decorated."

June watched the clouds circling the sky with growing concern as wedding preparations unfolded in a flurry of activity all around her.

When Martha Wilson received her invitation, she surprised everyone by offering to make the wedding cake—an offer they gratefully accepted. "I wasn't sure what to do about a topper," she announced, marching into the kitchen that morning. She deposited the cake unceremoniously onto the table.

"It looks very nice. Thank you so much, Martha." Edie smiled her gratitude at the staid, cheerless woman.

"I just didn't know what to put on top," Martha repeated, determined to make her point. "You know what I mean, though, right?"

"Of course," Edie said graciously, her eyes deliberately avoiding the scowl passing over June's face. "But it really doesn't matter."

Martha sniffed.

"I suppose not. We didn't have any of these types of weddings when I was young. No one ever heard of such a thing as two women getting married. Things have certainly changed."

Her tone made it quite clear that she did not think they had changed for the better.

"I know what you mean," Edie replied sweetly. "When I was in school, I got straight A's. Now I'm not even straight."

June choked back a laugh.

Martha, clearly at a loss, turned to depart. "I hope it isn't going to rain because it sure looks like it, doesn't it?"

Once she was out of their driveway, Doc chuckled to Edie and said, "You tell her, Edie girl!" Edie shrugged. "I read that somewhere and thought I would use it on just such an occasion."

"Good for you. Some people don't have much joy in them, do they?" The women nodded their agreement.

"It's a lovely cake, though," Edie conceded. "And it was nice of her to make it for us."

"It was very nice, but I really don't appreciate all her innuendos," June sighed.

"It's like giving a fellow a pair of pants and cutting the arse out of them, as my old Gramps used to say," Doc chuckled. "Still, it looks good enough to eat."

"It looks delicious," Edie agreed. "Does it have to have a topper, do you think?"

"I think a little circle of those wee sunflowers from The Patience Spot would look perfect on top of it, don't you?" Doc suggested. "I don't know much about these things, but can't you have whatever you want on top of your own wedding cake?"

The women did not see why not. It sounded good to them.

June's heart tightened with anxiety as a sprinkling of rain began. But just before the appointed hour, the sun appeared in a burst of glory from behind the grey clouds.

"Lo and behold, it's a rainbow!" Doc cried, pointing to the glorious arc of colour spanning the sky. "Special for you ladies. It's a wedding day miracle."

"This is like something you would read about in a story," Max said. "Honestly. No one would believe that would happen just when two people were about to get married and everybody thought it was going to rain."

"Write the story, Max," Doc urged him. "Write it down when you get home so you don't forget it. It's like magic."

"It is indeed," Edie breathed.

The esteemed task of walking Edie down the aisle—or rather, the path—to The Patience Spot had been delegated to Doc. This request had touched the old man right to the core of his being. He told her he was "pleased as punch" to do just that.

Edie exuded a timeless elegance, her beautiful hair swept back, with delicate white flowers scattered amongst her curls like tiny stars. Her brown eyes gleamed, reflecting her utter joy at the fulfillment of this special moment. The palest of blue gossamer gowns draped her small frame. In her hands, she clutched the jaunty sunflower bouquet bequeathed by Doc that very morning.

"You look so beautiful," Doc smiled down at her. "You look like somebody's fairy godmother."

"You look pretty dapper yourself, I must say. You clean up just fine."

"It's been a long time since I've worn this trusty old suit. It's seen me through lots of occasions, so it has. But none as happy as this one."

He squeezed her hand, tucking it into his arm.

"Are you ready?"

She nodded, standing on her tippy toes to deposit a kiss on his cheek. Then she inhaled deeply, smiled sweetly, and set forward to begin the journey to her new life.

They rounded the corner amidst a burst of applause, instigated by the Huckleberries.

June stood in The Patience Spot, clad in white pants and a light blue jacket, a sunflower tucked into her buttonhole. Her grey hair had been somewhat tamed into a bun, and her face beamed like a beacon of joy and love. She looked magnificent.

Nick stood beside her, grinning from ear to ear.

June had not realized how tall this dear boy had become, or how grown up and handsome he looked, until he donned his new dress shirt and pants. A wave of pure, unadulterated love and gratitude swept over her for the presence of Chrissy's boy. Her boy.

"Thank you for being my best man," she whispered to him.

"My pleasure," he nodded, sounding for all the world like Doc.

"And thank you, Jack," she reached across Nick to stroke the shaggy head of Jack, who sported a kerchief bearing the announcement, "Best Dog."

"Jack says it's his pleasure, too," Nick informed her.

Should she be worried about Nick thinking that he really could communicate with Jack on a human level? The thought passed through her head before passing right back out again at the sight of the breathtaking creature floating toward her on Doc's arm.

June Howard knew, right then and there, that this was exactly who she had been waiting for all of her lonely, loveless life.

Doc stepped back into the crowd after his very important task of giving Edie to June. As he gazed upon the two beloved women, he allowed himself to wonder why weddings were so often depicted by youth and tradition. What in God's world could be more beautiful than these two women standing before him, their love shining like a golden glow all around them? Shafts of sunlight streaked through the green of the pines, and the flowers bent their bright heads in silent benediction. It was a glorious moment as vows, short and sweet and full of hope and promise, were exchanged in voices breaking with emotion.

Doc came forward now, cradling Cracklin' Rosie.

"The Huckleberries and I are going to sing a little wedding song for these lovely ladies," he announced.

"At least he didn't say 'lesbian ladies,'" June whispered to Edie. "First time he's forgotten that adjective."

Edie giggled.

"But you can bet he was thinking it. What song are they playing?"

"No idea."

Doc strummed a little, then began singing to the melodious chords of "Rainbow Connection."

The richness and strength of Doc's voice, despite his age, always amazed June. Max, Dillon, and Nick joined in, their young voices mingling together in beautiful harmony. Jack, not to be left out, crooned along with a plaintive wail.

When they got to the last verse, Doc raised his hand, gesturing to the guests.

"Everybody, join in!" he sang out.

And they did. *"Someday we'll find it, the Rainbow Connection, the lovers, the dreamers, and me."*

Doc and the Huckleberries stood and bowed, amidst a burst of applause.

"For the lesbian ladies!" Doc announced proudly.

Chapter Twenty-Four

Once the official business of marriage had been attended to, everyone relaxed and allowed the party to unfold around them.

"The pressure's off now," Nick said, in a voice filled with relief. "Everybody can just eat and drink and have fun."

"Amen to that," Edie sighed. "Time to just enjoy ourselves."

Two long tables groaned under a plethora of food and drink as people wandered in and out of the house to partake of the feast.

The Huckleberries had put together a playlist from different eras of popular songs. Music boomed from speakers located on the lawn. Some people danced, others sang along. Some Laventra natives had stopped by only to pass on their well wishes but stayed for refreshments and companionship. It seemed that Doc had extended a warm invitation to everyone he'd seen in the village over the last few weeks. Many had taken him up on it.

Doc and the boys had strung Edison lights along the trees weeks ago. They twinkled now amongst the shimmering leaves. Several early stars glistened with cosmic blessings.

"This is just the way a wedding should be," Doc pronounced approvingly, gazing around the lawn at the crowd of happy people. He was tucked away to the back of the porch, balancing a plate of food on his lap and a glass of whiskey in his hands.

The boys had never seen Doc drink alcohol.

"I bet we'll hear some good shit from Doc after he's had a drink or two," Max whispered to his friends.

"Right?" Nick agreed. "We hear enough without it."

"Did you ever feel like getting married, Doc?" Dillon asked curiously, possibly hoping for just such a tale.

"Ah, boys, a wedding does make a person feel sentimental, doesn't it? Especially a happy one like this."

The boys nodded, then pressed eagerly, "Did you?"

Doc took a deep swallow, leaned back against the porch, and shut his eyes.

"Only once, I guess. But it was a long time ago. Funny you know, boys, when things happen to you when you're young, you think that you'll die from them. You think you'll never be able to go on, that things will never stop hurting."

"And?" prompted Nick.

Doc sat up. A hearty laugh erupted from his throat. "And then you get old, and it doesn't matter anymore. It's like it happened to somebody else. But I was in love once, madly in love. She was my Cinderella."

"What happened?"

"Things fell apart between us, so I took a job up here. They were in desperate need of a doctor at the time."

"That's why they took you, eh?" Nick ribbed him, gently poking his arm.

"Oh, you mean they must have been desperate to take me. I see. Yup, I guess they just took what they could get at the time. But I always liked it here. I never cared for the hustle and bustle of a big city. Anyway, it kept me so busy I never had any more time for romance."

"Ever again?" Dillon asked.

"Not really. I never met anyone else to compare to my Cinderella.

SHAGGY JACK

I'm telling you boys, the best way to get rid of problems is to outlive them. Just leave them in the dust. Then, after a while, you can't really remember too much about them anyway," he added quite cheerfully, taking a long swig from his glass.

Guests wandered in and out of the house, pausing to chat with Doc and the medley of boys and dogs perched across the end of the porch.

"Doc, you remember Ed and Marion, don't you?" June asked, materializing beside them to indicate a middle-aged, glum-looking couple. "Apparently, you invited them today, when you were at the bakery."

The words were pointed and directed at the old man.

"Ed and Marion?" Doc stood, a quizzical expression on his face. "I did invite a lot of people, it's true. But I must say it's Junie who remembers everyone. I don't remember a damned thing. Still, it's nice to see you."

The couple nodded curtly, preparing to depart.

"I heard they have all kinds of dysfunctional kids and dogs living here," Marion remarked to her husband, her gaze sweeping over the menagerie on the porch.

"Maybe *she's* dysfunctional," Doc murmured softly to his Huckleberries. But not quite softly enough.

The woman sniffed, turning her back, as Max piped up, "We put the fun in dysfunctional."

"That's a good one, Max. You should put it in a story."

"Doc, if I put everything you suggested into a story, I'd have a million of them."

"Good. Haven't you ever heard that truth is stranger than fiction?

I wish I'd jotted down all the funny things that happened to me as a doctor. Then you'd be able to read it and you could write a best-selling novel," Doc chuckled to himself. "It's interesting to listen to people, though. Some people, of course, have nothing useful to say, but some are quite entertaining."

"Like that Marion lady."

"Well, she wasn't exactly entertaining. Imagine her thinking we're dysfunctional."

"Right?" Nick exclaimed. "Even Jack agrees."

"Doesn't he always agree with you, Nicky boy?"

"Most of the time. Not always."

"Sometimes you hear interesting stuff when you just sit and listen," Doc told them, after a companionable pause. "If the people are interesting, that is."

"What if they're not interesting?"

"Then you hear Jack Shi—" Doc clapped his hand over his mouth. "Sorry about that. It's the Jack Daniels speaking."

"Jack Shit, Jack Daniels, whatever," Max laughed.

They sat in congenial silence and, as promised, snippets of amusing conversation drifted to their ears:

"I lent my brother my best suit so he could go to court and look good and maybe catch a break and turn his life around. My best suit, mind you. Went to attend his hearing in the courtroom and everything, just to show my support. And what do you know, he went and got convicted, and there went my best suit walking out of the courtroom and right out of my closet. Nobody better bloody well die or I'll be shit out of luck for a suit to wear to their funeral, I can tell you that."

SHAGGY JACK

"See," Doc whispered. "Interesting, right? Lots of stories to be told, Max, just open your ears."

"I'm telling you the truth," came another voice from the shadows. A female one this time. "A strawberry is *not* a berry."

"Duh," her companion said, voice full of disgust. "That's why it says 'berry' right in its name, I guess."

"I know what it's called, but it's not a berry. It's a modified receptacle."

"You're crazy, that's all."

"Why don't you Google it? And while you're at it, Google a banana because it *is* a berry."

"I don't have to Google it. I'm not an idiot. I know what I know."

"Actually, he is an idiot," Max announced as the couple wandered away, holding up his phone. "Because I just googled it and she's right."

"It's always good to be open to learning something new," Doc said. "I think I might have known that at one time. Maybe. I'm not sure, I don't remember now."

"You don't remember if you knew or you don't remember if you remember?"

Doc chuckled. "All of the above. Before Google came along, people just argued it out. Now you have proof right at your fingertips. No more arguing."

Dillon laughed, "Sounds like they were doing a pretty good job!"

"This is the kind of place where you might see a ghost, don't you think?" another remark floated up to greet their ears.

"Why do you say that?"

"It's kind of old and rickety. Ghosts would be at home here."

"Do ghosts realize they're dead, do you think? Are they sad when they find out they are?"

"I don't know, why are we even talking about this?"

"You brought it up."

"I did not."

"There you are," Doc laughed, as the voices faded away. "There's some things Google can't settle, after all."

"I'm asking you why menopause is called menopause? Why isn't it called womenopause?"

"Don't be ridiculous," replied a curt, female voice.

"It's a fair point," Doc reflected. "One I never thought of."

"And you are a doctor," teased Nick.

People began to depart amidst a sea of well wishes for a happy marriage and thanks for the wonderful party. An ensuing silence fell, comfortable and warm, enveloping the June evening in a sweet embrace.

"I suppose we'd better get inside and start cleaning up . . ." Doc sighed, without enthusiasm, leaning his head back against the porch rail and closing his eyes. ". . . in a few minutes."

"I'm telling you, my girl, I'm going places, I am," a young, eager, male voice broke the silence. The boys gazed toward the copse of birch trees where leaves rustled, indicating the presence of a young couple.

"You're going places, are you?" the girl asked, clearly unconvinced.

"I am, Sara, I am," he asserted, his words only slightly slurred.

"Only place I saw you going today was down to the laundromat."

"Oh, my mom sent me down there because our washing machine broke down. Took me forever because I had to go to the bank to

SHAGGY JACK

get change. She told me to get a roll of quarters. So I did but when I got there the damned thing only took loonies and credit cards, so I'm stuck with this roll of quarters."

"So that's why you were late? You were doing laundry? I've been waiting for you for ages."

"Sorry, sorry. Never mind that now. Come here and let me hold onto you."

"I'd like that," Sara's words floated softly into the evening air.

The night lay, still and peaceful, only broken by faint murmuring from the young couple.

"Oh, for heaven's sake." Sara's annoyed words broke the quietude. "I don't want to hug you anymore. All I can feel is that roll of quarters in your pocket and it's sticking into my leg."

A moan emitted from the depths of the birches.

"Sara, Sara! That ain't no roll of quarters."

Chapter Twenty-Five

Life at the boarding house flowed along on a wave of wedded bliss. Summer, autumn, and winter melted into another spring, their first anniversary, and the dawning of a whole new summer.

That year had been June's happiest ever. She knew that other people had experienced happiness like this, that it was indeed possible, even attainable. She'd read about it in books and seen it in movies. But it had always seemed to lie forever beyond her ken. She often said this to Edie when the two were snuggled up in their marital bed after nighttime had wrapped a sweet cloak of darkness around them. Only then did her inhibitions abate enough for her to whisper to Edie the wonder and joy that every day of living with her love meant to her.

Nick grew by leaps and bounds, stretching all the way up to a lanky six feet and two inches. He had grown into his features; his glasses remained quite securely on his nose (most of the time), and he was filling out. Sometimes, at odd little moments, June detected a glimpse of her long-lost sister in his laugh or the crease of his smile, and a wave of love swept over her, so strong it weakened her at the knees.

Jack grew too, if that was even possible. He had now reached the size of a small donkey. Edie said it was providential that Nick had also grown; otherwise, Jack would have surpassed the boy in height. It was rare indeed to see Nick anywhere without the accompaniment of his huge, shaggy companion.

Even Doc seemed to be holding his own. He still managed

to say the most inappropriate remarks known to man at the most inopportune moments, but most people overlooked this. He truly was such a cheerful, likable guy.

"This is a wonderful summer," Doc announced into the depths of a particularly warm afternoon. "I'm all taken over by it. I can feel the sunshine glowing inside of me."

"That's because it's almost thirty degrees out here," June grumbled. "Already. And it's only the end of June."

"Life is pretty good, though," Edie smiled. "We can have a rest in the shade, June, if you're too hot."

But nothing is ever perfect in this old world of ours.

My dear, departed mother used to say, "In this life, a little rain must fall."

It fell with a vengeance on the boarding house folk that particular day. As they stood admiring the sunshine, pondering the dawning and possibilities of the upcoming summer, a huge rainfall was rapidly approaching. Metaphorically speaking.

They had no idea, no warning. The day seemed ordinary, innocuous enough, like so many others.

But this one was different.

This one brought Garth Chapman.

Of course, no one suspected anything amiss at first.

An unknown car pulled up into the driveway, but this in itself was not unusual. The boarding house was the last on the end of a winding country road, and people often stopped to ask for directions.

But now an unsmiling man, perhaps in his early fifties, emerged from the car, gazing around with obvious contempt. His lips parted in a surly expression, beads of sweat glistened on his broad forehead, and his shirt buttons strained over a substantial paunch.

The scowling man approached the trio with long, deliberate strides. June felt an icy cold wave of foreboding overcome her, for no discernible reason.

"Can we help you?" Edie inquired, smiling tentatively at the stranger.

The man opened his mouth, but his reply was lost in a cacophony of pealing, boyish laughter and yelping dogs. Jack and the Huckleberries could always be heard before they actually appeared.

It was the last day of school and a cause for great excitement, whooping, and general commotion.

Careening across the freshly cut grass, the whole collection of joyful creatures came to an abrupt halt at the sight of the stranger.

Nick stood stock still, staring at the man, colour draining from his face.

"Garth!" he gasped.

The man spun around to take in the sight of the three boys and the huge, shaggy dog.

June hurried toward them, alarmed at the distressed expression on her boy's face.

"Do you know this man, Nick?"

Nick nodded silently, not taking his eyes off the stranger.

The man barked, "Of course he knows me."

He turned to June, extended his hand, and announced, "I'm Garth Chapman, Nicholas's father. I've come to take him home."

SHAGGY JACK

A collective gasp greeted the man's terrible, hateful words. A chill descended upon the entire world, sucking all the light and warmth from it.

"You are *not* my father! And I am *already* home!" Nick shrieked the words in defiance, his young body trembling like a leaf. "Auntie Bug is my home."

"Who?"

"Me. I'm his Aunt June. Chrissy was my baby sister."

"Well, you're big enough to be a home, for sure," the man snickered. "You don't look anything like your sister. *She* was some beautiful."

"Who are you? Exactly?" Edie moved close to June, gesturing for the shaking boy to stand beside them. Every fibre of her being reverberated with hatred for this man.

"Is he really your father, Nick?"

Before he could answer, the man cut in, his voice booming. "Next best thing to a father you ever had, right, Nicky?" He winked at Nick, who stared furiously at the ground. "Well, it's sure taken me a while to find you, my boy, disappearing like you did after your mom died. I wouldn't have known you now if I'd met you on the street. You've grown so bloody tall. This old aunt of yours must be feeding you, at least."

He motioned toward June with a chubby thumb.

Nick visibly clenched his jaw. "Auntie Bug—I mean Auntie June—takes very good care of me, and I'm real happy here."

"Glad to hear it. Glad to hear it," Garth bellowed. "You've been a long time away from home."

"I *am* home. I told you that. Mom and I never had a real home, and you weren't even there when she died. She would have died all alone if I hadn't been with her."

"Good for you, then. Good job. I do miss her, you know. And you." Garth advanced toward the boy, reaching out his arms, presumably for an embrace.

Nick backed away, clearly dismayed.

A low, warning growl erupted from Jack's huge throat.

"What the hell? What do you call *that* thing? Is it going to bite me?"

"That's my friend, Jack."

"He's never bitten anyone before," Edie said, smiling sweetly. "But there's a first time for everything."

"Ugly looking thing," Garth scoffed. "Looks like a big, old, grey dishcloth."

Doc, hitherto silent, cocked his head, considering.

Then he remarked, "He does a little, doesn't he? Or maybe a bunch of grey dishcloths stitched together."

Garth shot a quizzical look at Doc. "And who the hell's this old geezer?"

Doc, ever the gentleman, extended his hand to the appalling man. "This old geezer," he said, "is Jed McIntyre. I'd say it's nice to make your acquaintance, but it's really not. It's not nice at all."

"Like I care what an old wack job like you thinks," Garth scoffed.

"How do you know I'm a wack job?" Doc asked, his voice full of genuine curiosity. "I mean, you've only just met me."

The women sighed, shaking their heads in despair.

"I just know, is all. I've been around enough old dudes that are only running on a few cylinders to know one when I see one."

SHAGGY JACK

"Don't you dare talk that way to Doc!" Nick cried.

Jack emitted another low growl, just for good measure.

"Oh, Doc, is it? He doesn't even know his own name."

Doc drew himself up to his full height and replied with dignity.

"Doc is what my friends call me, and you, sir, are not a friend. And you're right, young man, I am declining mentally, for which I am extremely regretful. But I have not as yet lost my common courtesy—and I hope I never do—as you seem to have done."

Garth rolled his eyes toward Nick. "Again, he seems to think I care about what he thinks. What's going on here anyway? Is this a home for weirdos and stupid-looking dogs and dumb, teenage boys?"

"How dare you?" June gasped.

"Oh, I dare, lady. And Nicholas will be coming *home* with me."

Edie stepped toward him and stuck her index finger at his face, dainty brow furrowed in rage. "We'll just see about that."

He swatted at her finger, as he would an offending insect. "Won't we, though?"

"Yes, we will," Doc replied, his words firm and deliberate. "Our Nicky boy stays here with us. And I really do not like you, Mr.—what did you say your name was?"

"Chapman. Garth Chapman. And it doesn't bother me if some crazy old man likes me or not."

"I usually like everybody. But in your case, Mr. Garth Chapman, I'm going to make an exception."

"Well, I've already engaged the services of a lawyer," Garth announced, throwing back his head and guffawing. "I think that will be much more helpful than whether or not you like me."

He turned to leave, giving Jack a wide berth. His gaze fell on

Dillon and Max, standing wordlessly behind Jack and Nick like deflated balloons, all their former joy vanished.

"Who are you?" Garth asked, glaring at them.

Dillon stood transfixed, but Max offered his name.

"Max? Sounds like a bloody dog's name to me."

"I'm going to take that as a compliment," Max told him, staying true to his boyish spirit.

Garth shook his head in disgust and proceeded toward his car.

"I really don't like that man," Doc observed. "He's the kind of guy who steps in dog poop and then blames the dog."

As if on cue, Garth stopped short and, with a shout of revulsion, made a big show of wiping his large shoe on the grass.

"Dog shit!" he shrieked, thrusting an accusing finger in the direction of Jack. "I stepped in bloody dog shit!"

Doc grinned. "I rest my case," he told them.

"Couldn't happen to a nicer guy," June quipped, hoping the obnoxious man heard her.

The car reversed and sped away to the accompaniment of gales of laughter.

CHAPTER TWENTY-SIX

THEIR laughter was short-lived.

The boarding house folk worried. They worried and fretted and stewed. Their mental anguish squeezed every ounce of enjoyment from the long-awaited summer.

Did he have a leg to stand on?

Did he truly have a lawyer?

Should they request a DNA test?

How on earth could they fight this thing they didn't even really understand?

These questions bounced back and forth and all around the porch late at night, after Nick and Jack had retired to sleep.

"I just want to say one thing about a DNA test," Doc said, after endless bouts of conversation had spun round and round to no avail.

"Yes, Doc?"

"I want to tell you that you should never ask a question you don't positively know the answer to."

"What do you mean?"

"Many years ago, a woman brought her sixteen-year-old daughter to my office. The girl had been complaining about nausea and heartburn. She looked very shy and young sitting there. I asked her if there was any chance she could be pregnant. Her mother scoffed at me, very annoyed she was. But then I asked the girl if she'd ever had sex with a boy. She said she had, but she wasn't pregnant because her older sister had told her that you can't get pregnant if you have sex standing up. Well, guess what?"

"We can guess, Doc," June said, impatience threading through her words. "The kid was pregnant. But I don't see what a teenager getting knocked up has to do with what's going on right here."

"I think what Doc is trying to say," Edie laid a gentle hand on June's suntanned arm, "is that there's no one hundred percent way to know what a DNA test will show."

"Exactly."

Unexpected tears pricked at June's eyes, making her more irritable still. She had never felt this vulnerable in her life.

"Don't you think Nick is mine?" she whispered.

"I do," Doc nodded. "But we don't know for absolute certain. That's all I'm saying, Junie dear."

"He has Chrissy's St. Christopher medal." June couldn't bear how pleading and pathetic her words sounded, even to her own ears.

"I know, Junie dear. I know. But we can't base a whole case on that."

"A whole case? So we really have to go to court?" Edie asked.

June nodded glumly.

"It seems so. His lawyer called today when you were out. A Mr. Montgomery. Said he'd been trying to get us for a while, but there was no answer. He couldn't believe anyone still had a landline." June laughed bitterly. "I just wish I'd never answered the phone at all. Then I would never have had to talk to him."

"Ah, Junie dear, that won't solve this," said Doc. "I wish to God I was younger and sharper. I'd be much more useful to you in this terrible situation."

"Doc, you are just fine the way you are. Don't let anyone tell you any different."

SHAGGY JACK

The cruel words of Garth Chapman had departed from Doc's memory, but June and Edie remembered them. And they rankled.

"I've been putting out some feelers just in case he did materialize, this lawyer of his," Edie told them now. "I went to the school and explained the situation. Lots of people remember Nick, and they like him."

"And they know all of us," June agreed. "That helps. They know we've given Nick a good home."

"I'll just wait a few more days, give people a chance to think about it. Then I'll go in again and ask some more. Maybe somebody will be able to recommend a lawyer. I know there aren't any in Laventra, but there are quite a few in Dalton, I think."

Neither woman uttered aloud the worry that tumbled over and over in their minds—that lawyers were very costly creatures to retain, and that it was impossible to know if they were any good or not.

"He'll be an adult soon," June reiterated, for perhaps the hundredth time. "In two years, he'll be eighteen. Then he can do whatever he wants."

"Age of majority is nineteen in British Columbia," Edie said. "That's three years."

"But he doesn't live in British Columbia," June cried, sobs overtaking her now, as she buried her face in her hands. "He lives *here*. With *us*."

Doc and Edie exchanged looks of abject misery.

"Good news! Good news!" Edie dashed up the cobblestones,

magnificent white hair flying behind her. She was jumping up and down, unable to contain her excitement.

"Garth left?" Nicky asked.

"He got run over by a big truck?" Dillon chimed in.

"He got shot in the head?" Max offered. June caught the conversation from the kitchen and came out, wiping her hands on her apron.

"He left?" June asked.

Edie appeared quite deflated now. "I guess I should have led with my news because it's none of those."

"You found a lawyer?" Doc suggested.

"Yes, that's it. I found a lawyer, but that's not the best part. He's going to take the case pro bono."

"That's wonderful." Doc clapped his hands in delight.

"Why would he do that?" June asked, immediately suspicious. "Sounds fishy to me. Is he really an actual lawyer?"

"Yes, yes, June, he's a good lawyer by all accounts. I've asked around. He's in Dalton. His name is Dan Clark."

June and Doc both shook their heads.

"Don't know him."

"Doesn't ring a bell."

"Well, I, for one, am having faith in him. And you should, too, June. You and I are going to see him this afternoon at three o'clock."

"What? Today? I'm not ready."

"Well, get ready, my love. We have no choice. We have to do this. I'll drive."

Three o'clock sharp found the pair, with racing hearts and anxious faces, entering Dan Clark's law office.

"Mr. Clark will see you now," his secretary informed them

immediately. The lawyer's punctuality pleased June. His office looked official and welcoming enough. An immense wave of relief consumed June that he did, in fact, exist.

They were greeted by a burly, pleasant-looking man appearing to be in his early sixties. He wore a navy suit and a ready smile.

He ushered them into his office, where they sat and listened attentively as he proceeded to explain the ins and outs of a child custody hearing to them.

"Custody hearing?" gasped Edie.

"That's what it is, in essence. But I should correct myself; it is no longer called child custody. It was changed a few years ago to parenting arrangements. That was intended to remove any negative connotation with the word 'custody.'"

June nodded, not caring about proper legal terms.

Sensing her impatience, Mr. Clark continued. "This gentleman, Garth Chapman—"

"He's no gentleman," June interrupted.

Edie nudged her arm.

"Sorry," she mumbled, looking at her feet. "Please go on."

"Mr. Chapman feels that he has more right to Nicholas than you do, and that the boy should return to BC with him."

Edie nodded. "That's basically it, I guess."

"But he doesn't," June burst out, unable to contain herself. "He has no right! Nick doesn't even want to go back. He ran away, for God's sake. He made it all the way to Ontario on his own to find us. All the way from BC." Her voice trembled on the last words.

"I heard that," Mr. Clark remarked, shaking his head incredulously. "That's quite a feat for such a young boy."

"Doesn't that prove that Nick wanted to leave there? That he wants to be with us?" June continued, pleading her case to this man. "Shouldn't that count for something? I mean, he's sixteen now. Shouldn't he have a say?" She was terrified of being told that their case was hopeless.

"Oh, yes. He'll have a big say," said Mr. Clark, unruffled by June's outburst. He was used to this. Family law wasn't for the faint of heart. "But in the eyes of the law, Nicholas won't be an adult for another two years. I think I can help you ladies work this out, though. The court will always put the best interests of the child first. That's the biggest factor in their decision process—"

"His best interest *is* to be with us!" June interjected.

"I agree," Mr. Clark continued calmly. "It seems that it may well be in Nicholas's best interests to stay with you. I'd like you to bring Nicholas in so I can speak with him independently."

June and Edie nodded their agreement.

"Good," he nodded.

"I didn't even know this Garth guy existed until two weeks ago," June said, unable to keep the bitterness from her voice. "I wish I'd gone my whole life not knowing about him."

"Well, look at it this way. It will be settled once and for all after this," Mr. Clark smiled. "Think of what a relief that will be."

"I suppose," June admitted grudgingly.

"You really didn't know about Nicholas's existence until he showed up at your place a couple of years ago?" he asked June pointedly.

"No, I thought my sister had died a long time ago in a bus crash out west. And I never knew she'd had a child."

SHAGGY JACK

"Are you certain he is your sister's child?"

"Y-yes," June stuttered. "He was wearing the St. Christopher's medal I gave her years and years ago."

The lawyer nodded, considering this but offering no comment.

"He just turned up on my front lawn two years ago. Him and Shaggy Jack."

"Shaggy Jack?"

"Yes. They showed up at the same time."

"Jack is a dog," Edie explained.

"Oh, I see."

"A *big* dog," she continued.

"Okay—"

"A *really big* dog."

"Oh—"

"Probably the biggest dog you've ever seen in your life," June explained. "We figured out that he's a combination of Wolfhound, Newfoundlander, and maybe Leonberger. But mainly Wolfhound."

"Wow, he must be big."

"He's as big as a small pony. He's all grey and shaggy and silly looking."

"And Nick loves him so much. He thinks he's taught him to communicate. To talk."

"And has he?"

The women exchanged glances and shrugged, laughing.

"We don't know. We don't speak dog language."

June glanced at the man sharply. "You're going to think we're crazy."

"Oh, no. I'm a dog lover myself. I'd like to meet Mr. Shaggy Jack sometime. Maybe when this is all over, you could bring him in."

After a considerable pause, June asked a question that had been bothering her since Edie first told her about Dan Clark. "Why are you doing this for us, Mr. Clark? I mean, you don't even know us."

"I promise that I will explain all of that to you after we win this case. Because we *will* win it. And please, call me Dan."

June had always felt wrong calling professionals by their first names, but she wasn't about to argue.

"Now, I've been wondering what the incentive would be for Garth to look you up now and come all this way in an attempt to get Nicholas back," said Dan.

It was a good question. "I've been wondering that myself. I have no idea what he might be getting out of it. Because I don't think he has much affection for our Nick."

Chapter Twenty-Seven

JUNE and Edie became well acquainted with legal jargon and necessities for "parenting arrangements" that summer. They talked about, questioned, and debated things over and over until everyone was exhausted, physically and mentally. And no further ahead.

"I don't know why he wants me back there," Nick kept saying, despair in his young voice. "He must be getting something out of it, but I don't know what. My mom never had any money. If she had, we wouldn't have had to go to shelters all the time."

Dan had echoed this sentiment. He was making it his business to find out why Garth was making the sudden push to get Nicholas back out to the west coast.

The residents of the boarding house learned many new things that summer. Things they'd never thought any of them would need to know.

Apparently, a child cannot decide which parent he wants to live with, but as the child becomes closer to the age of majority, they have more say in where and with whom they live. Nick was brought into the lawyer's office to verbalize his side of the situation.

"If we end up going to court," Dan explained, "the judge uses a legal test called 'best interests of the child' to make decisions about parenting arrangements. Some of the elements they consider are Nicholas's safety (physical and emotional), the relationship between each of you and him, and Nicholas's wishes. And of course, if there's been any abuse."

He regarded Nick, who squirmed a little, clearly uncomfortable.

"Did Garth ever abuse you, Nick?" Edie asked softly.

"N-n-no."

"Did he abuse your mom?"

"No..."

"But?" Dan inquired, sensing there was more.

"I mean, he didn't hit us or anything like that. But he was mean. Not all the time. Sometimes he was nice, but that was worse, really. Because you never knew how long the niceness would last before he'd be mean again."

"How was he mean?"

"He said horrible, awful things. Doc always says that we should watch what we say because cruel words are like bee stings, and after you say them, the stinger stays underneath your skin. And sometimes it never goes away."

"Doc sounds like a smart guy," Dan observed. "So Garth hurt you and your mom with his words, is that right?"

Nick nodded.

"He hurt me like that, yeah. Sometimes he hurt me right to the bottom of myself. He made my mom so sad with his horrible moods. She always just wanted to make him happy. Doc says you can't make anybody else happy. You have to do that all by yourself."

"Again, excellent advice. The thing is, though, neither one of these ladies is your parent, Nicholas."

"Auntie Bug is," Nick cried. "She and Edie are like my mothers."

"I know you feel that way, and I commend that. But not in the eyes of the law. Maybe it's a good thing this happened after all. Then you'll have a legal guardian, and there won't be any more questions or uncertainty about it."

"Isn't that what Auntie Bug is? She's my mom's sister."

"To prove legal guardianship, you have to either have a court order saying that or a written deal with the other parent saying that."

"Well, I know my mom would want me to be here and not with Garth," Nick declared defiantly.

"I'm sure you're right, Nicholas. We just have to prove that. You'll get a chance to tell your side of the story, okay?"

Nick nodded glumly.

"May I ask you one more thing?"

"Sure."

"I'm just curious. Why do you call her Aunt Bug?"

Nick smiled at his aunt. June felt her heart swell and spill over with love. "Well, I used to call her Auntie June Bug, because my mom called her June Bug. Now I just call her Auntie Bug. My friends call her that, too. Because June bugs are beetles."

Dan looked puzzled, trying to make the connection.

"And the Beatles rock!" Said the trio.

That's when Dan understood. He grinned and said, "Well, nobody would argue with that."

The two women were forced to wait then. Just wait. June felt that she had used up every ounce of patience she possessed not to scream with frustration in the following weeks.

Finally, Dan contacted her to relay the information that Garth was indeed after monetary gains. He had researched her sister's background to see if there had possibly been any provision made for Nick and had unearthed the fact that Christy had left money for her young son.

"Apparently, your mom left a ten-thousand-dollar trust fund for you," June explained to her young charge after receiving this information from the lawyer.

"Ten thousand dollars!" Nick gasped. "I don't think that can be right. We never had any money. She died in a shelter."

"She must have wanted to keep it for you, Nick dear," Edie told him gently. "That's why she never told you. She wanted to keep it safe, just for you."

"But where would she get it from? She didn't work very much. She'd try, but she always ended up too stressed and could only lie in bed a lot." Nick lowered his eyes, clearly distressed by having to disclose this information.

June sighed. "Like our mother. Mom suffered from depression for years. She would never admit it, though. I think she was always afraid of the stigma attached to an official diagnosis."

Nick asked, "Is it a real thing? Can't you just try harder? I always wished she would."

"It doesn't work like that, I'm afraid," June said. "And yes. It is a real thing—a real disease. Right, Doc?"

"Clinical depression is very real," Doc agreed. "It can be crippling for some people, but things are better now. They have new medications that can help a lot."

Silence ensued, as June desperately tried to dispel the image of her beloved boy sitting beside his prostrate mother in some dreary, sad shelter.

"I think Chrissy might have gotten that money from our

grandmother. She bequeathed us both ten thousand dollars when she died. I hadn't thought of that before, but I don't think that was too long after Chrissy left."

"She must not have spent it then," Edie pointed out. "If she left it in trust for Nick."

"I wish we'd had it when she was living, that's all. It would have made life a whole hell of a lot easier," Nick sighed.

"But she wanted it for you, for when she wasn't around," Edie said gently. "She wanted to make sure you were okay. She must have been very unselfish, your mom."

"Garth thinks if he can be named as a guardian of Nick, then he'll have access to that money," June said. "Because it will be 'in trust' for Nick."

"Garth is a cockwomble!" Nick declared with feeling.

"A what?" Doc asked.

"A cockwomble. I read it somewhere yesterday on a social media post. It means a man who makes stupid statements and has a really high opinion of his own importance."

"That's him, all right," Doc agreed. "That's a good word. I used to tell my receptionist that a patient was NQR. You know, to be discreet."

"Oh, yes, we've all noticed how discreet you are," June said dryly. "What on earth does that mean?"

"Not quite right," Doc chuckled.

"Well, that's Garth, for sure," Nick declared. "A cockwomble and NQR together. And he's a liar too."

"Liar, liar, pants on fire!" Doc declared. "Hey, wouldn't it be neat if his pants *did* catch on fire?"

"How old are you again, Doc?" June asked, not amused. Nick's guardianship was nothing to joke about.

Doc didn't appear to notice her annoyance. "That's a darned good question, Junie dear."

He paused, considering his answer.

"Well, anyway, at least I'm not a cockwomble."

"Amen to that."

"Garth says he can't wait to go back to BC," Nick announced, as the days leading up to the hearing wore on. "I had to see him today when I had that appointment at the office. He calls Ontario 'Onterrible'."

"You're quoting him now?" June asked more sharply than she intended. This whole affair had worn her patience, her whole spirit, down to a nub.

"Of course not," Nick retorted. "I wish he'd go back, too."

June slumped into the chair, saying, "It won't be long now, anyway. That hearing is next week. We can all breathe easier when it's over."

"It's been very stressful," Edie agreed. "Even the dogs are restless and irritable. It's too hot and muggy, to boot."

"Just imagine saying our beautiful province is terrible," Doc remarked. "I think he's the terrible one here. All our provinces are beautiful, I might add. We'd never say that about British Columbia, now would we?"

"Oh, Doc, he doesn't care about being nice or which province is better," June sputtered, exasperated.

SHAGGY JACK

"I heard a story about two people from the States who were travelling across Canada," Edie jumped in, sensing a hitherto unknown tension rising in the stuffy kitchen. "They stopped at a little place in the prairies to get gas, and the man told the woman to go inside and ask where exactly they were. So the woman went in and asked the man behind the counter what the name of this place was. He answered, 'Saskatoon, Saskatchewan.' She went out to the car, and the man asked her what they said. The woman said, 'I don't know. They don't speak English.'"

The joke produced an obligatory chuckle, but it was short-lived. The prospect of the hearing continued to weigh heavily on the occupants of the boarding house. Except for Doc. He maintained complete and utter faith in the outcome. He knew deep down in his soul, he told them, that Nicky was meant to stay right there with them. He belonged at the boarding house where everybody loved him. No judge in their right mind would listen to Garth's story and rule that Nicky would be better off with him.

"Why, he's nothing but a cockwomble," Doc would pronounce. "Funny how that word stuck in my mind, eh, Junie dear?"

"Yes, when so many other more deserving words just fly right out."

"It's true," Doc nodded. "But don't you worry. Everything is going to turn out all right. I promise."

And it did.

The huge, life-changing moment arrived at last in the courthouse after many long, drawn-out weeks. Dan's summary was concise, professional, and compassionate, as he laid out his case for Nick. And the judge, after reviewing all of the facts, pronounced in his favour, awarding June Howard legal guardianship of Nicholas Benton.

Garth's face twisted into a sneer of disgust and rage as he turned to glare at the joyful boarding house gang.

But they paid no heed to him as they whooped with joy and grabbed each other in a group hug, squeezing into a beautiful, ecstatic embrace, tears and laughter flowing.

"That's just the way it should be now, isn't it?" Doc asked, literally beaming. "I knew it!"

"Maybe you're psychic, Doc," Edie teased him gently.

"Maybe I am. Wouldn't that be a turn-up for the books now, at my age?"

They all departed from the courthouse in high spirits, faces wreathed in smiles.

Garth Chapman emerged behind them, attempting a vain effort at conversation.

"Hey, you!" he called to them, in his greasy, Garth manner.

But not one of them, not even kind-hearted Edie, gave him so much as the time of day.

"This may come as a shock to you all, but I have feelings too, you know," he barked at their retreating backs.

They walked away through the courthouse doors to gulp the sweet, fresh air.

June turned and threw him the most contemptuous glare she'd ever mustered up in her entire life.

"Actually," she told Edie, linking her arm as they strode down the steps. " That does come as a shock to me. A huge shock."

Chapter Twenty-Eight

THE dust eventually settled around the remnants of the whole despicable affair, and slowly, with each passing day, the constant fear and threat of Nick being spirited away by Garth Chapman faded until it dissolved like the mist in the morning sun.

One bright day, several weeks hence, June received a phone call requesting their presence in Dan's office. All of them. Even Jack.

"You have to come too, Doc," June informed him. "He particularly requested your presence."

"Me? Oh dear, am I in trouble again?"

"What do you mean again?"

"Oh, I don't know. I just don't know why he'd want to see me. What's his name, again? This lawyer fellow?"

"Dan," Edie told him, for possibly the hundredth time. "Dan Clark. And he's been very good to all of us throughout this whole, terrible affair. He didn't charge us any fee for all his time and work."

"Well, he does sound like an awfully nice fellow. But he is probably looking for some compensation now."

"I think he just wants to get to know you better because our Nick speaks so highly of you. He wants Jack to come too. Come on, Doc. It's not too far. I can drive."

Doc chuckled. "Me and Jack. All the oddballs, eh? Okay, I better go then."

He loved Mr. Clatterbox, adorned as the old truck was in various stages of rust and multi-coloured letters. He found it extremely cheerful to ride around in him and prayed that his life would be over before he had to give up his colourful rattletrap. But he also realized that the truck was not exactly lawyer-worthy.

So they all arrived, very respectfully, in June's red Mazda, right on time for the appointment.

The receptionist had come to know June, Edie, and Nick over the course of the case, and so she smiled at the odd conglomerate, which now included Doc and the dog, as they arrived. She ushered them into the lawyer's office and closed the door behind them.

Dan had arranged chairs around his desk and gestured for them to take seats. Jack sat dutifully beside Nick, inseparable as always.

"You must be Shaggy Jack," the lawyer smiled at the huge creature, whose tail wagged furiously at the lawyer. "You were absolutely right. He is, by far, the biggest dog I've ever seen in my life."

Jack offered a massive grey paw to Dan, who shook it solemnly and with great respect. Nick, who was already indebted to the man, decided that he liked him very much.

"Hello, Dr. McIntyre," Dan turned to Doc, shaking the old man's hand warmly. "It's very nice to see you again."

"It's nice to see you too," Doc answered, not a trace of recognition in his voice. "If I met you before, I'm sorry, I don't remember. I'm getting old and senile."

Dan chuckled.

"No, really, I'm not joking. I really am. I diagnosed myself when I still had my practice going. That's why I decided to retire. And I have the best home I ever imagined now, with these lovely lesbian ladies and my Huckleberry friends and old Shaggy Jack and blind Leslie."

"Well, that's good to hear," Dan replied, clearly taken aback a little.

SHAGGY JACK

Nick wanted to whisper, "too much information," but refrained.

"It's wonderful. I'd like to settle the bill here, though. I tried to give Junie dear the money, but she wouldn't take it from me. But I'm sure you'll take it. I imagine that's why we're all here. To finish paying?" He looked around, seeking confirmation. June shook her head slightly.

"Doc, we don't owe anything. I told you that. Mr. Clark just requested a visit with us. And especially you."

Dan nodded his agreement, but Doc looked uneasy.

"Why's that, I wonder?"

"Before I begin, I'd like you to meet my daughter Emily," Dan told him. "I'll just call her in. She's a lawyer too, and now she practises in my office with me."

"Isn't that lovely?" Edie exclaimed. "You must be so very proud of her."

"Oh, I am. She's my pride and joy."

A tall, well-dressed woman entered the office.

"This is Emily," Dan announced.

Emily smiled warmly, nodding greetings all around.

"I need to tell you a story about Emily. My daughter," he repeated, supposedly for Doc's benefit.

"All right," June said slowly, exchanging glances with Edie. Neither of them had a clue where this unconventional conversation seemed to be heading.

Doc rubbed his hands in glee. "Oh, I love stories! I hope it's a happy one."

"The happiest one I've ever known," the lawyer assured him.

Before he began, the door opened and a beautiful teenage girl stepped inside. She had ivory skin, shining black hair, and huge, soulful eyes. Those eyes immediately sought out Nick. That boy blushed from the roots of his hair to the nape of his neck.

"Hi, Nick," she greeted him warmly. "I noticed you were here."

"Hi, Freya," Nick stammered. "What—what are you doing here?"

"Oh, this is my grandpa. And my mom," she explained, motioning to Dan and Emily in turn.

"Freya, we are having a meeting here," Emily chided. "You can't just barge in."

But Dan appeared unperturbed, regarding her with an indulgent smile.

"Oh, that's okay," Freya replied airily. "I'm leaving anyway. I just wanted to say hi. See you at school, Nick."

"Okay, see you," Nick croaked, his face still a dull shade of crimson.

Freya departed with a flourish.

Emily cleared her throat. "I apologize for my daughter. Go ahead and tell them your story, Dad."

"I live here in Dalton now, but when we first moved from the big city years ago, we lived in Laventra," Dan proceeded. "Emily was only five years old. We loved it there, so much fresh air, and the people were friendly. But the winters can be tough."

"They sure can," Edie nodded.

"Got that right," Doc agreed.

"Well, there was a terrible snowstorm in early December, the very first winter we lived there. Just terrible. You wouldn't believe that the sky could have so much white stuff in it. It never let up all day and all night, and we were in the evening of the second day when Emily got really sick. Just all of a sudden. She'd been playing that day and seemed all right, but when I came home from work, my wife said she seemed a little off. We didn't think anything of it, but then she got really hot. Her little face was scorching; her whole body was on fire."

"Terrible when your child is so sick," Edie murmured, into the ensuing pause.

"Especially when you don't know what's wrong," Dan agreed. "Anyway, I called the local doctor . . . Jed McIntyre."

"Me!" Doc cried. "Was it me?"

"Yes indeed, it was. I'd never met you before, but I called your office. Your secretary said you were done for the day. You needed to get home because the weather was horrible, and the snow was not stopping. They were closing the main roads because they were becoming impassable. I begged her to at least let me speak with you, so she went outside to see if she could catch you. I could hear her yelling for you over the howling of the winds. I waited on the other end of the phone, feeling quite desperate. I had no hope that you would come back and talk to me, but then you answered the phone. I told you how quickly Emily had gotten sick and about the high fever. You said that you'd swing by and see her on your way home."

"That sounds like Doc," June smiled.

"When you got there, she was convulsing. Full-blown seizure. My wife and I were terrified. We didn't know what to do. You turned her on her side and rubbed her back till she finally stopped. You told us to put cool washcloths on her head and keep her on her side. Then you used our phone to call an ambulance. I could hear you talking, and I knew that they weren't going to make it to our house. Not in that storm. And our side roads were closed. My wife was hysterical, but you were very calm. You told me to bundle her up in blankets and carry her out to your truck. It was a big, red Dodge Ram, and you said it was good in the snow."

"Ah, Josephine."

"Who?" Dan asked.

"Josephine. My old truck. I'm a Dodge man, you see. She was a lovely old girl."

June shook her head, incredulous at the quirky way his memory worked.

Dan just smiled, then continued with his tale. "Well, you got me and Emily into the back seat of your truck and told us to hang on. The ambulance would meet us at the highway, but we had to get there, and it was going to be tough going. The road to the highway was closed, but you took it anyway. I remember the truck slipping and sliding around. I was petrified. But not as petrified as I was of losing my girl. Emily was quiet by then, and that made me even more afraid. You asked me if I was a praying man. I said I really didn't know if I was or not. And you told me that, if I could, I should try to pray now. You told me that the good thing about praying is that even if you didn't believe in it, it never hurts to say a little prayer for those we love. I have always remembered that. Anyway, we made it to the highway, and who's to say that those prayers didn't help. We didn't have cell phones or anything like that back then, but the ambulance was there to meet us. It felt like the biggest miracle in the whole world. They took her from my arms and started working on her right away. They weren't going to let me go with her in the ambulance, but you insisted, and finally they relented. I can still see you standing at the side of the road, covered in snow, the wind whirling up around you, waving us on. We got to SickKids—just in time, according to the doctors there. Emily had bacterial meningitis and could have easily died or had permanent brain damage. It was touch and go for a few days, but as you can see, my daughter has grown up into a fine young woman."

Emily smiled at them modestly.

"Dan, that is a beautiful story," Edie said softly.

"It's true, every word of it. I just wanted you to know how very happy I was to have the opportunity to do something in return for this great man."

"I'm happy I was able to help," Doc said. "But I'm sorry, I have to admit to you, Mr. Clark, that I don't remember any of this. None at all."

"That's all right, Dr. McIntyre. It doesn't matter that you don't remember."

The lawyer stood and reached across the desk, smiling. He gathered Doc's old hands in both of his, clasping them warmly, his face shining with emotion. "Because I do."

Chapter Twenty-Nine

"Eat your carrots, boys. They'll make you look good in the dark." Doc uttered these prophetic words to the accompaniment of dinner dishes being passed around the table.

"They will?" Dillon inquired dubiously. "I thought they were supposed to be good for your eyes. My mom used to say that."

Doc grinned. "Your mother was right, of course, Dillon," he declared. "I was using that information loosely."

"Very loosely," Nick said, giving Doc a little nudge.

"Well, I just want you boys to eat up because we're going to have a little bit of a 'do' around Miss Chiminea. To celebrate the backside of Garth Chapman!"

"His backside?"

"Yes indeed. Some people bring pleasure by coming and some by going, and that, my Huckleberries," Doc lifted his finger in a knowing gesture, "is a well-known fact. So eat up your carrots. Then you can be easy on our eyes. Why don't you ask that lovely-looking girl with all the black hair from our lawyer's office over, Nicky? She seemed to think very highly of you, as I recall. Ask her to come by for a wee smash of music and a marshmallow roast sometime. Who could resist that?"

"I have asked Freya out already, Doc," Nick admitted.

"The beautiful Freya. I feel like she likes you a lot," Doc observed.

"Well, she doesn't want to go out with me."

"Did she say that actually?"

"No, but she had some stupid excuse. I asked her twice."

"Hmmm," Doc considered the matter. "Ask her out once more, Nicky boy. Just one more time."

He looked at the boy with such eagerness that Nick finally shrugged. "Okay, but if she doesn't go this time, I'm *never* asking again."

Doc nodded. "Fair enough. But I think this time will take."

"You don't know that."

"I'm pretty good at matchmaking. I knew Junie was a lesbian even before she did."

"Doc, you are incorrigible," June gave him a playful shove. "You had to borrow someone's phone at the store this morning because you forgot why you went, but you remember that you introduced me to my own lesbianism."

"Incredible, isn't it? And I was glad to borrow Mrs. Winthrop's phone because I wouldn't have wanted to forget these delectable marshmallows."

Happiness prevailed and lingered into the night, as twinkling stars congregated in the sweetness of the summer sky. Music, or a reasonable facsimile of music, drifted away and into the fields, all tangled up with the melodies of old and young voices and Jack's croons.

They were together. No one could threaten them now. It had been settled in a court of law.

Edie reflected that she should bake Dan something delicious for all his time, trouble, and kindness. She set her mind to choosing a recipe that might suffice.

June knew that she should go inside, that she should get Dillon and Nick off to bed and Max on his way home. She knew they should all retire for some sleep, even as the night air settled around them, enveloping them in its star-shot, velvety embrace.

But the leaves were stirring so gently in the evening breeze, telling tales of old. The last notes of birdsong echoed through the fading twilight. Nick was murmuring his low, special language to Jack. Dillon and Max sprawled out in comfortable silence, gazing at the patterns of fire sparks emitting from the chiminea. Edie smiled into the last embers, slowly toasting her marshmallow to golden brown perfection, pondering all the happy days that lay ahead.

Doc was spinning some outlandish story about God-only-knew-what. It didn't matter. It was enough just to listen to his pleasant, lighthearted words rambling along, tumbling over one another before they fell into the dark magic of the summer night.

Everyone she loved was here, right here.

Yes. She would linger a little longer.

Nick did ask Freya out one more time. The beautiful Freya, as Doc dubbed her, and thus she remained forever after. He had qualified, again, to Doc that this would be the last time in his whole life he would ask her.

"Guess what? She said yes! How did you know she would, Doc?"

"Well, Nicky boy, I know people. I don't always remember things, but I can still tell when a girl likes a boy."

"And you think Freya likes me?"

SHAGGY JACK

"Of course she does," Doc affirmed. "Why would she go out with you if she didn't like you?"

"Well, it's the third time. She said no twice already."

"Third time's a charm, my boy."

"We're going to see a movie in Dalton on Friday, but on Saturday, I'm gonna ask her to come out for a bonfire."

"One of our famous bonfires," Doc agreed, nodding eagerly.

"I hope she likes it."

"She will. Of course she will."

Freya did enjoy the bonfire. She helped gather kindling, she roasted wieners and marshmallows, and she sang along with Cracklin' Rosie.

In other words, she was perfect.

Life rolled along on a blithe wheel of happiness. The threat of Garth had been removed and firmly deposited back on the west coast. The whole world felt lighter and brighter. The kennels had been full every week, and the whole household was busy, feeding and cleaning and walking (and talking to) the dogs.

"I think the best thing to make in the summer is good memories," Edie declared one sunny afternoon.

"That's it!" Doc cried. "Write that down, Max."

Max nodded. He had taken to writing things down in the digital notebook on his phone every time Doc said this, which could be multiple times a day.

"That boxer in the last kennel snarled at me again," Nick told them, rounding the back of the house to plunk himself beside them. "I thought maybe he didn't like Jack, so I left Jack inside this time.

But when I went to feed him, he still snarled. I'll walk him later, but I'm going to put a no-pull, head-and-neck collar on him."

"He is pretty bad-natured, it seems," June agreed. "I'd have to say he's the worst-tempered dog we've ever boarded."

"Except for Rupert," Nick guffawed, doubling over and laughing. "Remember him?"

"He took the ass out of Max's pants!" Dillon cried with glee.

June frowned. "I didn't know anything about that," she said sternly.

"Oh, well, it was a while ago now," Nick said, giggling. "And it wasn't really Rupert's fault. Max was teasing him with a bone, holding it behind his back, and Rupert went to grab it."

"I was younger then," Max said defensively. "My mom was pissed about those pants though."

"I'm surprised we never heard about it," Edie remarked.

"Doc knew!"

Doc merely shrugged. "I don't remember. Sorry, Junie dear."

"Oh, that's your excuse all the time," June scoffed.

"Because it happens to be true," Doc informed her with great dignity.

"That wasn't the funniest part, though," Nick nearly shrieked.

"Shut up! Just shut up!" Max said, punching his friend in the arm.

Nick continued, ignoring his objections. "The funniest part was that he was going commando!" He could barely get the words out before he and Dillon dissolved into so much laughter that tears ran down their faces.

Edie and June exchanged puzzled glances.

SHAGGY JACK

"He wasn't wearing any underwear!" Nick and Dillon cried in unison.

Max rose from the porch, clearly mortified. "I'm leaving now. I'm fed up with all of you. Don't expect me back anytime soon."

"Sorry, man," the two boys protested, amidst a sea of giggles, but Max mounted his bike and peddled away in the direction of his house.

June said, "Now that wasn't nice." She was doing her damnedest to sound serious and not laugh.

Finally, the boys calmed down, and Nick returned to the matter at hand. "Rupert was different than this boxer, though. I feel like this guy's got a nasty personality. Even when we're being nice to him."

"Dogs are like people," Doc said. "There are some you just can't fix."

"But shouldn't we at least try?" It was clear Nick didn't like the idea of giving up on the dog.

"We should try, of course," Doc agreed. "Now, what about Max? I think you boys hurt his feelings."

"He'll be back," Nick declared.

"He said he might not be back for a while," Edie worried. She didn't like anyone's feelings to be hurt.

"He'll be back," Nick assured her, unfazed. It wasn't the first time the boys teased each other, and it probably wouldn't be the last.

They all lounged in the warmth of the afternoon, reluctant to move.

"Okay, I'm going to try with Mr. Boxer one more time," Nick announced eventually, getting up.

"Should I come too?" Dillon asked. "Would that make it better or worse?"

Nick shrugged. "I don't know. But you can walk Tripod if you want."

"Is that the three-legged dog? I haven't met him yet."

"Duh . . . yeah! That's why he's called Tripod."

"Does he walk okay with only three legs?"

"Yep," said Nick.

"It's surprising. Animals sometimes adapt better than people, I think," said June.

"That's why I love animals," Nick smiled. "They don't whine or complain. They just get on with things the best way they can."

"And they don't get offended when someone teases them about not wearing underwear," Dillon said. Both boys doubled over with laughter again, then departed to attend to the dogs.

The three adults continued to bask in the warm sunshine, enjoying the heady buzzing of the bees, the leaves fluttering in warm, sweet-scented breezes, and the beautiful, calming spell of summer magic.

"Well, I guess it's time I started thinking about putting together some supper. Are you guys getting hungry?" June asked, pulling herself out of her summer reverie.

"I was hungry earlier, but all I found in the kitchen was a bunch of ingredients," Doc declared.

"Ingredients? Ingredients for what?"

"Well, that's just it. I didn't know. They all seemed kind of random."

"Don't you worry, Doc," Edie assured him. "You have a little rest here in the sun, and June and I will see if we can make the ingredients into something for supper."

"You girls are amazing," Doc beamed at them.

"If you're hungry now, I can make you a sandwich," Edie offered.

"Oh no, that's fine. Just the prospect of supper is enough to keep me going."

"Like you don't get supper every night, Doc," June told him, smiling ruefully. "Like I've ever set a plate of *ingredients* in front of you."

"No, no, Junie dear. I would never, ever think that."

June turned and gave him a quick hug. "I'm only teasing you, Doc. And the next time you're hungry, just ask one of us. We don't mind feeding you any time at all."

"Ah, you're very good to an old man. I'm going to weed the sunflowers in The Patience Spot. Oh, just look who's here."

They all turned to observe Max pedalling down the cobblestones on his bike.

Doc grinned and waved, as if greeting a long-lost friend.

"I thought you were going to be gone for a while?" June dared to inquire.

"I *was* gone for a while," Max replied, with the manner of someone stating the obvious. "I went all the way to Laventra and picked up some chips for later at the bonfire."

"Very good. The boys are just around back at the kennels."

"Wonder if he has underwear on," Edie murmured to June. They both giggled, departing to the kitchen to begin the preparations of various ingredients.

Nick and Dillon emerged from the kennels with the boxer, subdued in his restrictive collar, and the three-legged dog in tow.

"Tripod!" Max cried in delight. "Look at him. He's doing all right now, isn't he?"

"Yeah. Come and help us, man. What took you so long?"

Chapter Thirty

June was so happy she found herself wishing it were possible to reach out and hold this summer in her hands, like a treasure to keep forever.

The boys were all working part-time jobs now, various shifts and days, but still spent many hours helping with the kennels and conglomeration of dogs who came and went at the boarding house. Some just came and never left. June had given up attempting to exert any measure of control over this.

Jack, of course, remained king of the canines, with Leslie a close second.

"It's good for the boys to care about animals," Doc told June. She'd been lamenting the state of her home, overrun, as it was, by a myriad of dogs.

"I know you're right," June conceded. "But I do think we need to have some kind of limit. Sometimes dogs just appear and stay for ages, and I didn't know anything about them. They never ask me if it's okay. They always ask you."

Doc thought about it and said, "I think they do that because I usually say yes and then I forget to tell you, Junie dear."

"Well, of course they do. They're not stupid," June retorted. "And they're costing me a fortune in dog food."

Doc hastened to say he'd been meaning to replenish supplies.

"Doc, I did not mean that. You are more than generous. You don't have to spend all your money on groceries and dog food."

"Well, now, what else would I spend it on? Anyway, where do you suppose my truck keys are?"

"Probably hanging in the ignition of Mr. Clatterbox, as usual."

"Ah, yes. If I leave them there, then I know where they are . . . Usually . . . Although sometimes I still have to look for them. I just hope nobody steals that gem of a truck."

The women exchanged smiles.

"Now, Doc, who in their right mind would steal that rattly old thing?" June asked.

Edie jumped in. "They wouldn't get too far now, would they, Doc? I mean, with 'Doc and the Huckleberries' written in rainbow letters on each door, it would be pretty distinctive."

"I guess it would, at that!" Doc appeared relieved. He called out to the boys, and they all piled into the ancient vehicle where the keys were, of course, dangling in the ignition.

"Where are we off to?" Max asked, always ready for an adventure.

"Off to get dog food. And whatever else strikes our fancy."

"It's my turn to drive," Nick announced.

Doc had been teaching the boys, one by one, how to drive a standard. Each time they departed, June had to make a supreme effort not to worry herself into a frenzy.

"Next, you'll be teaching Jack how to drive," she complained.

Doc considered this gravely, remarking that his legs were certainly long enough.

"Don't you dare, Dr. Jed McIntyre. I draw the line at that."

Doc grinned at the boys. "When she uses my whole name, she means business."

"You weren't going to do it, were you, Doc? Teach Jack how to drive?"

Doc shrugged. "We'll never know now."

They returned from the voyage with multiple bags of groceries, sacks of dog food, and cartons of ice cream. Doc's philosophy was that if you were going to go to all the bother of shopping, then you might as well stock up on ice cream.

After supper—and not before, at June's insistence—an array of ice cream flavours was produced, and bowls were handed out around the porch. Even the dogs received some, as Doc observed that it was hot for them also.

"All those years you warned people about what they were eating and advising them to cut down on sugar."

Doc considered this, scraping the sides of his bowl. "I did, didn't I, Junie dear? It seems such a shame now, doesn't it?"

"Look at those squirrels over there staggering around. Do you think they're sick or something?"

Nick indicated several squirrels, seemingly attempting to climb the crab apple tree, only to fall back and stagger around, then repeat the process all over again.

June threw back her head and laughed. "They're drunk, that's all."

"Drunk?"

"Yep. Every year, that old crab apple tree loses its fruit. Grandma used to pick them and make crab apple jelly, and I did too for a while. But I haven't for quite a few years now. So the apples just lie on the ground and ferment. I think it's the mold or the bacteria that causes the fermentation. Anyway, that produces the alcohol. When the squirrels get into them, they act drunk."

Nick looked doubtful. "Auntie Bug, is that true or are you just making shit up?"

"Watch your language, Nick. And my name is not Doc."

"Hey," Doc cried. "I don't make shit up!"

"Doc!"

"I was only quoting Nicky," Doc pointed out.

"But should you?"

"Probably not. I'm pretty sure I've seen some of those drunkards out at The Patience Spot, too. Maybe that happens to sunflower seeds, too."

June looked doubtful, but Max quickly confirmed that this could indeed happen. Google said so.

"Oh, it must be true then," June quipped.

"It says the sunflower seeds and shells on the ground can ferment," he continued, unperturbed. "And when the squirrels ingest bacteria from the seeds, they can appear drunk."

The world's smallest nature party entertained everyone for the remainder of the evening.

"We're eating ice cream and they're getting drunk," Doc declared. "What a great evening. Everybody's having a good time."

"Do people have birthdays after they're dead, do you think?" Nick posed the question solemnly to the three adults, as they sat enjoying their morning coffee.

The resplendent magic of autumn had transformed the countryside, turning maple trees into brilliant masterpieces of orange and red. The world rustled with the sound of their leaves, whispering ancient secrets to each other.

"I know it would have been Chrissy's birthday today, dear," June answered gently. "I always think of her on this date. I never forget that this is her birthday. Of course, for years, I thought of her on this day, and she was actually alive. I just didn't know it." Try as she might, June was incapable of keeping the bitterness from these words.

Nick sighed.

"Maybe she's not really dead now," Doc suggested, ever the optimist.

"She is, Doc, I saw her. I wish I hadn't, but I did. I wish I'd known Auntie Bug then. It would have been so much better for both of us. I feel like she was getting ready to come back here and see you. We talked about it, but then she died."

"It would have been nice," June agreed. "I wish I understood her reasons for never coming back, but I guess I never will now."

"I know, Auntie Bug."

"You should just try and remember her when she was happy, Nick. That's how we should think of people after they die. We should remember them laughing and having fun."

"Sometimes I wish I could see my mom one more time," Nick said softly. "Just once more."

"Me too," Dillon sighed, thinking of his mom, too.

"There's nobody like your mom," Doc agreed.

June reflected on this. She didn't feel that way, and she was quite sure Edie didn't either. People who shared that sentiment assumed everyone else had mothers like they'd had. June's mother had been distant and unaffectionate. June understood now that she had almost certainly suffered from clinical depression, but that realization was cold comfort.

"We could go visit my mom, you know," Doc declared brightly.

June, who had been lost in her reflections about mothers in general and hers in particular, startled a little at this outburst.

"Doc," Edie placed a gentle hand on the old man's arm, "your mom is dead now. You know that, right?"

"Oh, I know," Doc replied. "Don't worry, Edie, I didn't forget that. But I mean, we could visit her grave. It's not that far of a drive, a couple of hours, I think, and it's a nice, sunny day."

"Today?" June fairly shrieked. June had rarely given in to such a spontaneous act in her whole life.

"Why not?" Doc shrugged. "I wonder if good old Mr. Clatterbox would venture that far."

And, just like that, it was decided. Doc, Edie, June, and Nick took a road trip just because it was a beautiful day and Doc wanted to see his mom one more time. They threw together a makeshift picnic from leftovers in the fridge.

In the end, they left Mr. Clatterbox at home. June persuaded Doc that her little Mazda might be a better choice for the longer trip.

Dillon opted to stay home with Leslie. He had an English essay due, and there were four other dogs to walk and care for.

At the last minute, Jack jumped into the back seat, wriggling his enormous body between Nick and Edie.

"Jack wants to visit your mom too," Nick said to Doc.

Doc turned and scratched the shaggy dog's head. Jack was so big that he was able to occupy both the front and back seat simultaneously.

"And maybe we'll see my sweetheart's grave."

"Your sweetheart? Doc, we didn't know you'd had a sweetheart. Did she die young?" Edie asked.

"Far too young. She was so beautiful. I called her Cindy."

"Short for Cinderella," Nick recalled.

"We'll look for her grave too, Doc," June told him. "We brought enough flowers from the garden to put on two graves."

After much ado, several wrong turns, and a near collision at a turnoff where Doc said the yield sign was really "only a suggestion," they managed to find their way to a very isolated, very quaint country cemetery.

"I hope this is it," Doc said, appearing a little doubtful now. "It doesn't look like it used to."

"Neither do you," June retorted curtly. She was tired and hungry and cranky from the long drive. Her back was stiff, and if this wasn't the right one, she had no desire to pound any more back roads searching for other graveyards.

But Nick and Jack, bounding across the rows of graves, shouted (or in Jack's case barked) at the sight of a familiar name.

"Over here! Look, this must be your mom, Doc. Elizabeth McIntyre."

"That's her! You guys are geniuses! That's her!" Doc, full of excitement, hurried over to inspect the grave.

June groaned. "Really? Geniuses?"

Edie chuckled and reached for her hand. "You'll feel better when you've had a bite to eat. That was a long drive. And I put a bottle of our dandelion wine in the picnic basket. We can all have a little sip."

Nick had divided the flowers, and Doc gently placed a small

posy on his mother's grave. They turned, as one accord, to allow him to say a few words to her in private.

"She must have been so proud that you were a doctor and helped so many people," June said, after he had returned to join them.

Doc shrugged.

"I don't know. She wasn't forthright with praise or anything. She just never was very demonstrative. I always knew she loved us, though."

"You had siblings?"

"Yes, a sister. Connie."

"But where's Cindy?" Nick broke in. "We have flowers for Cinderella."

"Cinderella? Was that her real name?" June asked.

"Well, no. I don't think so. I always called her that because she was so much like a beautiful princess."

"Okay, well, what was her real name?"

Doc's face went completely blank, apparently searching his memory archives, which were limited on the best of days.

"What was Cinderella's last name? Can you look that up on your phone, Nicky boy?"

Nick pulled out his phone and googled. "It says her last name was most likely Tremaine. Does that sound right?"

"No," Doc shook his head sadly. "That's not it."

"Of course not," June erupted. "Because Cinderella is not a real person. She's a Disney character."

"I *do* know that, Junie dear, but that's all I ever called her."

"Maybe we can walk around until something looks familiar to you," Nick said. "Come on, Jack."

SHAGGY JACK

June groaned. "So, we're looking around for a grave of someone with an unknown name, hoping something rings a bell with your memory, is that it?"

"Right you are, Junie dear," Doc agreed, giving her a thumbs up.

The group decided to take a picnic break first.

June looked around her at the miscellany gathered on the old, worn, blue checked picnic blanket—Jack, taking up the space of a full-grown adult, one paw resting affectionately on Nick's outstretched leg; Edie, her beautiful white hair piled into a bun atop her small face, chestnut brown eyes crinkling with laughter in the afternoon sunshine; Doc, long and lanky and brimming with joy just to be here with all of them, happy to see his mother one more time; Nick, her beloved boy, glasses askew, body growing at an alarming rate, face beginning to showcase signs of the handsome man he would soon become; and her, squat old June Howard, thrilled to be here, right here, with all of them.

And, it must be admitted, I'm feeling much better after a bite to eat and a drink of wine.

Once the picnic was done and the basket packed away into the trunk, they took up the search for the grave of Doc's princess.

Of course, it would have been helpful if they'd had a name—first, last, or any name at all, really—June had muttered to Edie. This after wandering for the better part of an hour, to and fro and up and down the rows of old headstones.

"Talk about a wild goose chase, Doc!" she called to him, as he scoured each monument, Jack and Nick at his heels.

"You're right," Doc sighed. "Funny how I thought I'd never, ever forget. Now I can't bloody remember."

"It's all right, Doc," Nick reassured the discouraged man. "At least we got to see your mom and dad's grave."

"And my sister, Connie. Could we put the rest of the flowers on hers, do you think?"

"Of course we can, Doc," June said, pleased to see an end in sight to their futile mission. "I didn't see her grave, though. Is her name on your parents' headstone?"

Doc shook his head. "Sadly, no. She has her own stone. Over there."

The little group trooped over to a stone at the back end of the graveyard, small and indiscreet.

Constance McIntyre
1935—1959
Cherished daughter of George McIntyre
and Elizabeth Diallo McIntyre
Beloved sister of Jedidiah.

Doc knelt, fingering the stark granite tombstone and tracing the outline of the old, etched letters with utmost tenderness. "Ah, my wee Connie. She was such a dear sister to me."

"She died very young," Edie observed.

"She died the year I was born," June commented. "What happened to her, Doc?"

Doc rose, brushing off his trousers. He smiled his thanks to Nick as the boy placed the bouquet carefully at the base of Connie's grave. "I am not exactly sure. No one ever really gave me the whole story. I left home to go to medical school when she was still a teenager. But

SHAGGY JACK

I'd come and visit most weekends. We were very close. We always liked the same things, and we could talk about anything."

He paused. As of one accord, the little group sat down in a circle. It was clear there was an important story to be told. One that Doc would tell in his own time.

"My dad could be a very harsh man. It wasn't that unusual in those days. Things are different now, and I'm glad. But they used to say, 'Spare the rod and spoil the child.'"

"What does that even mean?" Nick asked.

"It means that if you don't punish a child physically when they do wrong, they won't learn what is right," Edie explained.

"You mean like beat them?"

"In my father's case, yes," Doc said, his voice saddened at the memory. "Unfortunately. My mom didn't agree, but in those days, women were wholly dependent on their husbands and had to go along with them. My mom was Flemish. She was born in Belgium. We used to tease her and call her 'a little bit McIntyre.'"

Seeing their blank looks, Doc laughed. "For Elizabeth. 'A little bit.'" He paused to let his joke sink in. After their obligatory chuckle, he continued. "Sometimes, if she was angry at him, she would say 'yes, a very little bit.'" He smiled at the memory.

"You were telling us about your Connie," Edie reminded him, gently interrupting his reverie.

"Ah, yes. My Connie. I tried to stay close to her because neither of my parents understood her. You see, she was a lesbian lady. Like you two." He smiled at Edie and June. "But in the '50s, it was unheard of and considered unnatural, something that nobody ever dared to mention. I think that my mother might have understood, but my father's opinions were hard and fast and immovable. I don't know for sure how they would have felt, though, because she never did tell them."

"She told you?"

He shook his head. "I think I just knew. And I let her know that I knew. We were always very close. And I didn't care about that. I would have loved her no matter who she fell in love with."

"You were ahead of your time, Doc," June observed.

Doc shrugged. "You love who you love."

They'd heard him say these words before. Edie rose and bent down to hug his thin shoulders. He caught her hand and gave it a squeeze.

"Connie loved another woman. I'm pretty sure that the other woman loved her right back, but as I say, it was such a different world back then. The other woman got scared, I think, and ended up getting married to a local farmer. Connie was never the same after that. When I graduated and set up my practice, I begged her to come and live with me. She was torturing herself by seeing this woman all the time. But she couldn't bring herself to leave. She kept saying that one day she would, but she just kept putting it off. Anyway, one Monday morning, my mom called to say Connie hadn't woken up. The doctor came and pronounced her dead."

"But what happened?" Nick breathed.

"No one ever said for sure. You can't imagine it, Nicky boy. It was so very different. So many things that you simply did not talk about. I knew she'd been depressed and I always thought she'd taken an overdose of medication, but I never found out for sure . . . and it was never spoken of."

"Poor girl," Edie said. "At least I'm glad she had you in her short life to love her and understand her and not condemn her for who she was."

"That's how I knew who you were, Junie dear. I was so happy the day that you lovely ladies got married. If only things had been like that for my Connie, she might still be alive and living with the love of her life. And I like the rainbow thing you have going on. Whenever I see a rainbow, I think of my sister." He shook his head wryly. "Silly, I know."

"I think it's lovely," June said softly.

They departed through the long grass of the old, forgotten cemetery, feeling closer somehow, a bond of past memories forged between them.

Strapped in, tired and spent, forty kilometres from home, Doc, who had appeared to be half asleep, suddenly lifted his head and called out. Even Jack startled at the cry, and June's car almost left the road.

"Susan! Susan McDonald!"

"Who?"

"Cinderella is Susan! I remembered her name."

June groaned.

"We're not turning around now. You know that, right, Doc?"

"Oh, I know that, Junie dear. I just take it as a personal triumph that my mind kicked in."

Chapter Thirty-One

"I know I always say this, but I really think that now would be a good time for us to seriously consider expanding our kennel and becoming a home for special dogs." Nick hadn't given up on his dream of helping more animals. Not by a long shot.

"Aren't they all special?" Doc inquired.

"I meant, like, dogs with special needs," Nick qualified.

"We already have that," June grumbled. "How many times must we go over this, Nick? If they're not blind, they're deaf and only answer to sign language. Or recovering from surgery. Or some trauma."

"So we're off to a good start then, is that what you're saying?" Edie inquired, her deep brown eyes sparkling with mischief.

"We could get a helpline for animals. For all pets. Remember we talked about it before?"

"*You* talked about it before," June corrected him.

"And we could have an on-call number for when an animal is in trouble," Dillon piped up.

"I'm not sure it works that way, boys," Edie told them. "Anyway, animals can't use the phone. Obviously."

But Doc took the topic and ran with it. "It would work if Nicky got his veterinary license. And people could call him if they had an animal in distress. He could settle down here as a veterinarian and look after all the special dogs around. We could all help him."

Doc's words tumbled overtop of one another, flowing on the tide of his enthusiasm.

SHAGGY JACK

Edie reflected on how wonderful it was that Doc foresaw a world so many years hence, where he continued to exist and participate.

"The boys haven't even graduated high school yet," June pointed out.

"No, but they're starting up their last year. And it's going quick."

"It is, Doc," Nick agreed, "but it takes a lot of time and money to become a veterinarian. I have the money my mom left me in trust, but I'd still have to apply for some grants."

Doc waved his arms about, unbothered by such trivial concerns. "I don't think that'll be a problem."

If only everyone saw the world through Doc's rose-coloured glasses.

"I *would* like to be a vet and help animals—all animals, but I guess I'll always love dogs best. See, Auntie Bug, so many dogs are affected from being abused or neglected. That's what I mean by special needs. If we set up a home like that here, then you and Edie could just pet them and give them affection. And that would be a form of their therapy. That would be a good job, right?"

June snorted. "As if I have all the time in the world to sit and pet dogs all day."

"Not *all* day. Just some of the day. You do that now, anyway, looking after all the guys who come."

"But they're not traumatized. They're just regular, everyday dogs."

"Sometimes it's hard to tell about trauma. It can be different for people, too," Doc said, after a moment's pause. "We had a man in our village, and he had what they used to call a 'soldier's heart.'"

"So he was traumatized from the war?" Edie queried.

"Yes. Now they call it something else. A bunch of letters."

"PTSD."

"Maybe. But it happened to a lot of soldiers when they came home from the war. They didn't act the same as they did before they fought. People used to think it was a mental illness. It was Dr. Jacob Da Costa who called it 'soldier's heart' and linked it to soldiers going through so much trauma."

"Doc!" Edie cried. "You remembered all that!"

"I did, didn't I?"

"Some days you amaze us, Doc," Nick observed.

"Some days I amaze myself," Doc said, delighted.

"Was this soldier with the bad heart a friend of yours?" June inquired.

"Not really, but I used to see him when I walked home from school, and sometimes we talked. He was always nice to me, and I was just a kid. But he always looked really sad, especially when he talked about the war. He's the one who made me want to be a doctor. I just thought that soldiers, of all people, deserved attention if their hearts were hurting."

"Did you ever have another patient with one of those hearts?" Max wanted to know.

Doc shook his head. "I don't remember, but I do know I had lots of patients who survived trauma. I tried to help them if I could. Not with pills, though. I only used pills as a last resort."

"I don't think pills would work for PTSD in dogs," Nick said. "I don't know for sure, though."

"I don't know how that works either. But if anybody can figure all this out, you boys can. I've no doubt of that. I can just imagine a big clinic with Nicky as the veterinarian and Dillon here assisting and looking after everything. And Shaggy Jack doing something, maybe helping in the kennels with the small dogs. And Max will be the journalist who keeps you in the public eye, so you'll get the recognition that you deserve."

Nick loved the sound of it all but knew better than to have dreams that big. "Ah, Doc, that's just a pipe dream."

Doc waved his unlit pipe above his head, grinning. "Don't forget what Old Smokey says. They're the best kind."

"I wish I believed all that was going to happen," Dillon sighed.

"Don't you worry," Doc reassured them. "I'll believe in all of you until you're able to believe in yourselves. I'm not going to stop. I'll always have faith in my Huckleberries.

"Now, come on. Mr. Clatterbox was requesting an outing earlier. Let's go get some ice cream."

"I'm almost afraid to say this, but Doc has been great lately," Edie confided to June. "His mind seems to be better than ever."

A lull in the busy day had allowed them a break for refreshments on the porch. Jack had just hauled himself to his feet and trotted down the cobblestones. The women knew that in twenty minutes exactly, he would return with Nick and Dillon in tow. And, quite possibly, Max as well.

The day compounded a perfect harmony of sights, sounds, and sensations of autumn's fleeting beauty. A gentle breeze caused the fallen October leaves to dance across the ground.

"I have to tell you, Edie, when Doc first came to live with me, I thought it would only be for a short while. I thought for sure that he'd have to be placed in a home or somewhere before too long. But that was almost six years ago now, and he's doing great. I mean, I don't think he could live on his own. He does still get mixed up and of course his memory is crap."

"True," Edie nodded. "And he'd get lost if he didn't have one of the boys with him."

"But just being here with us, he's great."

"And he does love it here, doesn't he?"

June nodded.

They both turned as the object of their tête-à-tête materialized around the corner of the house.

"It must be just about time for my Huckleberries to get home. I see Mr. Shaggy Jack's back end disappearing down the road."

"Yes, indeed. Who needs a clock when they have him? Would you like a glass of iced tea, Doc?"

"Ah, Junie dear, that would go down real nicely right about now. The Patience Spot looks great. I managed to pull a bunch of weeds out from around it, and some of those sunflowers are still holding up their brave, old heads. But some have gone to seed already. They'll be giving the birds a nice little feast. Very useful flowers, along with being so bright and cheerful." Doc sat down, brushing his hands off on his worn trousers as he gratefully accepted a cold drink from June.

"These are the most beautiful days, aren't they? These fall days. I guess, 'cause we know they won't last. I was just thinking when I was out back there, how nice this old world really is. Don't you think?"

The women nodded, smiling at the inherent joy that was Doc.

SHAGGY JACK

"And I was thinking about this couple that used to be patients of mine. Funny how little bits of things come back to me at odd times. I was pretty young, and they were some of my first patients. They've both died since then, so it's all right to talk about them."

June thought it was a shame Doc didn't always follow this guideline, often blurting out anecdotes about patients who were still very much alive. But she held her tongue.

"I can't remember their names, but they were an older couple. Anyway, they stayed married until the day they died, but they had some kind of a falling out in their sixties and stopped speaking to each other. They'd come in together and talk separately to me but not to each other, acting like the other one wasn't even there."

"That must have been awkward," Edie observed.

"And silly," added June.

"Yes, it was both of those things. I remember one day, the husband explained to me that he wasn't getting proper sleep. The wife said, 'Dr. McIntyre, could you please tell my husband that I don't appreciate him complaining to you that I sometimes pass gas in my sleep?'"

The women laughed.

"And had he?"

"Oh yes. He used to get quite a kick out of winding her up. He'd tell me the most embarrassing things about her because he knew she wouldn't answer him directly. Or I thought he got a kick out of it. The silence between them seemed to be more from her side than his."

"What a way to live!"

"I know. Bloody waste if you ask me," Doc agreed. "But the funniest part was that she started losing her memory."

He caught himself on his own words. "Okay, I didn't mean that was a funny thing."

"So what happened?" June prodded him after several seconds.

"Oh yes. Well, she forgot she was mad at him and started talking to him again."

They all laughed, just as shouts and barks heralded the arrival of their crew.

"That must have made it easier for you," June observed.

"For sure. And he was so much happier. But I always thought what a waste it had been to have missed out on all those years spent in anger."

"Did you ever find out what they were mad about in the first place?"

"No. I did ask once, but by then, neither one could remember."

"Oh, and here's Freya," Edie exclaimed in delight.

Freya had been a fairly regular visitor to the boarding house since Nick had asked her out that last time. The time that "took."

"The beautiful Freya," Doc nodded in greeting.

"I hope it's alright that I came along," Freya said, looking a little anxious. "Nick said it would be."

"Of course it is," June told her. "And please stay for supper. I've got a big batch of spaghetti sauce in the Crock-pot."

"I told you," Nick said to the girl, who smiled.

"Thursday is spaghetti night," Dillon pronounced. "And tomorrow's a PA Day, so no school."

"We should have a fire then," Doc declared. "One more fire before I put Miss Chiminea away till next summer."

The boys whooped with delight.

SHAGGY JACK

"Text your mom and ask her if it's all right for you to stay for a bonfire," Nick suggested. "We can drive you home after."

He turned to his aunt for confirmation.

"Yes, of course," she replied.

Doc was nodding with great enthusiasm.

"It will be too late for Mr. Clatterbox by then," she told him.

"I suppose you're right," he agreed reluctantly. "He goes to bed earlier than he used to. I'll have to take you out for a drive in Mr. Clatterbox sometime when it's daylight and we're both wide awake."

The beautiful Freya rewarded Doc with a dazzling smile. "Something to look forward to," she told him.

Nick felt his heart skip a beat, his eyes on Freya's face. He wondered if this was what it felt like to fall in love.

Chapter Thirty-Two

JUNE was jerked awake from a deep slumber, nearly propelling off the bed at the rough shoves of a huge, shaggy paw jabbing at her shoulder. Deafening barks echoed in her ears, reverberating inside the bedroom. She sat bolt upright, confused. The inky night abated as her sleep-addled eyes struggled to accommodate the darkness.

Edie shot up beside her, screaming, "What's happening? What's wrong?"

For something *was* wrong. Very wrong.

Edie's fingers fumbled for the switch of her small reading lamp, even as Jack wrenched on the sleeve of June's pyjama top with his teeth.

The two women dashed down the stairs, hard on the heels of the agitated dog.

The boys came piling down the narrow old stairway now, anxious and breathing rapidly, amidst the cacophony of barks and shrieks.

"The porch is on fire!" Edie cried. "Call 911!"

Nick's shaking fingers stabbed the dreaded numbers on his iPhone, his young voice ringing with terror as he gasped out the required information.

Dillon had somehow managed to locate the fire extinguisher in the kitchen. Glancing wildly around, he hesitated, uncertain what to do next. Leslie, gathered into the crook of his free arm, trembled in a terrified heap.

"Never mind, Dillon. Never mind. Come outside." June dragged

SHAGGY JACK

at the youth's arm. "We need to leave the house. The fire trucks will be here soon."

"Where's Doc?" Nick gazed around, his eyes wild with fear.

But Jack had not yet finished. He had vanished, only to return, ushering a bewildered-looking Doc down the stairs.

"Good boy, Jack. Good boy. Come on, Doc," Nick tugged at the old man's pyjama sleeve. "We have to get outside."

Doc allowed the others to lead him blindly out the back door.

"It's okay, it's okay, it's okay," June repeated the words over and over as she herded them out the back door.

"Yes, yes. It's fine," Edie's voice quaked. "I can hear the sirens. They're almost here."

"God bless them," Doc murmured.

God bless them indeed.

Laventra maintained a small but mighty crew of volunteer firefighters. Tears stung June's eyes as the firetrucks careened up the cobblestones, sirens blaring.

The firefighters performed their duties with competence and compassion as the small, terrified group of humans and dogs huddled together, looking on in horror. June stood, helpless and horrified, as the flames licked away at the porch of the only home she had ever known.

The outlines of Martha and Fred took shape out of the curtain of darkness. They had awakened to the blasts of sirens and the boom of trucks roaring down the country road and had rushed over. They each bore piles of blankets, which they proceeded to deposit on the shoulders of the shivering group. Martha even placed an old flannel over Jack's shoulders.

"I don't care about anything she ever said," Edie whispered to June. "I'll love her for this."

Doc placed his big hand on Martha's shoulder. "Thank you, Martha," he told her, his voice thick and broken. "Thank you both."

"I'm only doing what any good neighbour would do," Martha replied, in her usual brusque manner.

But for once, June didn't mind her curtness. "We appreciate it," she told her.

It took little time. Thankfully, the flames had been confined to the porch, and the house had sustained no real damage. When it was deemed safe to enter, the weary group traipsed into the kitchen amidst a prevailing acrid stench of smoke.

The men assembled in the kitchen, filling out the necessary forms, as they attempted to piece together some semblance of what might have happened. Edie produced tea and coffee and a plate of cookies, which disappeared in the blink of an eye. Clem, the fireman in charge of the scene, proceeded to make a report.

Questions chased themselves around the kitchen, but no answers were to be found.

Miss Chiminea had been put out thoroughly with several buckets of water. Everyone agreed on that.

"Who knows then?" Clem shook his head, after the discussion had been exhausted. "Sometimes embers will ignite combustible materials that can accumulate underneath a deck. Then they expose the rest of the deck to flame contact. Decking boards are always placed with a space between them for water drainage. So that can provide oxygen access, which makes an easy path for flames. Often, in a case like this, you never really know what starts these fires. This is an old house."

"It is that," June nodded, glad to be certain of something.

Doc, silent and shivering, opened his mouth to speak.

"Yes, Dr. McIntyre, right?"

Doc nodded abstractedly.

"I remember you. My mother thought the world of you."

Doc, clearly distraught, made no indication that he'd even heard the younger man.

"What is it, Doc?" Nick asked. "We're all good now. It's just the porch. The Huckleberries can rebuild it with you."

"Old Smokey," Doc stammered.

"What about him?" June asked.

Confusion passed over Clem's face. He'd heard the old doctor wasn't quite right in the head. Maybe it was worse than people thought.

"Doc," Edie's words were soft and firm. "You put Old Smokey away. It wasn't that. Don't worry. There's no real damage done, anyway."

Clem nodded kindly at the old man.

"There will be a more thorough investigation, of course, but Ms. Moon is right. The damage is just to the porch. It will probably be attributed to 'unknown causes.' The insurance will cover the cost of the porch."

Doc seemed only minimally mollified, but he attempted a weak smile.

"Thank you," he managed.

"It'll be a project for us," Nick told him brightly. "We needed a new summer project."

"Summer's all over now." The unaccustomed sadness in Doc, as he murmured these words, seemed to fill the country kitchen with despair.

The firemen prepared to depart. Clem stooped to tousle Jack's big, floppy ears. "I've never seen a dog this big. Or any dog that looked anything like him."

"Jack's in a size class all his own, that's for sure," June agreed. "It was him who woke us up."

"Saved the day, did you, buddy?" Clem smiled and pulled, of all things, a dog treat from the pocket of his big, bright coat. "You're a good boy."

"He's the best," Nick affirmed. "And he's really smart, too."

Because Jack had known who to awaken first and foremost: June, of course.

"I'm going to have to go and get that MAID," Doc announced, his words low and disparaging, one evening after supper.

Weeks had transpired since the fire, and the porch had been rebuilt as good as new. Better than before, truth be told.

"What's the matter, Doc?" June asked, placing a gentle hand on his arm. "You haven't been yourself since the fire. I know it was very traumatic at the time, but it's all over now. You don't have to worry."

"And you don't need a maid, Doc," Edie continued. "June and I can do more for you if you need more help. You know it would be our pleasure to help you with anything. Anything at all. I was a nurse, don't forget. I don't mind if you need extra help."

"No, no. I don't mean that. Not that kind of maid." Doc shook his head in frustration.

"You want a maid with nice legs, right, Doc?" Nick joked.

"Because you're a leg man," Dillon agreed.

Doc's gaze fell on the two, his eyes full of affection, as he emitted a soft chuckle. "You boys are silly. I only said something about that girl's legs one time. Only once. And you never forgot it."

"That's true," Max nodded. "We just like to tease you, Doc, that's all."

"But I'm not talking about that kind of a maid. I'm talking about the instant death person."

There was a collective gasp.

"Death?" Edie asked.

"Yes, it's been legal in Canada since 2016."

"Oh! MAID!" Edie and June cried out together, finally understanding. "The act that was passed for euthanasia."

"That's what I said," Doc replied, drawing himself up with dignity. "It's a great thing for people who are getting to the end of their life. Instant death. No pain."

"I'm not sure it's that great," June said. "And the 'I' doesn't stand for 'instant.' MAID stands for 'medical assistance in dying.'"

"But it *is* instant," Doc insisted.

"Well, yes, I suppose it is. But, Doc, why would you think that? You've loads and loads of years left in you. And you're so happy now with this crew." June waved her arm to include everyone, human and canine alike, gathered around the table.

"Well, it's because—" Doc broke off, his face a study of abject misery.

"What on earth is it, Doc?" Edie asked softly. "Whatever it is, we'll sort it out. Just tell us."

Doc sighed. "Funny how this old dementia works. So many times, I can't remember something even when I try really, really hard. And now something happened that I can't forget. But maybe it's just as well. Maybe it's the good Lord's way of letting an old man know that he's about done."

His hands shook, and his lower lip trembled as he slowly said, "It was me; I started the fire on the porch."

"What?"

"Oh, not on purpose, of course. It was the last night we had Miss Chiminea going. We all made sure that she was put out; that's how I know it had to be me. It was late, and I'd chased the boys off to bed. I decided, against my better judgement, to get Old Smokey out after he'd been put away, just one last time for a wee puff. It was such a beautiful night. That's all I remember. But it must have been a spark from him that set the fire. Not right away, but these things have a way of simmering. I did try to say that night when the fire people were here. I did, but no one listened."

"There's no way to prove that, Doc," June told him. "They did a thorough investigation and never found any cause."

"But that's worse because we don't know. And I truly don't remember. I mean, there's so much I don't remember every day, and I'm okay with that. Because it's so nice here with all of you. I never thought I'd endanger you." He closed his eyes, exhaling a deep sigh of defeat.

"I honestly don't think you did, Doc. We'll never know for sure, but you've told us now, so we'll keep a close eye on you when you have Old Smokey out. That would work, right? Is that okay?"

"June's right," Edie nodded. "We'll all be extra vigilant. Will that make you feel better?"

Doc nodded but still appeared uncomfortable. "I didn't want to tell you. I thought maybe you'd want me to move out when you knew."

"Move out? No way!" Nick cried. "You can't leave. We're your Huckleberries."

Dillon nodded his head vigorously in agreement.

"I'm very relieved about that. I've been so worried. I thought if I told you, then you might want to send me to that home over there out Dalton way. That Looney Acres place."

June laughed. "It's not Looney Acres, Doc. It's called Green Acres."

"Green Acres," Doc perked up. "You mean with Eva Gabor?"

"Pretty sure she's dead now, Doc."

"Oh, dear, too late for her then. Anyway, I'm happy to be able to stay here."

"Well, it's better than dying, that's for sure," Nick said, happy to be done with any thoughts of Doc leaving. "It's better than getting a maid to kill you."

"Animals in the wild search for a quiet place to go when they're hurt or dying. They're the smart ones." Doc sighed. "The big thing, I guess, is to know when the time is to get on your way."

"You wouldn't qualify for MAID anyway, Doc," Dillon said, seriously. "We talked about it in school last year. You have to be in your right mind or you don't qualify."

"Oh yes," Doc agreed, brightening visibly. "I forgot about that part. I guess because I'm not really in my right mind."

"Well, thank God for that," June declared, with a profound nod of her head.

Chapter Thirty-Three

Nick issued a request to June in November for permission to invite the beautiful Freya to their Christmas meal. The invitation eventually extended to her mother and grandparents, Max's parents, Dan Clark, and even the Wilsons.

"This is the best Christmas I've ever had in my whole life," Edie breathed to June.

"Me too," June agreed, planting a kiss on her beloved's rosy cheek. Their dining table was surrounded by happy people squeezed in at various angles.

The beautiful Freya and Nick, heads together and grinning widely, took turns placing tidbits on each other's laps for Jack. Fred and Dan appeared to be in some discussion or another. June hoped with all her heart that it wasn't about politics. Those dialogues never ended well, in her experience, but it seemed amiable enough for now. Even Martha seemed to be in good spirits, engaged in deep conversation with Max's mother and Dan's wife about some old-fashioned recipe for Christmas cake.

And Doc. Ah, dear Doc, he was his old self again, for which everyone was grateful. He grinned and laughed and ate heartily, and when the meal was over, he pulled out Cracklin' Rosie and led everyone in a Christmas sing-along.

Tears ran unabashedly down the cheeks of both women as Doc sang "I'll Be Home for Christmas" in his deep, beloved baritone.

"I'm so glad we're all home together," June whispered. "With Doc singing for us."

"Yup, me too. I'm glad he never found that instant maid he was looking for."

June laughed.

"He'll just have to stay here with us forever."

"That's fine with me."

"Me too."

But it was not to be.

One dreary morning, just as winter started to wane away, slowly melting the world into grey puddles of slush, Doc didn't come down for breakfast.

Trepidation crept into June's soul like a gust of ice-cold dread. She climbed the stairs and rapped softly on his bedroom door.

"Doc? Doc, are you okay?"

The unintelligible reply caught June's breath in her throat. Heart pounding like a trip-hammer, she held her breath and pushed open the door to find Doc sitting up, agitated, attempting to speak, not too successfully.

"It's okay, Doc." June sat on the bed, willing her voice to remain calm. "Slow down and try to say the words again."

"I haaa . . . haaa . . . sro . . ."

The garbled words fell on the morning air, scattering into the bedroom to lie like unwanted pebbles on the hardwood floor. June struggled to comprehend.

"I haaa . . . aaa . . . sro . . ."

"You've had . . . a . . . a stroke?!" June cried, working through

Doc's jumbled speech. "Oh my God. Are you sure? How do you know for sure?"

Edie scurried into the room, flannel housecoat trailing behind her, eyes full of concern. Both women strained to understand the distressed man's words, catching only bits and pieces of them.

He slurred as he spoke, but managed, "Dizzy . . . H-h-he-yaaa . . . can't ooove I . . . ight . . . arrr . . . ." He looked at his arm, attempting, it seemed, to raise it. It didn't budge.

"Smile for me, Doc. That's one of the tests." Edie said.

Doc's pathetic attempt at smiling would have been comical had it not been so tragic.

"I'm calling 911," June cried, springing to her feet. "Don't worry. It'll be alright, Doc. They'll send an ambulance. They'll get you fixed up, good as new."

A shriek erupted from Doc's lips. "Noooo!" He shook his head in a feverish attempt to be understood. "Pleeeeee! No!"

"They'll help you, Doc. I promise. I'm going to call them." June was pleading now, her anguished words breaking with emotion.

He grabbed June's arm with his good one. She looked at him in shock.

"No!" he slurred. Then he ejected a wail of emotion so profound that the old man was practically screaming.

"I don't know what to do." June almost wept the words as she sank down on the bed and buried her face in her hands.

Edie sat beside her and reached out to take Doc's timeworn hand in her tiny one. "Okay, Doc, okay, no ambulance. We don't want to upset you. Would it be all right if we call Dr. Sheridan, though? He could maybe come to the house and see you here."

Dr. Sheridan practised in Dalton, but he lived closer to Laventra, and he knew Doc quite well. She had no notion of whether doctors did house calls anymore, but it was the only solution she could think of.

Doc fell back onto his pillow, having exhausted what little energy he had. He weakly nodded his weary assent.

"Okay, you stay here, right here," June told him, full of relief that they had some course of action at last. "I'll call Dr. Sheridan."

She startled at the incomprehensible sound from Doc that might or might not have been defined as a chuckle. "What's that, Doc?"

"Don't . . . thin . . . I cuh oove if wann to." (*Don't think I could move if I wanted to.*)

The great effort these words evoked, coupled with the lopsided grin on his dear face, made June turn before he could witness the tears cascading down her cheeks. This caused her to nearly trip over Jack, who had crept in, unheard, and now lay quietly beside the bed.

June had no real faith that Dr. Sheridan would come, but after explaining the situation to him in short, halted sentences, that blessed man said he was on his way.

June led him to Doc's bedroom, where the others had gathered around his bed. Dr. Sheridan spoke of clot busters, carotid surgery, and rehabilitation. Throughout this discussion, Doc continued to jerk his head vehemently back and forth on the pillow.

Finally, Dr. Sheridan requested a private conversation with his patient. Reluctantly, the others piled downstairs to await the news.

He entered the kitchen, a half hour later, to face the sad little group assembled there.

Edie set a mug of coffee in front of him, accompanied by a

SHAGGY JACK

blueberry muffin, warm and buttered. He gratefully accepted both. "It's a stroke. Of course it is. Jed knows a stroke when he sees it, even if it is happening to himself. There are lots of ways to treat a stroke now, lots of treatments we could try, but he is very adamant that he wants none of them. His age is against him, of course, and he knows that. He knows that he wouldn't be able to drive anymore. He said something about huckleberries. Wandering a little in his mind, I guess. But even if he didn't want to be admitted to the hospital, we could still put in a feeding tube, since he isn't able to swallow anything. It would allow him to obtain medication and nutrition."

June's heart dropped like a stone. She didn't realize Doc couldn't swallow.

Dr. Sheridan continued: "That would buy him some time, but he doesn't want that either. He wants no intervention whatsoever, and he is very clear about this. Any further discussion is fruitless, not to mention upsetting to the poor guy."

"What happens then? If he can't swallow?" Nick asked, the strangled words barely escaping his mouth. He was staring down at the table, not trusting himself to face this man whom he now despised.

"He'll die. I'm sorry."

"But I don't want Doc to die!" Nick cried, looking around him wildly, as if in search of a solution somewhere. Anywhere.

"Of course you don't, Nick," Edie said, her words soft and gentle. "None of us do."

Dr. Sheridan rose. This wasn't the first conversation he'd had like this, and he knew when a family needed time to be alone. "I will see myself out."

The doctor looked at Nick with sympathy. "Doc is as fine a man as I ever knew. But I'm afraid, young man, it's not about what you want. It's about what Jed wants."

Home care offered to send a palliative nurse for a few hours each day, but June wouldn't hear of this. They could move Doc to hospice, but she wouldn't hear of that either. "This is his home. He belongs here. If he only has a little bit of time left, I want it to be here with us."

Everyone in the boarding house pulled together, ensuring that Doc never wanted for a thing. June equipped him with a little bell that he could ring if he needed assistance. Of course, Doc was loath to ring it, never wishing to bother anyone. He was able to get to the bathroom with a walker, just barely, and promised June that he wouldn't attempt this alone. He didn't have to. One of his Huckleberries was always there to assist him.

June had been forced to relocate Jack's food bowl to Doc's bedroom. The dog had taken up permanent sentry duty at the foot of his bed. Jack always knew where he was needed the most.

Doc, never a heavy man, grew smaller with the passing of each day. Despite his age, he had always been strong and wiry. He lay now, pale and diminished, swathed in the white flannel of his sheets, vanishing into a shadow of his former self.

They all gathered together after supper each evening, pulling in extra chairs to sit with him. They had grown accustomed to his halting manner of speaking, which had surprisingly become much clearer within a few days of the stroke. They could almost understand most of his words when they listened carefully enough.

"I wonder if your life flashes in front of your eyes when you die," he mumbled, gazing around at the people encircling him.

Max answered excitedly. "I know this, Doc. It happened in Vancouver. An eighty-seven-year-old man's brain waves were being studied for some test or other. Anyway, he had a heart attack and died in the middle of the test, so they got a recording of his dying brain waves. So now they have proof that your life *does* flash before your eyes before you die."

"That'd be nice," Doc managed the words slowly and with difficulty. "So many things I don't remember now. Bits and pieces. I hope they're the nice bits that come back."

"Of course they will be," Edie reassured him. "What would be the use of remembering the sad ones?"

Doc tried to nod. "You are s-s-o sen . . . sens-a-buh . . . Edie." He smiled that absurd, crooked half smile that had become achingly familiar to them all. Then, closing his eyes, he sank back into the bed, exhausted. His head lay on the crisp, white pillowcase that had, that very day, hung out on the clothesline and now smelled of the sweet springtime that Doc loved so much.

The next morning, just as the daylight beckoned to the night to abandon darkness, just as the pink and purple beauty of dawn washed the sky, leaving it aglow with brilliant sunlight, just as the birds sang their beautiful herald of melody to the breaking of the day, Doc slipped away.

June awoke with a start, feeling a subtle, inexplicable shift in her world. She and Edie crept from the bed and hastened down the hall, hand in hand, filled with foreboding, hearts thrumming madly in their ears. The three boys, hearing them, exited their rooms, and they met, as one, in Doc's room.

Those who loved him best in the world gathered in a silent circle of grief around his bed.

Jack had crawled onto the bed at some point, and he lay there now, his massive head resting beside Doc's. One huge grey paw covered Doc's wasted arm, and it appeared, for all the world, to be holding his hand.

Doc lay, white and still as marble, aglow in the first golden rays of morning light.

A peaceful smile covered his beloved, lifeless face.

Chapter Thirty-Four

A heaviness descended on the boarding house. The whole world had shifted on its axis, and nothing seemed to lift the veil of sadness prevailing there.

"I can't believe I would miss that silly old man so much," June muttered, wiping her eyes as she picked up Doc's mug.

Edie took the mug from her, patting her hand in sympathy. "Maybe we should put this one away," she suggested, smiling at the caption sprawled across the mug. It read: *In my defence, I was left unsupervised.*

June sank heavily onto the kitchen chair and clutched her coffee. "I can't do that yet. I just can't."

"That's fine. You don't have to. Ever. We can just keep using it. Doc would like that." Edie soothed June.

"Yes, he would," she agreed. "He was tickled pink when Nick gave him that silly mug." Both women sat sipping their coffee in silence, sad yet smiling at the memory.

"Doc's mug," Nick declared, entering the kitchen, Jack at his heels. "He liked that thing, didn't he? I got it at the dollar store because I thought he'd get a kick out of it."

"He loved it. He sure did. He always liked a little joke, and if it was on himself, all the better. It wasn't about where you got it or what you paid for it." Edie said.

"No, you're right. Doc never seemed to care about money, did he? Which reminds me, Auntie Bug," Nick rummaged around in his jeans pocket, finally producing a tattered-looking envelope with June's name sprawled across it.

"Doc said I should give you this after he died. He said it was important. I had to look around his room for a long time before I found it. It was after he had the stroke, and he couldn't remember exactly where he'd put it."

"That might not have been the fault of the stroke," June remarked, with a wry smile.

"True. Anyway, I forgot till now. Sorry. I think it's his will or something."

"Good thing I didn't wash those filthy jeans when the paper was still in your pocket."

"They're not filthy," Nick protested. "I was going to get another few days out of them. Anyway, I'm glad I remembered because Doc really wanted to make sure you got it. And now you have," he concluded.

June had serious doubts regarding the legality of such a ragged bit of paper, entrusted to a teenage boy, but she held her silence. Her eyes scanned the few words, nodding.

"It's not his will, thank God. It just says that his will is in the care of Dan Clark. I don't know how that could have transpired. This is the first I've heard of this, but it says we're to contact Dan and go from there."

"The beautiful Freya's coming over after school. We can ask her."

"No, this is official business. We'll have to contact the office. If there really is a will . . . Doc may have gotten a little muddled about that. I don't know when he would have gotten to the office without Edie or me. He hasn't driven much these last few months.

SHAGGY JACK

Poor old Mr. Clatterbox is going to seize up from lack of use. Or disintegrate into a pile of rust in the driveway," she added ruefully.

"Anyway, I don't know if Doc had many possessions to worry about. I don't think he was very wealthy. His clothes were basically rags. I had to hound him to buy anything new for himself. The only thing he had to his name was that old Dodge truck."

But June Howard was proved to be wrong. Very wrong.

Doc, indeed, had been wealthy. He had left behind a veritable fortune.

"It makes sense," Dan told the women after explaining the legal facts to them. He grinned at their dropped jaws and shocked faces. "I don't suppose he was a big spender."

"He was always more than generous with groceries and anything we needed," June said. "But he sure never seemed to spend anything extra."

"Which is exactly why he saved so much," Dan pointed out.

Doc was as generous in death as he had been in life. Dan had written the words out verbatim as Doc had dictated them to him. It was like listening to the man himself. The reading of his final words was bittersweet, punctuated with tears and laughter from the women. *"I always said I'd like a soft landing when I die, but I couldn't have asked for a softer landing than to end up at the boarding house with you, Junie dear."*

These opening words tugged at June's heart. She would be forever grateful for the time Doc had spent with all of them.

Money had been left to Edie and June—an incredible amount of money. More than enough to totally modernize the old boarding house. He even made specifications for the work that should happen. He knew they wouldn't have accepted it from him in life, but now they needed to get to work and get it fixed up. New roof, new siding, new windows and doors, new furnace, air conditioning. Only suggestions, he said, but he hoped they would heed them. Oh, and maybe a drilled well so people didn't have to use the same bath water. Just in case.

It would be good to have these in place if they really wanted to launch a veterinary clinic there. When Nicky and Dillon were all done with their education, of course.

He mapped out the funds that Nicky would need to become a veterinarian. He'd looked into it, or he and Dan had, and Nicky would require two to three years of a college degree in health science and a four-year university degree in veterinary science. Guelph seemed to be the best school. But it was up to the boy to choose, of course. There was more than enough money to ensure this happened.

Dan had cautioned Doc that Nick needed good marks to be accepted and that it was a long, gruelling course ahead. But Doc had entertained no doubts about Nick's ability to acquire this. None at all.

There was money set aside for Dillon, too. Doc thought he wanted to be a veterinary assistant, but whatever he chose was fine with him. And the boarding house would be the perfect place for a vet clinic. It already had so many kennels and rooms. But only if that's what everyone wanted. Most of all, he wanted everyone to be happy. In any case, the money was there for them to use in whatever way they wished.

He left money for Max's education, also. He thought that Max would probably take a course in writing. Maybe a bachelor's degree

SHAGGY JACK

in linguistics or journalism. But no matter what he decided on, he wanted Max to continue writing because he was so good at it. Doc loved Max's stories and poems. He was never to forget that he had a God given gift. And that he'd won the Maple Leaf Competition when he was still young.

He'd had a housekeeper, Yolanda, for many years, who had brought up a young boy on her own. Yolanda was dead now, poor woman, but he left some money to her son, who still kept in touch with him. Or had before he forgot to correspond with people. But it still counted, Doc pointed out.

He'd even commissioned an artist that Dan knew to paint a big sign for the future Veterinary Clinic. The letters were to be multi-coloured, like rainbows.

"Rainbows for the lesbian ladies," he'd explained to Dan.

It was to depict an image of Jack, or a reasonable facsimile, and say:

Shaggy Jack's Veterinary Clinic
All animals welcome.

He'd told Dan that this dedication was due to the fact that Jack had saved the boarding house from fire. A fire possibly started by Old Smokey.

If none of these plans transpired and they didn't need the sign, then that was fine, but he wanted it to be available if it was required. He would leave that part in Dan's capable hands.

Last but not least, he wanted Nick and Jack to go to Tom's Meat Market. Tom allowed well-behaved dogs in his store. He wanted

Nick and Jack to pick out the biggest, juiciest roast in the whole market and present it to Martha Wilson.

He had explained to Dan that this was "so she'd stop harping on about Jack stealing her roast when the poor thing was only a starving pup." However, Dan had chosen to omit this last remark. Especially since Fred Wilson was one of the witnesses to the signing of the will.

That was how Doc had managed it.

Dan and his family had been invited out to the boarding house for Christmas dinner. Doc had approached him, stating that he needed help with his present will. His old will had left everything to the SPCA, and he wanted to change that, although that good society still figured in his bequeaths. But he had so many more people in his life now, he was happy to say. And he wanted to make sure that his Huckleberries were looked after. So they'd waited for a day when the ladies were known to be gone for a few hours. Fred had picked him up, driven him to Dan's office, and witnessed the will.

Edie and June left Jack at home when they presented Martha with her roast of beef. She remained unsure whether she should be offended by this beyond-the-grave gesture or not. She did, however, manage to portray her disapproval at the whole idea of Doc's new will and the involvement of her husband. "Isn't it kind of like breaking rules or something to have been allowed to write that will? I mean, we all know that Doc wasn't in his right mind. That was certainly common knowledge."

June bristled at this criticism of their beloved Doc, but Edie replied in her usual calm fashion. "I suppose you might have a point, Martha. I guess it's kind of like how Doc broke a lot of rules, driving on roads closed by the township, when he saved Mr. Clark's daughter so many years ago."

Martha sniffed her disapproval. "Oh, well, one lies and the other one swears to it."

"Somethin' like that," Fred agreed blithely. His day had been made by the appearance of the delicious-looking roast.

But Martha was not prepared to let it go at that. "I guess I just don't understand any of it," she told them. "How you all lived together the way you did. And I sure will never understand about gays living together."

"That's all right," Edie told her, throwing her the sweetest of smiles. "We're not asking you to live with us."

She could almost hear Doc's chuckle reverberating in her ears.

Chapter Thirty-Five

Doc had wanted to be cremated. He had told Dan this and had specified it in his will. He left the residence of his ashes up "to the ladies." He had complete and utter faith that they would find the best place for him to rest.

Time stretched along until the school year ended; the last year the Huckleberries would attend high school. It seemed a fitting time for Doc's celebration of life. The end of an era.

Edie and June decided to hold the event at the Laventra Community Centre.

June had asked Dan if he would host the celebration. "Kind of like a master of ceremonies."

Dan said he would be deeply honoured to do just that.

So the date was set for the last day in June. The morning broke on the wave of a beautiful, pink dawn kissing the country meadows. The loveliest of months and the loveliest of days. The sun beamed in the bright sky, the gentle breezes whispered to the new leaves clinging to the tree branches, and fields brimming with white daisies shone in star-studded glory.

June's heart swelled at the sight of so many people gathered together to pay tribute to Doc. Even though he'd been retired for quite a number of years now. Even though he might not indeed have recognized many of them. Even though they may have witnessed him driving erratically with three teenage boys and one very large dog. Still, they came to remember and honour him.

Dan thanked people for attending, then proceeded to relay the story of his daughter Emily and the meningitis scare. He told of the frantic ride through the closed roads in Doc's old truck and the subsequent, terrifying drive to SickKids.

"I wouldn't have my daughter or my beautiful granddaughter, Freya, if it hadn't been for Dr. McIntyre," he concluded.

Everyone applauded heartily.

"Are you supposed to clap at a celebration of life?" Edie whispered to June.

"I don't see why not. I don't suppose it matters," June said, thinking that Doc would certainly approve. "It's not a conventional one. Kind of like Doc, I guess."

When the applause died down, Dan asked if anyone else wanted to say a few words or had any memories they wished to share.

Dr. Sheridan came forward, stating that he'd known Doc for many years. He remembered him as a compassionate and competent doctor. He spoke of how tireless he'd been, caring for his small community, making house calls when it was almost unheard of to do so. "When I first came to Dalton, I even heard of him delivering a baby right in his office when his secretary was out at lunch. It was a long time ago now, though, so I'm not even sure if it was true or not."

A woman, sporting a huge smile and wild red curls, jumped up, waving her hands excitedly in the air. "It's true!" she cried. "That's me! I'm that baby! My mom told me the story lots of times. She wanted to come today, but she's not too well, so she sent me instead. Anyway, it was forty years ago almost to the day. She went to see him for her regular appointment. I was her fifth kid. She wasn't due for over a week. He helped her up onto the table to examine her. He told her she was nine centimetres dilated and she was going to have the baby right then and there. He bustled around for a few minutes, getting gloves and stuff. Then he put his hand on her shoulder and told her, very calmly, that she had two things to do for him. She had to say a little prayer and give a great, big push. And I was born right then and there! When his secretary came back from lunch, my mom was lying on the table with me in her arms. He'd clamped the cord, delivered the afterbirth, and had me all wrapped up in a big white towel. Mom said his secretary looked like she was going to faint. He picked me up to show her that everything was okay. Then he asked my mom what name she had picked for me. She said, 'Matilda.' He thought that was a great name and he took me over to his secretary, singing 'Waltzing Matilda' before he deposited me back in my mother's arms."

Everyone laughed. It was so very Doc-like.

Others rose, one by one, reiterating tales from when Doc had cared for them. Some were elderly, some quite young; all were grateful for the care they'd received at his hands.

Dan assisted an elderly woman to the front to share her story. "When my husband died, Doc came to be with me so I wouldn't be alone. He stayed all night on my couch until my son arrived from Quebec City, and then off he went to his office in the morning to work the whole day. He said that the Good Lord has a book with everyone's name in it, and every morning He turns a new page over. If your name is on the page for that day, then it's just your time to go." She returned to her seat as another woman rose and began to relate her memories.

"When my dear boy, Stephen, was born with Down syndrome, he told me that he was glad he had me for a mother because he would need a good one. And that, sometimes, children come with challenges to show all of us how to be better people. He helped me for years, getting my son all the resources and assistance that he needed. And he always treated him with great dignity and talked to him with respect and affection. Stephen thought Doc was just a really good friend for years until he figured out that he was our doctor. Doc used to come by to visit sometimes on his way home and throw a baseball or a football to him. Stephen's doing just fine now, and I know I owe so much of that to Doc." Stephen's mother, looking careworn from life, smiled as her voice broke on her last words. A middle-aged, swarthy man gave her a hand down as he took his place at the front.

"My mother was Yolanda, and she kept house for Doc for many years. She was a single mom and always struggling. I never knew my dad, but I considered Doc to be like a grandfather. He was so good to my mom. She always said it was the best day of her life when she read the ad in the hardware store that a country doctor was looking for a housekeeper. He paid her well and never minded if she brought me along. If I was sick or had something on at school, she never had to worry about asking for time off. I think he attended every one of my Christmas concerts. When I got older, I'd cut the grass and do odd jobs for him, and he always slipped me money for that. When she got too old to do housework, he still sent her an income every week until she died. And I was informed by Mr. Clark that he has left me a sum of money in his will, as well. I owe him so much." Tears glistened in the eyes of Yolanda's son at these last words. He slipped down, making way for another elderly woman who spoke in a clear, concise voice.

"Years ago, my husband had a heart attack, and Doc told him to go home and rest. George said that was easy for him to say now, wasn't it, because he had to go out and shovel the snow off our roof or it would bloody well collapse. Doc said he wasn't to get on that roof, and that was the end of it. He told him to hold his horses and wait, and that when he was done at the office, he'd come over and shovel the roof off himself. George scoffed at him and said he highly doubted that would happen. Doc said, 'By George, you just wait and see. I'm a man of my word.' He was making a joke of George's name, you see." She paused to give people a chance to appreciate this.

"I had grave doubts myself that he would come," the old woman continued. "Just because he was always so darned busy. But sure enough, after supper, we heard something up on the roof. I went out to look and there was Doc, shovelling off our roof. I can still see him in his bright red toque, whistling away. He told me it sure was a nice view from up there."

When the room settled into a semblance of silence, Edie rose.

"A man of his word," she said softly. "I loved that about him. Even as he got older, to the best of his ability, he meant what he said and said what he meant. He was the dearest, kindest man I've ever known, and I'll be happy for the rest of my life that I got the chance to know him and love him. I read a quote the other day that reminded me of him.

"Sometimes you find people who have sun inside them . . . It's not just their smile but their entire presence just brightens your world. They have an internal being that shines so bright it feels like sun warming your soul."

Nick, Max, Dillon, and Jack now proceeded to the front, armed with various bits of paper. Nick counted down from three, then the boys began to sing, their youthful voices filling the little centre. *"Come and listen to a story 'bout a man named Jed."*

A wave of laughter rippled through the crowd.

Martha Wilson, whom June and Edie had the misfortune of sitting right behind, turned to them, shaking her head in disapproval.

"I never heard of such a thing at a celebration of life. Beverly Hillbillies? That's appalling! And I have no idea why that monstrosity of a dog is even allowed in here," she hissed at the women.

"Jack was one of Doc's favourite people," June hissed back.

"He's not a *'people'*," Martha retorted. "He's a dog."

"Shh," Edie cautioned. "I'm not sure Jack is aware of that."

Martha, giving up, abruptly turned her back on the women.

"Doc used to sing that when we were driving together in Mr. Clatterbox, only he'd sing the whole song about finding oil in the hills. But we just wanted to sing the first line because this *is* a story about a man named Jed."

"Well, thank God for small mercies," Martha muttered.

"She just can't help herself," Edie whispered to June, who was gritting her teeth to keep from saying something she would regret.

"Doc taught us lots of things," Nick was saying. "Things we never would have known if it wasn't for him."

"Like Dodge Rams are the best kind of truck ever made," Max jumped in.

"Here, here!" cried Bert Lozier, the local Chrysler dealer.

"We've heard some people talking today about Doc praying," Nick continued. "I don't know if he did or not. The only time we ever heard him pray was when his truck acted up. He'd say, 'Lord

Tunderin' Jesus, Mr. Clatterbox, could you please help me out here and turn over so we can get going.'"

"He taught us that it was legal for women to marry each other in Canada and that lesbian ladies were the best because you should be able to love whoever you wanted to," Max said.

The boys seemed to be taking turns at this. Doc's beloved Huckleberries.

A smattering of applause echoed around the room.

"And that it was legal in Ontario for women to go topless. Because women get hot in the summertime just like men do. Also, a woman breastfeeding her baby is the most beautiful sight in the world."

This last came from Dillon and brought much more applause.

More mothers than lesbians in the room, June surmised.

The boys seemed to be on a roll now, one following the other with regales of memories.

"He taught us to always have a condom because it was better to not need one and have it, than to need one and not have it. You might have to pay for that for the rest of your life."

This was met by a disapproving "Harumph" from Martha.

"He taught us about fiddleheads and how they looked so nice first thing in the spring. Also, they are superfoods because they have antioxidants in them. He sometimes fried them up with garlic lemon butter for us, and when we ate them, he told us we were 'super Huckleberries.'"

Dillon's voice choked a little on these last words, but he quickly composed himself. The boys had decided that they would make

SHAGGY JACK

Doc proud, and not cry and whine about his passing, but celebrate everything that had been wonderful about him.

"He said we should always notice those little blue butterflies that fly all over the puddles after it rains. He called them 'peri twinkles' because they are periwinkle blue, and he said they brought happiness. I know that's not their proper name, but we like Doc's name."

"He showed us what fireflies look like. They really are beetles and are black with red heads, but Doc wanted us to know what they looked like in the daylight so we wouldn't kill them, mistaking them for something else. When you see them in the day, you'd never believe they could light up like they do at night."

"And when it's going to rain that the leaves on the trees turn inside out because they want a drink. And he always knew just exactly how long to boil maple syrup."

"And if we ever get lost, we just have to remember that the moon rises in the east and sets in the west, just like the sun. So if you know that, then all you have to do is point your right hand to the east, and your face will look north."

"He told us about a maple leaf bra that was coming out for hockey fans. Lots of support but no cup."

Groans echoed in the room. The boys were on a roll now.

"One day," Dillon piped up. "We were in town with him, and Nick said, 'Look at that dog with one eye.' So Doc covered one eye and looked at the dog."

Laughter erupted.

Martha Wilson sniffed her displeasure, turning to remark that this whole event was very disrespectful. "More like a comedy show than a celebration of life," she muttered at one point.

"Doc would have loved it," June responded, her tone sharp, leaving no room for negotiation. She had grown tired of Martha's dull, negative attitude.

"He would," Edie agreed.

Then added, in a whispered aside to June, "They were going to tell the one about the nuns, but I talked them out of it. I said this one would be more respectable."

"The nuns?"

"You know. The nuns riding their bikes on the cobblestones."

"Oh, I'm glad you did. Martha would have fainted dead away."

The boys had stopped speaking but remained on the little stage, Jack in their midst, seemingly loath to step down, to let go of this last bit of Doc.

Dan, sensing this, spoke gently into the ensuing silence.

"It's so nice that you shared all this with us, boys. Doc would be proud of you. How lucky you were to have known him as you did. I personally did not know that those beetles with the red heads were fireflies. I think we tend to think all flying insects will bite us. I'll be on the lookout now and won't swat them when they land on me.

"Doc was an amazing example of how someone can age and lose some of their abilities but still keep going strong. He was quite open and honest about not remembering things. So he never got offended. He just didn't remember any slights, real or imagined. It's a lesson we could all use today, in a world where people are offended so very easily."

He turned to the boys, smiling warmly. "Do you boys have anything else you'd like to share with us?"

SHAGGY JACK

"Is it okay?" Dillon asked. "We just have a few more little things he taught us."

"You bet it is, Dillon."

Several people clapped, eager for more memories of Doc.

"He taught us to always be kind. At least do your best to be kind. And to be kind, especially to nasty people, because they need it the most."

"Sunflowers are the best flowers because they're always happy. And they're the most cheerful flower because they track the sun."

"The plant that grows in ditches around here, with bright orange flowers, is called jewelweed. And Doc showed us, if you take off a piece and hold it underwater, that the leaves turn silver. It's really neat. But it's useful too, because if you take a few leaves and mush them up in your hands, then the leaves give off sap. And you can use the sap for poison ivy to take the itch away."

"And to listen to the black sheep in the family because they usually tell the truth about how things actually are."

"And every family has one weirdo. If you don't know who it is, then it's probably you. But it's okay to be a weirdo. The most important thing is to be yourself."

"We were his Huckleberries," Nick announced. "If you live around here, I'm guessing you've seen his truck, Mr. Clatterbox. He always said a huckleberry was just the right one, the perfect match. Jack was one, too. Because Jack was not just a dog to Doc."

"No matter what we were talking about, if Doc thought it was a good story, he'd tell me to write it down," Max continued. "I want to be a writer, but Doc was a natural storyteller. He always had a fun story to tell."

"The inappropriate ones, they were the best ones," Nick interjected.

Max nodded. "For sure. I'd have a book already if I'd written down everything that he told me to. But someday I'm going to write a book called 'Doc and the Huckleberries' and I'm going to dedicate it to him." (In years to come, Max did write a book entitled just that. It became a bestseller and won a very prestigious literary award. But that's a story for another time.)

Amidst a round of applause, the boys and Jack retired to sit amongst the crowd.

Dan concluded the celebration and announced that everyone was welcome at the boarding house for refreshments and fellowship.

Then he told Max, "I have absolutely no doubt that you will write that book. Doc had endless faith in all you boys. According to Jewish tradition, everyone dies twice. The first time is when your heart stops beating. The second time is when your name is uttered, read, or thought of for the last time. It's nice to think that you will be keeping Doc's memory alive, Max."

Chapter Thirty-Six

WHAT to do with Mr. Clatterbox became somewhat of a dilemma. June would have (or thought she would have) been happy to take it to the scrapyard and run it over the scales for the price of the scrap metal. But the boys protested vehemently. Mr. Clatterbox had been such a big part of Doc. Couldn't they keep it and give it the occasional ride down the back roads for old times' sake?

This, June flatly refused to consider. No one was to drive that rickety, old box of rattling nuts and bolts ever again.

It had been Edie who suggested parking it over in front of the copse of birches and maybe decorating it with some bird feeders and birdhouses. June finally conceded to this, considering it to be the lesser of two evils.

Edie went to the hardware store where she had them manufacture and inscribe a metal plaque in Doc's honour, to mount on Mr. Clatterbox's side panel. It read:

In loving memory of Dr. Jed McIntyre.
Our beloved "Doc"
When I die,
Don't place my
Wasted husk
In a wooden box
Buried six feet under
Where I can't feel the rain.
Bury me in a

Field of sunflowers,
With their
Faces continually
Turning toward
The rays of the sun.
I want my soul
To become the petals.

The boys carted in a load of topsoil to scatter around Mr. Clatterbox's tires, where each planted a sunflower. The three plants grew tall and strong, nodding their bright, beautiful heads toward the sun.

Jack "watered" the sunflowers every time he happened to pass by them.

"Doc would have laughed at that," Nick observed, pointing at the dog as he unceremoniously lifted his leg in the direction of the plants.

"Yup," Dillon agreed. "He always said, 'when you gotta go, you gotta go.'"

Nick chuckled. "Sometimes he had to stop when we were out, but he always went into the bushes or woods to pee. He was very respectful like that."

"He used to tell us, 'Nobody wants to see that thing, boys. It's private. That's why they're called your privates and never show it to anybody unless they ask.'"

"'And they have to ask *really* nicely,'" Max concluded, as all three boys dissolved into laughter at the memory.

"Oh dear," June sighed. "Do we need to know that, I wonder?"

Edie shrugged, smiling. "It's not bad advice, though."

SHAGGY JACK

The sunflowers continued to grow in spite of, or perhaps because of, Jack's regular irrigation system. They multiplied freely, numerous seedlings springing up on all sides of Mr. Clatterbox.

The birds gratefully partook of their seeds, pecking some, dropping many, thus increasing the number of new sprouts. But they also spread because sunflower roots are aware of each other and have been shown to work together to share nutrients.

That's why sunflowers are the very best flowers.

Doc could have told you that.

And so my story has come to an end. It's been my great pleasure to share it with you.

"They lived happily ever after" is such a cliché, but it can happen, in my humble opinion. We can make it happen. After all, that's how sayings become clichés.

June and Edie spent many pleasurable hours laughing and talking, as the steady stream of days and months and seasons tumbled over them, weaving the tapestry of a beautiful life together with sweet threads of love and joy.

They grew older, weathering the occasional tempests of life. But their days, for the most part, were peaceful and full of quiet happiness. They watched and waited, full of patience and pride, as Nick excelled at university, eventually earning his Doctor of Veterinary Medicine.

Dillon, Max, and the beautiful Freya (Freya, they now knew, was in for the long haul) travelled the four-hour trip to Guelph with them to attend his graduation ceremony.

Tears streamed down both women's cheeks when Dillon and Nick informed them that they would keep Doc's dream alive and set up their own veterinary clinic right there at the beloved old boarding house. Dillon, already a vet tech in Dalton, had put in his notice and would take up duties with Nick at the end of the summer. His heart still lingered there, full of fond memories.

They were sure to have lots of business, Nick explained to the delighted ladies, because so many people already used the boarding kennels.

And so it was that June, Edie, Jack, and Freya sat on the porch, waiting, on the last day of a beautiful series of spring days, for Nick to return home for good.

Jack had aged and didn't walk as quickly as he once had, but he remained treasured and beloved.

The ladies had, with the assistance of Dan, unearthed the sign commissioned by Doc so many years ago. June had not wanted to tempt fate by hanging it prematurely. But now that Nick was truly qualified after so many gruelling years, she and Edie hung the multi-coloured marquee on the front porch, hearts overflowing with pride and joy.

Shaggy Jack's Veterinary Clinic
All animals welcome

It seemed to take forever until Nick finally pulled up in his blue Dodge Ram truck.

Jack rose slowly, tail thumping a mile a minute, and started down the porch steps.

SHAGGY JACK

The women stood, all three brimming with pride and overflowing with joy, at the sight of their very own veterinarian.

Nick parked the truck behind the shed and withdrew his old bike from its depths.

"Why on earth is he driving that rickety old bike?" June wondered. "Today of all days."

Freya groaned. "Oh, he's going to make an entrance. He's going to tell that silly old joke of Doc's," she sighed. "He thinks he's funny."

"Hey, beautiful Freya!" Nick clunked down the cobblestones, a huge grin plastered on his beaming face, glasses hanging haphazardly by one ear.

"Have you ever come this way before?"

THE END

ABOUT THE AUTHOR

BARB Bissonette is a retired nurse of many years, who has enjoyed writing since childhood. She has won prizes for her short stories, including the Melody Richardson Writing Contest, the BDO Writing contest of York Region, and the 2021 Orillia Readers' Choice Award as Favourite Local Author.

Barb lives in the beautiful village of Washago, Ontario. She loves children, dogs, and all things nature. This is her seventh novel. You can find her at *www.entouragemedia.ca/barb_bissonette* and at *barbbissonette.wixsite.com/home*.

www.ingramcontent.com/pod-product-compliance
Lightning Source LLC
Chambersburg PA
CBHW011126070526
44584CB00028B/3800